City of Betrayal

The Genovese Family's Springfield Crew

By Nicholas Anthony Parisi

ISBN: 979-8-9913436-0-2

I wish to express gratitude to certain individuals in my journey; some are family, some I have met along the way, some played a significant role during my formative years, and many I am fortunate to consider friends.

(In alphabetical order)

Anthony "Bingy" Arillotta, former capo of the Springfield Crew and made member of the Genovese Crime Family

The family of Adolfo "Big Al" Bruno, former capo of the Springfield Crew and made member of the Genovese Crime Family

Rex Cunningham, former Springfield Crew associate and bookmaker, loan shark, and notorious enforcer

Mario Fiore, alleged made member of the Genovese Crime Family and the oldest living gangster in America

Fotios "Freddy" Geas, former Springfield Crew associate

Ty Geas, former Springfield Crew associate

Gaetano Milano, former made member of the Patriarca Crime Family

Frank "Franky Pugs" Pugliano, alleged made member of the Genovese Crime Family and Patriarca Crime Family associate

"If it weren't for informants, the public would know nothing about the inner workings of La Cosa Nostra."

-AUTHOR NICHOLAS ANTHONY PARISI

Prologue

The night was quiet; the streets of Springfield, Massachusetts, were illuminated by the soft glow of streetlights. In the South End section, a police detective named Maurice Kearney sat in his patrol car, listening intently to the static-filled police radio. Suddenly, the dispatcher's voice cut through the silence, urgency laced in her words.

"We have a shooting down on Winthrop Street. We need an ambulance fast because the guy is in tough shape."

Homicide detective Thomas Malidi also heard the dispatch.

"Al Bruno just took about eight to the body at the Mount Carmel Italian Club."

Hearing this, homicide detective Thomas Malidi's heart raced as he jumped into his car and sped towards the scene. As they arrived, the duo was met with a chaotic scene. Al Bruno, a prominent figure in the community, was still there on the ground. He wasn't moving.

The smell of gunpowder hung heavy in the air, the only sound being the distant wail of sirens. Without hesitation, another officer rolled Bruno onto his back and began administering chest compressions, desperately trying to revive him. At that moment, Kearney's eyes met with the officer's, and in a silent exchange, it was clear that all efforts were in vain.

"Ah, he's dead. He's gone," the officer shook his head, his words heavy with defeat.

They ripped his shirt off, revealing the holes in his chest. Blood gushed out of him from just about everywhere, painting the ground a deep crimson. He lay motionless, clutching onto his cigar as if it were his last lifeline.

The cigar hung limply from the lifeless hand of the man sprawled on the pavement. He was no ordinary victim of murder. Adolfo Bruno, better known as Big Al, was the boss of Springfield's Italian mafia. Two years ago, he had reveled in the glory of being the most powerful mobster in town. But now, his lifeless body lay in a pool of blood, a stark contrast to the glitz and glamour he once exuded.

The police were baffled by Bruno's death.

Mob hits were rare in Springfield, and for a boss to be ruthlessly gunned down was almost unheard of. It had been nearly 80 years since the last boss was killed, back in the days of prohibition, when Giuseppe "Joseph" Parisi had taken out Carlo Siniscalchi less than a mile away. The parking lot was now a desolate crime scene, filled with the echoes of a notorious past. The air was thick with dread, and the faint smell of cigar smoke lingered, a reminder of the man who had met his untimely demise. As the police combed through the evidence, they could only speculate on the events that led to Big Al's downfall. It was a shocking turn of events that left the entire city in disbelief.

In the ruthless world of the mafia, taking the life of a "made" man, especially one as revered as Big Al Bruno, carries heavy consequences. Being made comes with certain privileges, the most coveted being protection from any harm, even from other made men. Therefore, eliminating a made man is not only an act of violence but also a bold risk that could ultimately cost you your own life. One would assume that someone daring enough to take such a risk must have something significant to gain. Perhaps power, wealth, or something that could make the risk seem worthwhile.

John Gotti took that risk and orchestrated a hit on Paul Castellano, his family's boss, in 1985. This bold move led to Gotti becoming the new boss of the Gambino crime family.

When Al Bruno was murdered, investigators immediately assumed that the shooter had everything to gain. They believed it was an inside job and that the gunman was a member of the mob who sought to take over Bruno's profitable rackets and claim his power.

However, their primary suspect did not fit into these assumptions.

Table of Contents

Chapter 1

Wiseguys on the Rise

Aldolfo "Big Al" Bruno was a larger-than-life gangster who dominated the room with his imposing presence, leaving no doubt about his position in the underworld. His signature fat cigars were a constant presence, adding to his confident persona. He had a way with words, often cracking jokes to the press, but his extensive political connections truly solidified his power. He had been telling people he would be the boss his whole life. It was his ultimate goal, the thing he wanted the most. He wanted to be "the guy."

Born on November 24, 1945, in Bracigliano, Salerno, Campania, Italy, Adolfo Bruno left his homeland at ten and settled in Springfield, Massachusetts. He quickly adapted to his new surroundings and took various odd jobs to support himself and his family. Young Adolfo was determined to make a living, from shining shoes to delivering newspapers. His family's restaurants, Bruno's Pizzeria and La Casa di Lisa, became a second home for Adolfo. He spent countless hours working alongside his family, learning the ins and outs of the business.

As he grew older, Adolfo moved to the Feeding Hills area of Agawam and the picturesque grounds of Oak Ridge Country Club. His simple home provided a peaceful retreat from the city. Adolfo was an avid golfer and spent most of his free time on the green, honing his skills and enjoying the company of his fellow golfers. But Adolfo's love for golf went beyond just a leisurely activity. He used his passion for the sport to make a difference in the lives of others. He sponsored golf tournaments to raise funds for those affected by cerebral palsy, a cause close to his heart.

Aldolfo, now going by the Americanized name of Al, was a masterful salesman with a charm and charisma that could sell ice to an Eskimo. His powers of persuasion were unmatched, and it was no surprise that he quickly became the top salesman at Carando Foods. He could have easily been a multi-millionaire just sticking with the major Italian food distributor, but that wasn't enough for him. Bruno's ambitions went beyond just selling food. He wanted more and would do whatever it took to get it.

His sales job allowed him to interact with restaurant and bar owners and gave him access to the seedy underworld of gambling. Bruno was a natural networker, and he quickly built a vast web of ties in the sports betting world. Some of these connections were in deep debt and desperate for money, and Bruno saw an opening. He became a loan shark, preying on those who were already in a vulnerable state. With his smooth talk and persuasive ways, he could convince anyone to take a loan from him, no matter the high interest rates or consequences. Bruno was a complex guy with a magnetic personality that drew people in, but also a dark side that could be ruthless and calculating.

It was during that time that he caught the attention of Salvatore "Big Nose Sam" Cufari and the infamous Scibelli brothers - Franky "Skyball," Albert "Baba," and Anthony "Turk," the most prominent crime bosses in Springfield for decades and the ones in charge of the Springfield crew's territory under the Genovese crime family from New York. Their headquarters was Cufari's restaurant, Ciro's, which he opened in 1948.

Big Nose Sam was in charge of the Western Massachusetts operations and had a record of over a dozen arrests dating back to the 1920s, when he was shot by police while trying to run a bootlegging roadblock in Granby, Connecticut.

In 1914, Cufari left his hometown of Reggio Calabria, Italy, and immigrated to the United States. He eventually became a citizen in 1927, but in the 1950s, he fought intensely to maintain his American citizenship.

In 1924, Cufari was taken into custody on Christmas Eve for stabbing a service station attendant in Enfield, Connecticut, who later refused to identify Cufari as the culprit. No charges were ever pressed, which appeared to be a recurring theme for the notorious Big Nose Sam.

In 1940, the Genovese family appointed him as Springfield's first modern-day mafia boss. The New York crime family had arrived in the mid-1920s after Giuseppe "Joe" Parisi eliminated the "King of Bootleggers," Carlo Siniscalchi. Vito Genovese sent Antonio Miranda, brother of his Consigliere, Micheal Miranda, to take control of Siniscalchi's illegal alcohol empire.

In 1957, Big Nose Sam's presence was felt at the infamous "Little Apalachin" summit in upstate New York. He was a formidable figure, feared by many. Years later, in 1972, Sam received a summons from a U.S. Senate Committee. They were investigating the organized crime's control of cleaning product sales to Boston and New Jersey labor groups. But Sam was not one to be easily intimidated. He rejected the summons, a bold move that showed his defiance and power. Sam was not one to play by the rules. He and his fellow gangsters were behind distributing the locally-produced "Poly-Clean" to unions. It was a strategic move to maintain "labor peace" in exchange for their support. But to Sam, it was just business as usual. He was a mastermind, always thinking one step ahead.

In the streets of Springfield during the 1960s and early 1970s, four young men were making a name for themselves in organized crime. Al Bruno, Amadeo Santaniello, Tony Liquori, and Victor DeCaro were not just friends; they were a tight-knit clique of wise guys on the rise. Their actions spoke louder than words, as they were involved in traditional organized crime rackets such as street lotteries, truck heists, illegal sports betting, and casino junkets.

This young crew was not afraid to get their hands dirty and make a name for themselves in their dangerous world. Their tight bond and fearless actions made them a force to be reckoned with.

In September of 1968, Victor DeCaro found himself in handcuffs after an altercation outside the Living Room Lounge in Agawam. It all began when Ralph Ramsdell and his female friends were asked to leave a booth because the bar's co-owner, Amadeo Santaniello, was on his way, and they were sitting in his usual spot. As Ramsdell, his wife, and his sister were leaving, the round of drinks they ordered arrived. The waitress told them to pay for them before leaving, and they refused, walking away without touching their drinks.

Waitress Gladys Heath recounted, "I went to the back of the bar and talked to Victor DeCaro. He is almost always in the place, and Amadeo, the owner, is his brother-in-law."

Victor went after them to ask them to pay. A fight broke out between DeCaro and Ramsdell, culminating in a violent punch that sent the man tumbling down a flight of concrete stairs, his head bouncing off each step. Unaffected by the man's fall, DeCaro stood at the top of the stairs and called to another man.

"Get him out of here and use the pay phone across the street," he shouted.

Ramsdell suffered a fractured skull and died the following day.

In 1970, his actions finally caught up with him. The verdict was handed down: 8-12 years for manslaughter. But two months later, he found himself in a place he never expected - a minimum-security forestry camp. This was not the usual fate for someone convicted of such a severe crime. The prison officials were taken aback, admitting it was highly unusual.

Chief Public Defender Edward McBride Jr. said, "The mechanics to do that thing had to be high-powered. It has to come from someone who had some pull. I would think it would have to come from the legislature." McBride did not speculate which legislator would have stepped in on DeCaro's behalf.

Why was he being treated differently?

It wasn't long before the truth came out. The jurors had access to a newspaper that revealed his true identity - the son-in-law of notorious mobster Skyball Scibelli, the underboss of the Springfield crew. This revelation was enough for him to appeal his sentence. And it worked. In October 1971, after only serving two and a half years, he was released from Walpole State Prison.

As he walked free, the taste of victory was bittersweet. Rumors began circulating that he was having an affair with Big Nose Sam Cufari's most recent wife.

Months later, on the evening of May 18, 1972, Victor DeCaro found himself in the company of his father-in-law, Skyball Scibelli. They were at Ciro's Restaurant, the headquarters of mob boss Big Nose Sam in the South End of Springfield. As they sat enjoying their meal, DeCaro received a call from his close friend and fellow gangster, Amadeo Santaniello, who needed a replacement bartender at their Living Room Lounge by the Agawam riverfront. Skyball offered to drive DeCaro to the bar since Victor did not drive and dropped him at the club's back door.

That night at the Living Room Lounge was a turning point that would change everything. The setting, with its dimly lit interior and the gentle flow of the nearby river, masked the sinister events about to unfold.

DeCaro was never seen alive again.

His fate was sealed when he crossed the line and cheated on Skyball's daughter with the wife of another gangster, despite Scibelli's repeated warnings. As a result, Skyball was forced to carry out a contract on DeCaro under the orders of their bosses back in New York. And so, DeCaro's lifeless body was found two months later, floating in the Connecticut River, bound, beaten, and riddled with bullet wounds. The once powerful and feared mafia enforcer met his end in a sleeping bag dumped in the river.

The killing of 29-year-old Victor DeCaro remains one of the most infamous and unsolved crimes in the history of Western Massachusetts. According to underworld circles, two of Cufari's hired guns, Anthony "Skip" Delevo and Franky Campiti, were waiting for DeCaro to appear at the bar that fateful evening. Despite being suspects, they were never formally charged due to a lack of incriminating evidence.

Others point to Francis "Franny" Soffen, who is serving time for the murders of fellow bank robbers Gary Dube and Stephen Perrot.

When Dube testified against him before the grand jury, Soffen's paranoia took hold. He knew that Dube's betrayal would not be the last. His friend and partner in crime, Stephen Perrot, would surely follow suit. And so, in desperation and madness, Soffen silenced Dube and Perrot forever.

However, the disappearance of Vincent Palmieri, Gary Dube, and Victor DeCaro within weeks of each other in 1972 raised suspicions that Soffen was somehow involved. They all followed a similar pattern, with the victims being executed in a manner typical of old-school gangster hits - shot in the head and dumped in nearby rivers. Vincent Palmieri went missing on May 1, Gary Dube disappeared on May 8, and Victor DeCaro on May 18, 1972.

Dube, a bartender from Feeding Hills with a criminal past, ran with a rough crowd. On June 23, 1972, his body was found by a deckhand on a ferry traveling between Rocky Hill and Glastonbury, Connecticut. It was wrapped in plastic, and his feet were bound with a sheet. Bullet wounds covered the back of his head, and his body was splattered with lime. Investigators noted an empty gun holster still attached to his hip. His body was not discovered until six weeks after his disappearance.

Palmieri, a father of nine, met his demise when four bullets were pumped into the back of his head. His body was eventually discovered on June 1, 1972, in a remote river in East Barnet, Vermont, approximately 350 miles away from his home on Staten Island, New York. His body was found by a worker at a sewage treatment facility, who noticed his decomposing body dressed only in pants, socks, and boots. An autopsy revealed that Palmieri had sustained three gunshot wounds to the back and side of his head, presumably from a small-caliber weapon.

The lone common thread between them was the firearm that ended their lives – a .38-caliber Smith & Wesson pistol. Ballistics analysis by the Connecticut State Police matched the gun used to kill DeCaro to the one responsible for the murders of Dube and Palmieri.

Franny Soffen, who maintained close connections with high-ranking members of the Italian mafia in Western

Massachusetts, died behind bars as the cases remained unsolved.

DeCaro was seen as a rising star among the younger gangsters, and his killing had a profound impact on the local mob scene. Many believe that if he had not been killed, Al Bruno would not have risen to power and become the infamous mobster he was. DeCaro was on the path to becoming a "made" man in the Genevese crime family, potentially even the boss in the future.

Chapter 2

Making His Bones

With a ruthless demeanor and slick charm, Big Al Bruno quickly became a force to be reckoned with in the East Coast mafia scene. Under the guidance of the rough-around-the-edges Skyball Scibelli, Bruno honed his instincts for traditional rackets and rose the ranks in the 1970s and 1980s with a ferocious hunger for power.

In 1976, the public first heard of Big Al Bruno's involvement in organized crime.

He was named as a suspect after 31 bookmakers in Greater Springfield were nabbed alongside members of the criminal underworld. During this operation, authorities seized $200,000 in cash and betting equipment from one of Bruno's offices. As the case was trialed, federal agents tied Big Al Bruno and his associates, including Skyball Scibelli, to the infamous "Vito Genovese Crime Family" and the "La Costa Nostra."

Fueled by a burning desire for respect and wealth, Bruno became a mastermind of sports gambling and extortion, overseeing the operations of the Scibelli brothers. His connections and alliances stretched far and wide as he built valuable business relationships with wise guys across the country.

Big Al had no qualms about getting involved in the dangerous world of organized crime, getting his hands dirty with mob "wet work." Bruno was a triggerman responsible for the 1979 assassination of notorious Springfield gangster Antonio Facente. He took pride in his role and bragged about it to his associates.

Two years prior, Antonio Facente was freed from behind bars after a successful appeal of his 1972 conviction for the high-profile gangland slaying of Springfield liquor store owner William Griffin. Facente had allegedly killed Griffin over an unpaid debt between the two men. The conviction was overturned due in part to the use of ethnic slurs by Matthew "Matty" Ryan, the district attorney, during the trial.

However, Ryan and Facente also clashed over more personal matters.

When Tony Facente returns to Springfield, he becomes romantically involved with Matty Ryan's daughter. Ryan is a prominent State U.S. attorney, wielding control over the entire Western Mass region. He is a formidable man with numerous connections and associates in Washington, D.C. Ryan is upset with Tony screwing his daughter and feeding her cocaine. He turns to the mafia for assistance, requesting that they handle Tony and keep him away from her.

Big Nose Sam attempted to sever Tony's ties with Ryan's daughter, but his efforts were unsuccessful. Tony continued to sell coke and run around with her.

The sun had just crept up over the horizon when Matty awoke to the smell of freshly brewed coffee. As he made his way to the kitchen, he found Tony Facente sitting at the table, dressed only in his boxers, sipping on a steaming cup of coffee.

"Good morning, Matty," Tony greeted him with a wise-ass smirk, his words dripping with sarcasm.

Matty felt his temper flare up at the sight of Tony's cocky attitude. He had had enough of his wisecracks and decided to take matters into his own hands. Without a second thought, he marched down to the mobsters' headquarters, demanding that they put a stop to Tony's behavior before things got out of hand.

Skyball Scibelli, a notorious and dangerous man, stepped forward and warned Tony, "Back off, or else we'll kill ya; this is your last warning."

But Tony wasn't one to back down easily. In a daring move, he pulled out a gun and aimed it directly at Skyball.

"I don't listen to you, I don't answer to you, I don't answer to nobody. I'm my own man. You guys don't tell me what to do," he declared defiantly.

The tension between the two men was intense, each daring the other to make a move. Tony's risky and audacious move defied someone as threatening as Skyball. But it was a testament to the kind of person Tony was— bold, fearless, and always ready to take a stand for himself.

That was just the kind of person he was—crazy, but with a set of steel balls.

Skyball had to report back to Big Nose Sam. It was clear that this guy wasn't listening. Tony had revealed that his brothers from Calabria were coming, and he would soon have his own crew. The situation was escalating quickly. They needed a plan. But this guy couldn't just be given a beating. He was uncontrollable and dangerous. He'd come back and kill you and your family; he'd slaughter everybody, so they made the plan to murder Tony.

It was their only option. They went back to him under the pretense that they would make him. They needed someone like him - wild and unpredictable - to make their organization more feared. Facente thought he was getting straightened out with the local Springfield crew of the Genovese crime family.

He arrived at the Mount Carmel Social Club in the South End of Springfield, dressed in his finest suit and feeling invincible. Al Bruno greets him outside and leads him down to the club basement. Waiting for him in the dimly lit cellar are Cufari's henchmen, Skip DeLevo and Jake Nettis, viciously striking him with Louisville Sluggers. They brutally beat and tortured him for daring to point a gun at the underboss Skyball.

To ensure he can never seek revenge, they raise their weapons and fire multiple rounds into his body. Lying lifeless on the floor, Al Bruno approaches and presses his gun against Facente's head, blowing a gaping hole into it.

Delevo and Nettis are livid. Bruno's shot creates a big mess on the floor and the walls, with blood spraying everywhere. His head, now gushing blood like a fire hose, had to be plugged with a baby diaper. The trio then tosses Facente's limp body into the trunk of a car, with Felix Tranghese driving it to a secluded parking lot on the outskirts of Springfield.

Subsequently, authorities discovered Tony Facente's diaper-wearing corpse in the trunk of his Chrysler Cordoba. Tony had been brutally tortured and shot six times, with a second diaper stuffed into the cavity in his head.

The ambitious and rising star, Big Al Bruno, boasted about committing this grisly murder to gain favor with Hampden District Attorney Matty Ryan. Despite being implicated in Facente's death, Bruno was never formally charged, and all records containing informant statements regarding the incident remain sealed in Hampden County Superior Court, under the jurisdiction of Matty Ryan.

"Making his bones" and receiving a button, Big Al Bruno rose to top lieutenant for the Scibelli's. A skilled and influential figure in organized crime, Bruno frequented the mafia scene along the eastern coast, mingling with and conveying messages to leaders of crime families in New York, Boston, Providence, Connecticut, New Jersey, Philadelphia, and Northeast Pennsylvania.

One year later, a patrol officer in New Britain, Connecticut, noticed a 1977 Lincoln Continental repeatedly driving around the Willow Street welfare section of town. He observed that the rear license plate was hanging down, barely attached by a single bolt. The officer pulled over the vehicle and discovered a bolt-action shotgun lying on the passenger floor. Further investigation revealed a shotgun on the back seat with six 12-gauge rounds, a loaded .38-

caliber revolver, a high-standard .22-caliber derringer with 13 magnum rounds, and a blackjack.

Anthony Delevo, Jake Nettis, and Felix Tranghese rode in that car, the same three that murdered Antonio Facente and discarded his body.

The authorities were never able to uncover the reason behind the trio's possession of such a dangerous arsenal. But, soon after his release from prison, Felix Tranghese "received his button," officially becoming a member of the Genovese's Springfield Crew, sponsored by Big Al Bruno.

Despite never becoming a made member himself, Amedeo Santaniello played a small role in one of the more infamous botched mob slayings in New England mafia history. The bungled 1981 hit targeted Joe Maruca, a bookie, thief, and henchman for the Bufalino crime family.

Russell Bufalino controlled the northeastern Pennsylvania and upstate New York regions. According to syndicate higher-ups, Joe Maruca was suspected of skimming sports gambling earnings and "eating alone," or keeping it to himself, rather than sharing with other members of the Bufalino crime family in Binghamton.

As a result, he was marked for death. Seeking assistance, the Bufalino Family turned to their deep ties with the Genovese clan, who then assigned Skyball and his crew to carry out the hit. Scibelli then delegated the task to Big Al, along with Springfield mafiosi member Jake Nettis and Hartford mob associate John "Sonny" Castagna, to carry out the murder.

Bruno had met Maruca once before, in the company of Skyball, when the three were on a gambling junket to Curacao.

Two meetings were held to plan the killing during the summer of August 1981. Bruno, accompanied by Skyball, talked with Sonny outside Geno's Barber Shop on Main Street, Springfield. Skyball mentioned, "he had something he wanted him to do for him."

Castagna joined Bruno and Skyball a few weeks later at the Venezia Restaurant on Dickinson Street, which Amadeo Santaniello owned. During this meeting, Skyball elaborated on the plan's details, including Nettis' involvement. As they sipped on drinks, Big Al and Skyball reviewed Al's role in the plan.

Castagna first met Skyball Scibelli and Big Al Bruno in the late 1960s when Bruno was working as Scibelli's driver, and Castagna was a frequent visitor to the Living Room Lounge in Agawam. He especially enjoyed going on Sunday nights when bars in Connecticut were closed.

The plan was to have Ellis Klepfer of Endicott, New York, send Joe Maruca to West Springfield in the guise of meeting with a man called "Mike Demarco" and collecting a debt. Klepfer was an associate of Anthony "Guv" Guarnieri, an organized crime leader in Binghamton, New York. Jake Nettis, masquerading as "Mike Demarco," was a physically imposing enforcer and assassin. The two met at Howard Johnson's on Riverdale Road.

Their following encounter would occur at an Agawam barn owned by Big Al's brother, where Maruca was to inspect some stolen goods. "Mike Demarco" would drive Joe to Bruno's farm. It was there they would kill Maruca.

Before the planned attack, Al Bruno and Skyball informed Castagna that he, Cosmo "Pinky" Panarelli from Worcester, and Anthony Delevo would be posted nearby to assist in placing Maruca's body in a car trunk and disposing of the corpse after the hit. Castagna was instructed to use a plastic sheet to wrap the body to minimize blood on the floor.

Sonny and Al changed their clothes at the Venezia Restaurant in case they became bloodied in the attack. Castagna changed into a sweatshirt and old pants while Bruno wore a black jumpsuit over his clothes and taped his shooting hand. They then left their jewelry, wallet, rings, and identification so that nothing could be left at the scene to link them to the crime. They gave the items to the restaurant's owner, Amedeo Santaniello, to hold for them as they departed to kill Maruca.

Bruno gave Castagna a gun and a pair of fur-lined gloves while he armed himself with a .38 caliber handgun. Then, Bruno drove the blue delivery truck to the barn, arriving around 7 p.m. They then reviewed the plan again, with a few hours remaining before the target's arrival. However, their wait was interrupted by a fierce thunderstorm.

On that rainy August night, the car carrying Jake Nettis and Joe Maruca pulled up to a barn in Agawam around 9 p.m. As they arrived, Nettis gestured for Maruca to wait while he turned on the lights. Maruca's glasses were blurred from the rain as he ran from the car to the barn at Nettis' request. They were in rural Agawam, where Maruca had been brought to inspect a shipment of hijacked canned tomatoes. As the rain pelted down, Maruca's vision was obstructed by the water droplets on his glasses. He could barely make out a shadow moving in the distance.

Suddenly, a bullet grazed the top of his right ear.

Maruca flinched and turned to see Nettis standing behind him, holding a gun with the muzzle still flashing. Panicked, Maruca lunged for the door, trying to escape the danger. But before he could make it past Nettis, he was hit multiple times - in the ear, the right side of his jaw, his right forearm, and his right bicep. As he struggled to break free, he realized that Nettis was the one who had shot him. The hit was meant to be fatal, but the second gunman, Big Al Bruno, "froze" at the last moment, unable to pull the trigger. In that split second, Maruca's life was saved, but he was left reeling from the betrayal of someone he had trusted.

Gunfire erupted from the other side of the barn. Maruca's heart raced as he shoved past Jake Nettis and stumbled down the grassy slope toward the dark country road. The sound of shots rang out, causing him to drop his glasses and the knife he had been carrying. A sharp pain seared through his leg as a bullet struck him. Amidst the chaos, someone shouted, "Get the car. Get the car."

Meanwhile, inside the barn, Castagna's senses were on high alert. He heard three or four gunshots but couldn't decipher how many shooters there were. He was supposed to wait for Bruno's signal to leave his hiding spot, but it never came. Fearing the worst, Castagna rushed to the doorway. Castagna knew something was wrong when he didn't see a body on the floor. He had been instructed to use a pillow to absorb blood, but it seemed unnecessary now. With a sense of urgency, Castagna darted outside.

Al Bruno and Jake Nettis were chasing the guy down the hill. They were shooting at him. The scene was chaotic, with bullets flying and voices shouting. The tension was intense as Castagna took in the frantic scene before him. The setting was a picturesque country road flanked by rolling hills, but now it was marred by violence. As Al Bruno and Jakie continued their pursuit, their guns blazed, their voices filled with rage. Castagna could feel his heart pounding in his chest as he watched the dangerous scene unfold. It was a moment he would never forget.

Although Jake Nettis shot him in the head in the barn and five more times while chasing him down an embankment, Maruca just kept running.

Ignoring the blood trickling down his leg, Maruca sprinted towards a nearby house, his heart pounding in his chest. With desperation, he pounded on the front door, hoping for someone to answer. When no one did, he grabbed a lawn sprinkler and hurled it through a window, shattering the glass. The sound of a car approaching made Maruca's stomach drop. He knew his attackers were not giving up. Bullets whizzed past him as he ran towards the next house.

Marcia McKenzie's 11-month-old daughter was trembling in her arms, her tiny body shaking with fear from the violent thunderstorm raging outside. Marcia heard a loud, frantic pounding at the back door as she tried to soothe her. Her heart raced, thinking it could be her husband returning home. Without hesitation, she opened the door, only to be met with a sight that made her blood run cold. A man, covered in blood, forcefully pushed his way into her home. His eyes were wild and desperate as he pleaded for help.

"Please, I won't get blood on anything. Just let me sit in a chair in the middle of the room," he begged.

Marcia's instincts kicked in, and she quickly dialed 911 for help. But when the police called back to verify her location, she couldn't contain her panic.

"There's a man here; he's dying in my kitchen! Why are you calling back?" she screamed into the phone. In the chaos, Marcia's eyes landed on something glinting in the dim light of her kitchen. She cautiously approached and realized it was a bullet lodged in the weathered barnboard of her front door. The reality of the situation hit her like a ton of bricks – this was no ordinary night.

Meanwhile, Al Bruno's complexion had turned ghostly white, his nerves clearly on edge as he trembled with fear. Both men knew that they had fired shots at Joe Maruca, but the exact location of the bullets was uncertain.

"They must have hit him a few times," Castagna recounted, his voice filled with adrenaline.

The chase had ended, and the men gathered to discuss their actions. Jake Nettis believed his shots had also struck Maruca, his words laced with a mix of pride and fear.

Sonny Castagna's clothes were caked with mud and dirt, evidence of the intense chase up the hill. He struggled to catch his breath, the result of years of smoking three packs a day. As he emerged from the hill, he felt like he was on the brink of death.

As the tension settled, Nettis sped off, leaving Castagna and Bruno to seek refuge in a nearby barn. They quickly changed their clothes, trying to shake off the intense encounter. The three men then went to Casa di Lisa Restaurant, owned by Bruno's brother in Agawam. Bruno handed the guns to Skyball at the restaurant, who then passed them on to another man. The exchange was done with a sense of urgency, a silent acknowledgment of the gravity of their actions.

Sergent Gary Nardi rushed to Maruca's aid after the shooting on South Westfield Street. He urged Maruca to keep talking, desperate to keep him conscious. Maruca, struggling to stay alive, asked Nardi if he was going to die. The next thing Maruca remembered was waking up in the emergency room at Baystate Medical Center in Springfield. He was surrounded by Agawam and state police, bombarding him with questions.

Maruca, determined to withhold information, refused to reveal who had sent him to Springfield or his attacker's name, only referring to him as "Mike Demarco." He even tried to throw them off by initially identifying his attacker as "DiCarlo." Maruca feared it was a "hit" and didn't want to start fingering anybody until he knew what was going on.

Within 24 hours of the shooting, Maruca spent 45 minutes to an hour with Officer Alan Collins, trying to develop a composite drawing of the perpetrator. Collins watched as Maruca's tired eyes scanned the page, making slight changes here and there.

"I'm satisfied with this," Maruca said, but Collins could tell he wasn't. Collins wanted to spend more time perfecting the drawing, but Maruca insisted he would take care of it himself. The drawing didn't resemble Jake Nettis at all, and he didn't tell them anything.

After nearly 48 hours in the hospital, Maruca checked himself out, determined to take matters into his own hands. He promised, "I'll take care of this myself." With a sense of determination in his step, Maruca left the hospital, ready to seek justice for the shooting.

Agawam Police Officer James Lewis visited Casa di Lisa restaurant in Agawam to inform Frank Bruno of a distressing event. A man had been attacked in the barn adjacent to his home, where his in-laws were looking after his children. The barn was situated within 100 yards of Al Bruno's residence. Upon hearing the news, Frank was taken aback.

"I can't believe it," he exclaimed. In disbelief, he quickly called his home and, after hanging up, told Lewis that his in-laws were unaware of anything happening.

"They heard nothing. They don't know anything. They were watching TV."

As Officer Lewis made his way out of the restaurant between 9:30 p.m. and 10 p.m., he encountered a man entering wearing a brown shirt with white polka dots. Later that night, another officer informed Lewis that this man was Big Al Bruno, the reputed second-in-command of the Mafia faction in Western Massachusetts.

Officer Alan Collins later discovered a bullet lodged in the side of Frank Bruno's house, with two more found in the front of the house at 932 South Westfield Street, where Maruca sought refuge.

Maruca lived in fear, worried that he might face another attempt on his life. He waited three months until Anthony "Guv" Guarnieri reassured him that there would be no consequences.

During the initial incident, Jakie Nettis accused Bruno of "chilling" in the barn. When you say "chilling," it means freezing, not doing the right thing. Jakie then registered a beef with Frank "Franky Pugs" Pugliano of West Springfield, causing a big stir.

While all the other members had already established their presence elsewhere on that particular night, Pugliano found himself in a dangerous position due to his lack of knowledge of the plan. "Pugs" was somewhat of an outcast among the small group of eight or nine "made members" in the Greater Springfield area, as his loyalty primarily lay with Raymond Patriarca and his crime family in Providence, Rhode Island, despite being a soldier in the Genovese family.

A sit-down was arranged in Springfield to mediate Pugliano's grievance and Nettis' claim that Bruno had failed to carry out the execution. Franky Pugliano, Skyball Scibelli, Jakie Nettis, Big Al Bruno, Sonny Castagna, and others attended. Big Nose Sam Cufari presided over the meeting.

When the Springfield meeting failed to resolve the situation, Pugliano planned to seek satisfaction from mobsters in New York. Franky Pugs informed Skyball that he intended to go to New York to file a complaint. Skyball warned him not to escalate the situation, but Franky remained resolute. He told him he wouldn't be intimidated and would go to New York.

Eventually, Patriarca family soldier Billy "Wild Guy" Grasso became aware of the situation and confronted Franky Pugs.

"You need to make an issue out of it. How come everybody in Springfield knew about it, and you didn't know about it? This wasn't the right thing to do. You could have been in serious trouble over here," Grasso advised him.

Grasso urged Pugliano to complain to "The Commission," comprised of the bosses of the five New York

Mafia families and the dons of the Chicago and Philadelphia families. Its function is to resolve disputes arising between families. The complaint was referred to New York, but Grasso failed to speak on Franky Pugliano's behalf.

Grasso promised to back Pugliano but did not, and that caused ill will between the two that would come back and sting Grasso in the future.

Later, during a dinner at an Atlantic City casino, Big Al confided his concerns to the Scarfo family's underboss, Phil Leonetti, and Mafioso Larry "Yogi" Merlino. He expressed his fear of retaliation from the now 80-year-old mob captain Skyball Scibelli, who was not happy with him for the failed assassination attempt. Skyball was upset because the target survived and felt he would have a problem.

Bruno, who was also known by the alias "Mr. Brown," had crossed paths with Phil Leonetti many years prior when Phil had a meeting with Baba Scibelli, brother of Skyball Scibelli, at a Philadelphia restaurant owned by Philip "The Chicken Man" Testa. The two were introduced as members, "Amica Nostra," or Our Friend. This particular greeting was reserved for when one member of the Mafia was introduced to a third member by another member.

They quickly became acquainted, discussing matters concerning their respective families, including Bruno's and Leonetti's. They even socialized together in Fort Lauderdale, Florida, alongside Germanio "Jerry" Sarno from Springfield, at a residence and on a boat owned by Leonetti's uncle, Nicodemo "Little Nicky" Scarfo, who was the boss of the Philadelphia crime family.

Scarfo had his sights set on taking over the Bufalino territory in northern Pennsylvania and western New York state, and he even approached Louis "Bobby" Manna, consigliere of the Genovese crime family, to discuss the matter. During the early 1980s, Leonetti also assisted Bruno and Scibelli when they faced a labor issue in their gambling junket business. They resolved the problem with the help of a union official from New Jersey, who intervened on their behalf.

In the spring of 1983, the infamous Big Nose Sam Cufari quietly relinquished his position as leader of the Springfield mob. His once powerful physique, now weakened and partially paralyzed from a stroke, had left him unable to maintain control. Despite rapidly declining health, he attempted to maintain a semblance of power, but it was clear that his time as a feared and respected leader was over. Forced into semi-retirement, he retreated from the public eye, his presence now a mere shadow of its former self.

Taking his place was Francesco "Franky Skyball" Scibelli, who was joined by his two brothers, Albert "Baba" and Anthony "Turk," and "Big Al" Bruno.

Multiple prison sentences marked Skyball's rise to regional boss as prosecutors became more aggressive toward organized crime. He was reminiscent of an earlier era, often wide-eyed at the mere mention of "the syndicate" or the Mafia, and constantly complained about his sentences and the media's scrutiny.

Skyball Scibelli, the eldest of four brothers, grew up in the city's South End. He graduated from the former Howard Street School and remained a well-known figure in the community. He was notorious for his explosive anger and his powerful influence over those involved in the illegal bookmaking business, which was a key source of income for organized crime groups.

Dubbed "The Scholar Group," Skyball Scibelli and Andrew Pradella possessed an unmatched talent for predicting the outcomes of professional and college sports, making them highly valuable to bookmakers nationwide. Their expertise was utilized in setting betting lines.

In Vincent Teresa's 1967 memoir "My Life in the Mafia," Skyball Scibelli was mentioned for his exceptional handicapping skills and the fear he instilled in anyone who posed a threat to him.

That same year, a Life magazine article linked Pradella and Skyball to Boston Celtics legend Bob Cousy, who was then coaching at the College of the Holy Cross.

In one conversation recorded by federal investigators, Skyball Scibelli tells New York Genovese crime family boss Anthony "Fat Tony" Salerno, "We're doing good up there running the thing. You got me? I'm doing a good job for you."

In November 1983, Salvatore "Big Nose Sam" Cufari, the reputed boss of organized crime in Western Massachusetts and Northern Connecticut, passed away after a prolonged illness.

Over 1,500 people attended his wake, and a procession of 100 cars, including five loaded with more than 250 floral arrangements, made its way from the church to St. Michael's Cemetery. During his funeral, a relative shared with mourners how Cufari had contributed to constructing a convent for Italian nuns at Mount Marie in Holyoke. However, there were doubts whether it was a genuine act of remorse for Skyball's past transgression. Two decades prior, a Roman Catholic nun dropped a dime on Skyball for running an illegal gambling ring from the telephone booths at Providence Hospital in 1961.

Another speaker mentioned how Cufari had aided immigrant workers in securing employment and generously donated a whole floor of furniture to the Brightside orphanage in West Springfield.

In the wake of Big Nose Sam's passing, investigators into organized crime pinpointed Big Al Bruno as a lieutenant within the Genovese crime family, headquartered in New York City.

With his larger-than-life personality, Big Al was a fixture in the South End neighborhood of Springfield, where he owned several restaurants, bars, and nightclubs notorious for their ties to the mob. His influence also extended to Hartford, Connecticut, where he oversaw the gambling operations for the local faction of the mob.

Referred to as second-in-command to newly appointed family leader Skyball Scibelli, Big Al Bruno worked closely with Amedeo Santaniello. Under Skyball's direction, Amedeo managed the family's policy lottery operations and supervised gambling activities in various parts of New York on behalf of the Springfield crew.

In the same year, Big Al was a key figure in a gambling, drug, and pornography ring in Worcester County, along with over 50 others who were targeted in a crackdown on organized crime. As part of "Operation Big League," wiretaps revealed that Bruno never had to seek approval from Skyball before making decisions. In a bookmaking scheme, Bruno was also linked to Carlo Mastrototaro, second-in-command to Raymond Patriarca.

Soon after, Bruno, along with his right-hand man Anthony Liquori and Amedeo Santaniello, were arrested for forcefully taking control of an independent gambling operation in Albany and Schenectady, New York. Albany has always been a bunch of "cowboys" until the organized crew from Springfield stepped in. The operators primarily took bets on football games and horse racing and ran an illegal daily numbers lottery.

The Springfield crew's expansion into the Albany area was approved by the National Crime Commission in New York City as a trade-off for losing gambling operations in Hartford and New Haven, Connecticut, to the Patriarca family years ago. Big Nose Sam brokered this arrangement at the Monte Carlo restaurant in West Springfield, Massachusetts, which Franky Pugs owned. Al Bruno, under the supervision of the ailing Skyball, oversaw the takeover.

Meanwhile, Anthony Liquori, who had relocated to Albany, managed the crew's bookmaking and numbers operations as Bruno's representative. Amadeo transported gaming profits back to the Springfield crew as an intermediary and courier between Bruno and Liquori.

Bruno's assertive rise in the criminal hierarchy resembles Scibelli's ascent years earlier when Big Nose Sam suffered a stroke. While Scibelli used to make all gambling decisions under Cufari's guidance, Bruno now held that authority under Skyball.

One year later, Bruno, Liquori, and Santaniello, along with Paul Pizzuto of Pittsfield, are arrested and extradited by the state of New York to face trial for the forceful takeover. Governors Mario Cuomo and Michael Dukakis orchestrated the extradition. Other participants in the takeover include "Fat Paulie" DiCocco, his father Paul "Legs" DiCocco, and Peter DiCocco, all from upstate New York. This event highlights the collusion between various figures in the state. Rick Songini goes on the lam and has not yet been apprehended.

Federal authorities pinch Amedeo for managing Skyball's lottery operation in upstate New York. Santaniello pleaded for leniency before the judge, expressing his lack of previous run-ins with the law.

"I've never been in trouble before," Amedeo told the judge. "If I can get a break, I'd really appreciate it."

Despite his appeal, he was sentenced to 18 months in prison. Anthony Liquori, on the other hand, was found guilty of running an unlawful gambling enterprise and received a one-year prison sentence.

Meanwhile, Skyball was handed a 6-year term for his involvement in the racketeering scheme. Big Al Bruno, described by his lawyer as "an inveterate gambler," admitted to racketeering charges in January of 1988 and was given a 5-year federal prison sentence.

Shortly afterward, Mario Fiore was busted for running a bookmaking and racketeering operation.

During his prime, Fiore was a part of Big Nose Sam's entourage and oversaw the gambling and travel operations of crew bosses Skyball and Baba Scibelli. This included arranging chartered airplane packages to and from Las Vegas in the 1960s and 1970s before legalized gambling was available in Atlantic City. These junkets, departing from Bradley Airport, transported players from Springfield to the Dunes in Las Vegas or other international resorts. The agreement was that the gamblers place large bets in exchange for a round-trip flight, accommodations, and meals.

Fiore conducted his operations from the World Tours office, working with Andrew Pradella and his son Andrew Jr. However, the Las Vegas Gaming Commission eventually revoked their permits to operate due to their connections to organized crime figures. Notably, Skyball Scibelli had accumulated a massive gambling debt at the Dunes casino. Although Pradella had advocated for the casino to extend credit to Skyball, he later claimed he couldn't reach him for repayment. It was later revealed that Pradella was paying Scibelli a monthly salary as an employee of the junket service.

Less than a year later, amid serving his federal prison sentence, Big Al was able to maneuver, through his "connections," a controversial 14-day "unsupervised" leave to travel abroad for his father's funeral in Salerno, Italy. This was a highly uncommon event and a significant violation of official Federal Bureau of Prisons protocols. The circumstances surrounding Bruno's approved furlough immediately came under scrutiny by law enforcement. However, the subsequent investigation went nowhere.

Chapter 3

You Won't See Him Anymore

Over the years, two rival factions of organized crime, the Genovese and Patriarca families, have thrived in New England, raking in substantial profits from traditional rackets such as illegal gambling, extortion, and loansharking. Despite their illicit activities, they have maintained a peaceful coexistence and amicably settled beefs, often with the intervention of ranking members of the Mafia in New York City.

The Genovese family's presence was established in the 1920s, with the Patriarcas later entering the scene from Worcester.

The Patriarca family oversees Mafia affairs across New England and manages the West Springfield operation led by Frank "Franky Pugs" Pugliano. Traditionally, the West

Springfield group has been allowed to operate, although strict boundaries have been set.

On the Springfield side of the Connecticut River in the South End, Skyball Scibelli has been pulling the strings since 1983, wielding control over the local faction of the Genovese crime family headquartered in New York City.

After the death from a heart attack of "Old Man" Raymond Patriarca in the summer of 1984, his son Raymond "Junior" Patriarca, who was seen as weaker and less capable, took over as the leader of the La Cosa Nostra family that dominates most of New England. With the support of the powerful Gambino crime family in New York, he could keep the peace within his organization.

However, in 1987, his original second-in-command, Ilario "Larry Baione" Zannino, was sentenced to thirty years, weakening Junior's position. He appointed Billy "Wild Guy" Grasso as his new underboss to solidify his control.

During the 1970s, Billy Grasso united the Bridgeport Independent Refuse Collectors Association members and laid down the law.

"If there are any attempts to compete, we will equip trucks with enough muscle and send them into Bridgeport. There will be arms broken and bodies in the river," the independent haulers were told.

These reckless words ultimately led to his downfall, as Grasso was convicted of extortion and conspiracy, leading to his incarceration at the federal penitentiary in Atlanta for a 10-year term.

Surprisingly, Grasso found himself sharing a cell with Raymond Patriarca Sr., a notorious bootlegger from the

Depression era who had built the most powerful criminal organization in New England, the Patriarca crime family.

"The best thing that ever happened to me," Grasso later told an associate, "was when they sent me to Atlanta."

Patriarca arranged for the transfer of Grasso from the Colombo crime family to his organization so he could oversee Patriarca's rackets in Connecticut. Grasso was groomed in the mob by the Colombo's Connecticut capo, Ralph "Whitey" Tropiano, a former triggerman for the notorious Murder, Inc. crew in New York.

However, in 1980, when Whitey returned from retirement to the chaotic underworld of Connecticut, the Patriarca mobster was none too pleased. Eventually, Grasso made a trip to Rhode Island to discuss the need to take care of Tropiano with Patriarca.

"Whitey is bad for business," Grasso argued, "and he brings the FBI with him wherever he goes; the Feds are always up his ass."

Raymond Patriarca, never one to shy away from sanctioning murders and never pleased with the New York families' freely operating on his turf, essentially exclaimed, "What ya' waitin' for!"

On April 2, 1980, Whitey was in his old neighborhood of Bath Beach, Brooklyn, where he'd grown up and made his bones for La Cosa Nostra. At 2:25 p.m., he was walking down 63rd Street with his nephew when suddenly, two cars screeched to a halt, and two masked gunmen with stockings over their faces leaped out and blasted away. The nephew managed to escape unscathed, but Whitey was mercilessly riddled with bullets in the head, back, and stomach.

After walking free from prison in 1988, Francis "Cadillac Frank" Salemme was put in charge by "Junior" Patriarca to oversee the Boston wing of the crime family. In essence, Junior utilized Grasso and Salemme as his protection against Beantown's underworld figures, including Vincent "Vinnie" Ferrara in the North End and his top ally, esteemed "OG" Joe "J.R." Russo from East Boston. These individuals did not respect the younger Patriarca and wanted him out of the picture.

Despite already earning millions of dollars from bookmakers in eastern Connecticut, the ambitious "Wild Guy" Grasso set his sights on expanding his territory to include Springfield and parts of Worcester, which the Genovese family had long controlled. He began enlisting members of the Springfield crew, including Gaetano Milano, William "Hot Dog Billy" Grant, John "Sonny" Castagna, and his stepson John "Jackie" Johns.

Grasso cleverly secured Sonny Castagna's allegiance by paying off a debt he owed to Scibelli and Bruno, known loan sharks in the area.

In 1970, Sonny Castagna bombed a Glastonbury grocery store, for which he was never charged. He served a six-year prison sentence in the late 1970s for manslaughter, resulting from a dispute in a bar where a man was bothering another man and his wife. Castagna and Thomas Forni initially planned to fight outside the bar but drove to a nearby park instead. Castagna claims that the fight never occurred and that he asked Forni for a ride back to the bar. However, during the car ride, Forni suddenly pulled out a .357 Magnum and lost control of the vehicle, causing it to crash into a telephone pole. The gun went off, injuring Forni, who later passed away.

Castagna told this version of events.

Following his parole release, Castagna worked for six months in construction before catching the attention of Skyball Scibelli and Big Al Bruno, who "sent for him."

This led to Castagna becoming involved in picking up numbers for the duo and shylocking, lending money at excessively high interest rates, typically ranging from 3 to 4 percent per week. However, Skyball and Big Al extended loans to Castagna at a lower interest rate of 1 to 1 1/2 percent weekly, subject to their ever-changing attitudes.

"It depended on what mood they were in at the time," Castagna says.

Castagna had a falling out with Skyball and Bruno when he "put a beard on the shy," adding a phony name to his list of those who owed him "juice." He did this to conceal the money he had siphoned from the loan pool to cover his gambling losses.

Once this was uncovered, he had multiple meetings in the Greater Springfield area to try and resolve the matter.

"I was afraid at the time," he admitted. "Getting killed, my legs broken, or getting hit in the head with a bat."

Castagna was approached on Asylum Street in Hartford by Francesco "Franky" Campiti, who informed him that Skyball and Big Al were looking for him. Campiti suggested he "go away for two or three days" while the problem was sorted out.

Campiti, who is currently serving prison terms totaling 40 to 60 years for heading a cocaine distribution network, is "with" Franky Pugliano.

Castagna, who disappeared for three to four days, received word from Campiti that Billy Grasso from New Haven was assisting in resolving the beef.

He described his relationship with Grasso as very "to the point" because he was an "associate with Springfield" and had become embroiled in activities at the Southend Social Club in Hartford, where he ran a Greek dice game called "barbute" for Grasso and Americo "Rico" Petrillo. The "house" would take a 2 to 2 1/2 percent cut from each winning bet, and since people would bet against each other, there was always a winner. On average, during good weeks, they would split $13,000 to $14,000, but one week, the "chop" or percentage amounted to $55,000. Castagna would hand over the profits to Rico Petrillo every 7 to 10 days.

In the mid-1980s, Castagna was making a living by "swindling, doing whatever he could do." In late 1986, he struck it lucky with a win of $300,000 to $400,000 at Atlantic City casinos. However, Castagna quickly blew all of it and exhausted all his available credit within four or five hours.

In addition to this reckless behavior, he also set up a sports betting operation in Hartford under the guidance of Salvatore "Butch" D'Aquila. Castagna recounted losing $11,000 in a game of barbute to John "Fast Track" Farrell, whom he called a "mechanic," skilled at using marked cards and loaded dice.

Along with Castagna, Billy Grasso recruited his stepson, John "Jackie" Johns.

Jackie was instructed in August 1986 to meet with Grasso and Salvatore "Butch" D'Aquila Jr. on a Sunday evening and meet with a man driving a white Cadillac with Florida registration.

"We gotta do something Sunday," Grasso proclaimed. Johns understood that to mean that someone was going to get hurt. Someone was in trouble.

At a supermarket parking lot, the group met with the driver of the white Cadillac. Later, at a doughnut shop, Grasso gave Jackie gloves, cautioning him always to keep them on. Richard Beedle, Grasso's top henchman, led them to a garage in Hamden near his home. Butch D'Aquila stood guard, given orders to sound the horn if someone approached.

Beedle warned the others, "Be careful. There's nosy neighbors."

Grasso led the group through the dimly lit garage and tumbled into a newly dug grave. Salvatore Caruana, the driver of the pristine white car, quickly popped open the trunk. Inside, a lifeless body was wrapped tightly in plastic, its neck bearing the marks he had been choked. Johns gingerly removed a piece of twine from the victim's neck as they stripped him down. Together, Johns and Grasso dragged the body to the open grave and tossed him in, covering him with two 50-pound bags of lime.

The dead man was Theodore Berns, a prominent Boston hotel executive who was rumored to be having an affair with Caruana's wife. The gruesome scene was a testament to the consequences of infidelity.

Following the burial, Jackie noticed Caruana dining with a lady at a Middletown restaurant, but they didn't exchange words, only stared at each other. Johns informed Grasso about the encounter and stated, "I saw that guy that we did that thing with."

Grasso responded, "You won't see him anymore."

Caruana, a major marijuana smuggler for the Patriarca family, fled in 1983 while under investigation for drug-related crimes in Boston. He has been missing since 1987, and many veteran law enforcement officials suspect he may have met the same fate as Berns, who was buried in a secret grave beneath the residential garage in Hamden.

In 1990, an informant led the FBI to the garage, only to find that someone had already unearthed the old graves, the big bones removed and replaced with a new concrete floor. The garage owner, Richard Beedle, was a former gang member of Irish bank robbers who had retired and become a locksmith. He believed he would have ended up beneath his garage if he had not cooperated with Grasso.

During the fall of 1988, Jackie Johns was laying down sod near the sidewalk outside Franco's Restaurant, a popular lunch spot for Hartford judges. Grasso was overseeing the placement of the turf when Eric Miller pulled up in his brand-new Chevy Blazer. Miller wanted to know what a big-time gangster was doing working in the dirt.

"After you finish your work at the restaurant, would you also trim my shrubs?" Miller joked.

Jackie playfully fired back, clowning with a friend about their national origins and religion. They were busting balls and just hangin' out on the corner. Miller and Jackie were familiar with each other from the Hartford Boxing Club on Charter Oak Avenue, which Miller managed and trained fighters for.

Grasso was filled with fury, believing that Miller was disrespecting an up-and-coming gangster on the fast track to becoming a sworn soldier in the Patriarca family.

The two were pulled apart, but as Miller made his way to his truck, Grasso continued to hurl expletives at him. In a fit of rage, Grasso charged towards Miller, and he grabbed a sod knife, threatening to gouge out one of Miller's eyes. Sonny Castagna arrived, and he and Johns tried to restrain the two and calm the situation.

However, Grasso lunged at Miller with the knife. In response, Eric Miller swung a big roundhouse punch, which connected with Billy's jaw and knocked him cold in front of a group of stunned onlookers at one of the busiest intersections in the South End. People who were inside Franco's rushed out to see what was happening.

When Grasso finally came to, he said he wanted to "bang" him, slang for shooting.

Grasso was embarrassed when the former boxer Miller remarked on how ineffective Grasso's blow had been, further enraging the underboss of the Patriarca Crime Family. Any guy affiliated with the mafia is aware of the unwritten law that striking a made member of La Costa Nostra is a death sentence. Consider it official; you can bank on it.

Jackie says Grasso probably made the call.

"I talked to him every day," he said. "I knew he was gonna kill him. He wanted me to find out where he went at night."

In late December 1988, Miller's lifeless body was discovered on Ledyard Street in Hartford, Connecticut, in the front seat of his car, bearing multiple gunshot wounds to the head. His girlfriend was the last person to see him alive and claimed that he left their apartment after receiving a call from Johns on the night of his death to get some food.

Upon discovering Miller's body, Grasso coldly remarked, "See what happens to a tough guy. That's my game."

No one has been charged with that crime.

Billy Grasso enlisted the support of a Springfield loyalist, William "Hot Dog Billy" Grant, who owned Augie and Ray's on Silver Lane in East Hartford.

Castagna and Grant opened the Paradiso Cafe in Hartford, where high-stakes poker games were held. Skyball Scibelli and Big Al Bruno had a "piece." Castagna received 25% of the profits, Grasso and Hot Dog Billy split another 25%, and Scibelli and Bruno claimed 50%. In addition, Grant ran an illegal numbers pool, with Castagna earning 30%, Grasso and Grant splitting 25%, and 45% going to Springfield.

After that, Grasso recruited a Springfield associate named Gaetano Milano. According to two associates familiar with Grasso, he did this to spite the Springfield Genovese crew. Milano served as an intermediary between Billy Grasso and Franky Pugs, hand-delivering messages that could not be trusted over the phone.

One Saturday afternoon, Gaetano was contacted by his friend Louie Failla, who informed him that Grasso wanted to see them the following day. Milano is perturbed as Sunday is reserved for his family, and his team, sponsored by his bar, Club 57, had a touch-football game planned for that day.

Their orders were clear: meet with Butch D'Aquila at a mini-mall in Connecticut.

Once there, they quickly jumped into another car with Grasso and Rico Petrillo and sped off to an undisclosed destination. Upon arrival, they were ushered into a room where Billy Grant and three others sat at the edge of a bed. Standing before them was Anthony "The Saint" St. Laurent, who revealed a gun from his leather jacket and declared that no one would leave alive. As Milano's initial reaction was to jump up, Grasso tactfully stepped on his foot, signaling him to remain calm.

That day marked the formal initiation of Gaetano Milano, Hot Dog Billy Grant, Louis Failla, and three other men into the ranks of the Patriarca crime family as "made men."

Billy Grasso envied the close relationship Gaetano and Billy Grant shared with Alphonse "Allie Boy" Persico, the underboss of the Columbo family. While Persico was on the lam, taking shelter in a West Hartford hideaway with Billy Grant, they formed a strong bond. However, in 1987, a fugitive squad from the U.S. Marshals Service traced Persico's whereabouts and raided the hideaway, catching him off guard while cooking sauce in the kitchen.

Shortly after, Billy Grant mysteriously disappeared, and it is believed that he was killed on a weekend when he had planned a graduation party for his sons. Milano knew "in his heart" that Grasso was responsible for Grant's murder, stating that he had a "gut feeling" about it.

According to Milano, Grasso once looked Gaetano in the eye and, with a lowered pair of glasses, declared, "Billy Grant is weak." He also insinuated that Grant could have been eliminated at a different time if he had known about the party.

"If he had known, he might have waited till Monday or Tuesday," Milano revealed. "That's the kind of heart he had."

Later, Gaetano is summoned to a meeting with the notorious Wild Guy Billy Grasso in Connecticut.

Immediately, he reaches out to Franky Pugs, expressing his unease. And Gaetano's apprehension is not unfounded. Could it be because Grasso was responsible for the death of his closest friend, Billy Grant? Franky Pugs advises him that he has no other option but to attend the meeting, as avoiding it would surely result in a death sentence. So, with heavy reluctance, Gaetano goes down to see him.

The following day, they come face to face. Thumping his chest, Grasso states, "I'm gonna break your cherry." When Grasso tells him this, he intends to have Gaetano kill someone for him. He then concludes with, "Standby."

Grasso informs Milano that he will first deal with his girlfriend's, Pia Ferro's, ex-husband, followed by a trip to Boston to confront the three renegades: J.R. Russo, Bobby Carozza, and Vinnie Ferrara. Milano rushes to a nearby payphone to warn Franky Pugs that Grasso is making a move. In Boston, Pugliano meets with Pinky Panarelli and J.R. Russo to discuss Grasso's scheme. Ultimately, Vinnie Ferrara makes the crucial decision that Grasso needs to go.

Grasso's aggressive actions had provoked the Genovese faction, led by Skyball Scibelli, to make a beef with the "Commission" in New York. This was partly driven by the rival Boston mafia faction's plea to take Grasso out. The notorious Wild Guy was already embroiled in a fierce internal battle within the Patriarcas, pitting Boston against Providence.

Gangsters from Hartford, Springfield, and Boston, fearing they were on Grasso's short list of victims, decided to strike firs

Chapter 4

It's All Over

For nearly three decades, Franky Pugs and Sonny Castagna have been inseparable friends, running illegal casinos and hosting illicit card games right under the nose of Billy Grasso. At one point, Franky daringly went on the carpet in New York to protect Sonny from being "banged out," a term commonly used in organized crime circles to refer to murder. One day, while driving through the busy streets of New York City, Franky Pugs proudly showed off the exact spot on Mulberry Street where he was inducted into the Genovese Crime Family as a soldier.

During May and June of 1989, Castagna and Pugliano owned a rigged underground casino in New York City, each with a 10 percent stake. The illicit activities of the establishment resulted in payouts of $15,000 to $35,000 a night. As part of their scheme, Larry Cupidi utilized his

New Haven limousine company to transport players to the casino located on West 36th Street in New York City for the rigged blackjack and crap games at which they lost large sums of money.

On July 12, 1989, Cupidi was one of the 30 individuals attending the Manhattan game when FBI agents suddenly raided it. Despite no arrests being made, everyone present was photographed. However, Castagna had suspicions that Cupidi may have disclosed information about the crap and blackjack games. Shortly after the raid, John "Fast Jack" Farrell, in a wiretapped conversation, warned William Vuotto, the vice president of marketing at Caesar's World Casino in Atlantic City, to be cautious.

"So, all I'm tellin' ya is be on your toes. Ya hear me?" Fast Jack Farrell told Vuotto. "I don't know if there's any leaks, this or that. Sonny says Larry's the leak, that limo guy."

Vuotto, Farrell, Castagna, Pugs, and Failla were all business partners at the casino.

An intercepted conversation also discussed that the Patriarca and Genovese families maintained a presence in Worcester and Springfield.

"That was in fucking Worcester. I followed them fucks, Chester. Chester was in fucking Worcester," said Franky Pugliano.

Asked Failla, "What's Chester's last name? Iacone?"

"Yeah," Pugliano replied. I think he mostly went south, from New Haven to New York City."

Farrell asked, "Chester is with Raymond Patriarca, right Frank? He's a captain with Raymond."

Failla responded, "Captain, right," Pugliano grunted, "Yeah."

Chester Iacone is a name that Angelo Iacone uses interchangeably with his given name. Iacone owns East Side Package Store on Shrewsbury Street and is a captain with the Providence-based Patriarca Family.

As Franky Pugs and Sonny strolled the streets of New York City, Pugs probed Sonny about his sentiments towards Grasso while they were guests at the prestigious Plaza Hotel. Pugs' questions assessed if Sonny could be approached if Grasso were killed. It was evident that Pugs' questions carried a weighty implication.

While walking on Broadway, Franky asked him, "How's Billy Grasso?"

"He's crazy as ever. He's nuts," Sonny told him.

"Maybe someday somebody will jump out of a bush and shoot him in the head."

"It wouldn't matter to me one way or the other," and the two kept walking.

In May 1989, Franky Pugs once again sought out Castagna, accompanied by his son, Jackie Johns, during a reception at the Somers Inn in Somers. Also present were Louis Pugliano and Frank Colantoni, who were celebrating the christening of Milano's newborn child.

In a private conversation in the parking lot, the men discussed Billy Grasso's becoming a real problem and that Grasso wanted to kill several people associated with them. Franky Pugs was still reeling from Grasso's lack of support during a sit-down in New York when he lost a beef about the Maruca hit.

"How do you feel about killing Billy Grasso?" Franky asked.

"It's all right with me," Castagna answered.

They were going to Boston that night seeking permission to kill Grasso from Patriarca caporegimes Joseph Russo, Robert Carozza, and Vincent Ferrara.

"This thing will be taken care of; all you have to do is worry about the law."

The notorious North End crew from Boston used the ongoing animosity between the Patriarca crime family's underboss, Billy Grasso, and the Western Massachusetts faction of the Genovese crime family to gain approval to "bang out" Grasso.

The true motive behind their actions was Grasso's decision to put a contract out on Vinnie Ferrara.

The Grasso hit was sanctioned by the infamous boss of the Gambino crime family, John Gotti. Little did they know Gotti harbored deep-seated resentment towards the Wild Guy for withholding information about the murder of Hot Dog Billy, a business partner in which Gotti held a 50% stake.

But, the "contract" had a due date.

"If it weren't done by Friday, the Boston crew would come down and do it themselves, even if they had to go into his house. Whoever wasn't falling into line with Boston would get taken care of."

Following the initial gatherings, it was conveyed that Franky Pugs would not participate further in the plot to kill Grasso. Gaetano was the sole "made" member of the remaining five individuals.

The group devised three schemes to eliminate Grasso. However, each plan was ultimately abandoned.

On one occasion, Gaetano Milano and his long-time friend, Frank Colantoni, visited the Bowl-A-Rama in

Newington, Connecticut, a bowling alley frequented by Grasso. The idea was for Sonny and Jackie to shoot or stab Grasso when he parked his car at the back of the building, with Gaetano and Colantoni waiting on standby on the other side. However, the plan was abandoned when they spotted Grasso entering through the front entrance, which was highly unusual for him.

The initial idea was to carry out the remaining plans at various restaurants.

One of these plans involved using a stun gun to immobilize Grasso behind the Monte Carlo Restaurant in West Springfield. After incapacitating him, Grasso would be transported to a waiting cargo van for execution, and his body would be disposed of in Connecticut. To ensure the success of the operation, a car was strategically parked near the van, and Jackie Johns was ready to pounce on Grasso with the stun gun.

However, their plan was thwarted when Grasso, who typically "went around" on Sundays, was accompanied by a waitress from his Hartford restaurant to the Monte Carlo. This forced them to abort the mission. Instead, they went to Milano's house, where a graduation party was underway for Milano's sister, Christina, a recent East Longmeadow High School graduate.

The other aborted plan was at Franco's Restaurant in Hartford, which Grasso owned. Jackie Johns was to fire shots at Grasso from a passing car as he walked to his usual spot across the street in a nearby bank's parking lot. However, the plan was quickly abandoned due to heavy traffic and Jackie's notoriety in the area.

Both schemes were deemed "too public" for the hit.

On the morning of June 13th, 1989, the group of five men gathered at Valle's Restaurant in Hartford, braving the rainy weather to discuss the disposal plan for their victim's body.

They traveled to the site in two separate vehicles, ensuring its suitability for their grisly task. The van they had borrowed from Claudio Cardaropoli, driven by Milano, was caked in mud and required cleaning before their intended target, Billy Grasso, could be picked up. The vehicle's exterior boasted front and back bucket seats, a rear bench seat, and tinted windows, all of which had been meticulously chosen for their purpose.

Jackie Johns was assigned to hide behind the rear bench seat, armed with a gun, in case Rico Petrillo arrived with Grasso. Johns ensured that Petrillo did not intervene in the planned attack. Sonny and Colantoni were to ride together in Colantoni's vehicle, monitoring Milano as he picked up Grasso from the Ramada Inn and then trailing the van. Once Grasso was eliminated, Castagna and Colantoni were tasked with disposing of the body.

Shortly before 1 p.m., at the Ramada Inn in Wethersfield, Gaetano Milano, Louie Pugliano, and Jackie Johns were gathered, eagerly awaiting Billy Grasso's arrival. Across the parking lot, another car sat parked, occupied by Frank Colantoni and Sonny Castagna. Notably absent was Franky Pugs, a member of the Genovese family who could not be present at a killing that his own family did not approve.

The three men loitered by the van at the front of the hotel, anticipating Grasso's arrival. Gaetano Milano, an associate in the Springfield mob and recently inducted made member of the Patriarca family, had cleverly deceived Grasso, the underboss of New Haven, Connecticut, into believing they were meeting with high-ranking Worcester wiseguy Carlo Mastrototaro, to mediate a beef over cigarette and vending machine territories in Springfield.

Castagna and Colantoni positioned themselves on the opposite side of the street from the Ramada Inn, their eyes fixed on the van where Louie Pugliano and Gaetano Milano were stationed. At the same time, Grasso emerged from behind the hotel, seething with anger. Grasso stood, cursing and bellowing at the three men for choosing an exposed location where anyone could see them meeting together. Milano's ploy to provoke Grasso and throw him off was evident in his decision to make him endure the downpour for thirty long minutes.

Nervous that Grasso might spot them, Castagna and Colantoni ducked out of sight briefly.

After his outburst, Louie Pugs took the wheel while Gaetano opened the sliding door for Grasso to enter. However, Grasso refused and insisted on sitting in the front seat, which was highly unusual for a wise guy. It seemed Milano watched too many old mob movies where the front passenger was at risk of being strangled with a piano wire. Grasso eventually settled in the front seat, with Milano seated behind Pugliano, the driver. Meanwhile, Jackie Johns had already slipped into the back of the van, carrying a bag containing silencer-equipped .22 caliber revolvers.

The surveillance vehicle and van occupants couldn't hook up with each other as they remained concealed from the Wild Guy's sight. When they arose, Grasso and the crew were already gone. Colantoni believed he caught a glimpse of the van departing and attempted to pursue it but was unsuccessful in locating it. Their task was to trail the van and take care of the body after they threw him out. They were responsible for grabbing Grasso's keys, cash, and belongings and disposing of his clothes. However, the duo was ultimately unable to trace the van's whereabouts.

Moments earlier, Louie Pugliano had departed from the Ramada Inn, driving the van onto Interstate 91. Milano handed Grasso a newspaper containing an article about a local gambling bust. While Grasso was engrossed in the article, Gaetano leaned over and fired his .32-caliber handgun, delivering a fatal shot to the base of Grasso's skull. Jackie sprang out of the back seat, grabbed Grasso by the hair, and yanked his head against the headrest. Jackie then brandished his .22-caliber handgun, pointed it at Grasso's head, and asked Milano, "Should I shoot him again?" as the van sped down Interstate 91.

"It's all over," Milano declared.

Milano held a towel to Grasso's neck to soak up the blood from the gunshot wound. Johns clasped Grasso's head to prevent him from slumping forward and assisted in covering the bullet wound with the towel. Louie Pugliano altered course and headed towards the riverbank of Wethersfield Cove.

Johns put on gloves, grasped Grasso's legs, and, together with Milano, carried Grasso's body to the riverbank. There, they retrieved the keys and cash from his pockets.

Frank Colantoni and Castagna, having lost sight of the van, proceeded directly to Rocky Hill, the intended location for disposing of the body. Unable to locate the van, they drove to Abdow's Restaurant in Enfield, which had been designated as a meeting point after the murder. Approximately five or ten minutes later, the van arrived at

Abdow's, with Milano informing them, "It's all done." Colantoni and Johns then took the van to clean it, using a hose to spray the interior and a vacuum cleaner to dry it. Meanwhile, Louie Pugliano departed in an old "beater" car.

Castagna and Milano entered Abdow's Big Boy, a local restaurant, and indulged in some sandwiches. Before heading across the street to the State Line Package Store, Milano took the time to make two phone calls. Once there, he purchased $90 worth of lottery tickets, selecting the number 613 - a significant date that marked Billy Grasso's passing. This was a numerical reference for June 13th.

Later, Milano's 20-year-old girlfriend, Lisa, who had a child with him as his teenage babysitter, picked them up from the liquor store. As they returned to Milano's place, he made two more phone calls, freshened up, and changed his clothes before leaving with Castagna in a car. As they drove, Milano asked Castagna to dispose of a pair of shoes, one at a time, by tossing them into the woods.

Milano stopped the vehicle at a secluded area surrounded by trees and instructed Castagna to get out and toss a small plastic baggie containing a shell casing into the nearby woods. Castagna complied, walking a short distance from the road before discarding the bag. As he looked on, he noticed that the shell casing had traveled further down a ravine than the bag.

Then, after driving a short distance, they turned left into the Springfield Sportsmen's Club in Monson. Milano parked the car and proceeded to the shooting range. Following some conversations, he returned to the pistol area and fired his automatic weapon. Milano had a specific goal: to have nitrates on his hands. This was a standard test used by law enforcement to check for the presence of nitrates, which are released upon firing a weapon. Afterward, Milano disposed of a bag of clothing in a dumpster behind a Friendly's restaurant. They then made their way to Colantoni's house.

Two days following the murder, a meeting was set at Monte Carlo Restaurant to inform Louis Failla, a soldier of the Patriarca family, about Grasso's death. Louie Pugliano was also in attendance. During the meeting, Frank Pugliano instructed his brother to disclose the news of Grasso's murder to Failla. Next, Louie provided a detailed account of the killing of Grasso.

Grasso's dead body was discovered by two fishermen on the shores of the Connecticut River in Wethersfield three days after he was murdered. While trying to fish after rainfall made it difficult to mow lawns, two landscapers stumbled upon the body around 2 p.m. on June 16. As one of the fishermen attempted to cast his line, it got snagged in a tree. After cutting the line, he climbed the tree to retrieve his bobber, and from his elevated position, he spotted the body lying in poison ivy. The pair then drove to a nearby office building and requested the assistance of a secretary to notify police.

At 62 years old, Grasso's death left behind a legacy of bloodlust, terror, and paranoia. As the second-in-command of the Patriarca family, he was a suspect in numerous gangland homicides spanning decades, including the 1988 killings of his loyal associate, Billy Grant, and promising boxer, Eric Miller, in the New Haven area. However, Miller's punch to Grasso in front of Franco's Restaurant in Hartford sealed his fate. In that moment, the young man was marked for death – anyone who dared to strike a man in Grasso's powerful position was doomed.

"Billy got power drunk; everything was his, even when it wasn't, and he had no right to claim it was in the first place," one informant is quoted in an FBI intelligence report discussing Grasso's demeanor at the time of his death.

On the same morning, mere hours before Grasso was rubbed out in Connecticut, a hit team from the North End crew attempted to gun down infamous New England mob figure Francis "Cadillac Frank" Salemme.

Salemme was aligned with Grasso and the Providence branch of the crime family in a power struggle against Ferrara and the Boston faction. Despite being shot multiple times, Salemme managed to survive in the parking lot of an International House of Pancakes in Saugus, Massachusetts. He sought refuge in a nearby pizza parlor before fleeing to California, waiting for the dust to settle.

Salemme had served as a contract killer for Patriarca during the 1960s, ultimately serving a 15-year sentence for car-bombing a lawyer on Patriarca's orders. Grasso and Salemme reaped significant rewards from their connections to Raymond Patriarca, the notorious head of the New England mafia, for nearly 30 years.

On July 10th, renegade capos Joe J.R. Russo, Vinnie Ferrara, and Robert Carrozza gathered with Gaetano Milano, Sonny Castagna, and Jackie Johns at Santarpio's, a pizzeria in East Boston to discuss the assassination of Grasso. After the incident, they had been avoiding public appearances.

However, when Russo noticed they were being watched, he loudly exclaimed, "State police!" prompting Gaetano, Sonny, and Jackie to leave abruptly through a back exit.

After the murder of Grasso, J.R. Russo and Vinnie Ferrara attempted to forcefully oust Junior Patriarca from his position of power during a tense and emotionally charged meeting in the back room of a Providence jewelry store. With tears streaming down his face, Junior was given an ultimatum by Russo: step down, or he would personally kill him.

Eventually, the Gambino crime family from New York intervened, and John Gotti ordered Russo and Ferrara to cease all violence and reconcile at John Gotti Jr's Labor Day wedding on Long Island, where both families were in attendance.

At the wedding, Gaetano and Franky Pugs watched as John Gotti made his grand entrance, flanked by two men in front, two behind, and two on each side. Later, Gotti summoned Gaetano to meet with him. Milano tells him it's an honor to meet him. Gotti then inquired about Grasso's potential involvement with the feds, to which Milano replied he doubted it. In response, Gotti slammed his hand on the table and shouted "il topo," which translates to "rat" in Italian. His men immediately sprang into action, but Gotti calmed them down and reassured them that everything was all right. The festivities continued as if nothing had happened.

Following a brief ceasefire and a major RICO case against Ferrara and other leaders of the Patriarca family, resulting in widespread arrests, Salemme emerged as the boss of the New England mob in the early 1990s. He tirelessly worked to eliminate any remaining loyalists to Ferrara, leading to a series of changes within the organization.

Grasso's death set in motion a series of realignments and organizational changes, including Nicholas Bianco's ascension as the new underboss.

Two months later, the Patriarca family decided to have their members in Connecticut and Gaetano Milano answer to Matthew "Good Looking Matty" Gugliemetti, a "capo regime" or captain in the Providence organization, instead of appointing a leader in Connecticut. This directive caused frustration among the Connecticut members, who felt they were denied the right to present their grievances to the organization's "consigliere," or advisor. They believed it went against the Mafia's code of conduct.

After his trip to Connecticut, Matty met with Gaetano Milano and Louis Failla to discuss whether Patriarca would appoint a successor for Grasso. The next day, upon returning to Providence, Guglielmetti met with Nick Bianco before returning to Connecticut for a second meeting with Failla, Milano, and Americo "Rico" Petrillo.

During this meeting, they were informed that no capo regime would be designated for Connecticut. Instead, they were to report to Guglielmetti, and all proceeds collected would be funneled back to Rhode Island, where the bosses would decide how much, if any, would be sent back.

Following the abrupt meetings held after Grasso's death, a truce between Patriarca, based in Providence, and three of his captains in Boston eventually brokered. Among the three captains, Joseph "J.R." Russo was appointed as the family's consigliere, or trusted advisor, while Patriarca also consented to expand the family's membership by four individuals from Boston.

In reassurance to Sonny Castagna, Vinnie Ferrara told Sonny, "It's going to be all right. Don't worry about nothing. You guys will all get made over there." Castagna, Johns, and Louis Pugliano were to be inducted into the Mafia, joining Milano and Frank Pugliano as "soldiers" or "made members."

Russo's recent promotion to consigliere was seen as nothing more than a "token job."

Carrozza and Ferrara disapproved of Russo's decision to accept the position, stating, "You shouldn't have even taken the job as consigliere. They wanted to appease you." It seemed that the higher-ups were trying to placate him.

However, their efforts were short-lived as Russo, along with Vinnie Ferrara and Bobby Carrozza, was arrested on charges of extortion and thrown into jail without the possibility of bail not long after the induction ceremony on October 29, 1989, in Medford. With these Boston captains or caporegimes behind bars, the figures in Springfield and Hartford were left without sponsors.

Gaetano Milano, a "made" member of the Patriarca Family who had achieved a certain level of power through his connections, had his sights set on becoming the capo regime, or "captain," of organized crime in Connecticut.

However, he was not satisfied with his boss's decision. The next day, Milano and Failla discussed Guglielmetti's instructions, which designated Bianco as the person to go to in case of any disagreements with Guglielmetti. The FBI recorded this conversation through a device planted in Failla's car.

"Who in the fuck are they to tell us we can't go directly to Boston to see the consigliere," Failla said, referring to the traditional procedure of having the consigliere, or counselor, mediate disputes.

Failla said, "'I was fucking ready for war."

Milano responded, "Did you practice drawing if someone came?"

Said Failla, "I didn't practice, but I knew I could move pretty fucking fast. I had some suspicions. You're right, Gaetano."

"What about me, Louie?" asked Milano.

"I would never come to you and put you in a position where somebody would see us, and that guy would bang you out."

Chapter 5

Breaking Omerta

Members of the New England Mafia were no longer willing to risk a lifetime behind bars. The once unbreakable code of silence was shattered as they chose to betray their associates. This sudden shift was evident in the large-scale investigation into organized crime, where wiretaps and informants were now providing crucial evidence against the group. It was a rare occurrence in the history of such investigations where authorities were able to identify those responsible for an organized crime murder or hit.

The once loyal members of the Mafia were now turning on each other, trading their silence for freedom.

Gaetano Milano, Frank Pugliano, Louis Pugliano, and Frank Colantoni Jr. were indicted by a federal grand jury for the murder of Mafia underboss Billy "Wild Guy" Grasso. These four suspects were taken into custody on August 20,

1990, based on a criminal complaint charging them with conspiracy to commit murder and murdering Grasso. They have been in custody without the right to bail since then and could face a lifetime in prison if convicted.

Additionally, three Mafia members in Boston, Joseph "J.R." Russo, Vincent "Vinnie" Ferrara, and Robert Carrozza, all members of the Patriarca Crime Family based in Providence, were identified in the murder as unindicted co-conspirators in the crime.

Despite being indicted in March 1990 with 20 other members of the crime family, Milano's mother, family, and friends have remained resolute in their belief of his innocence in Grasso's murder. His supporters were convinced he had been framed by turncoat gangsters who had cut deals with federal prosecutors. To help cover the mounting legal fees, a fundraiser was held on Memorial Day at Chez Josef in Agawam, attended by approximately 300 people. The event aimed to "honor and support" Milano, a naturalized citizen and graduate of Longmeadow High School. Both federal and state agents closely monitored the banquet, organized by "Friends of Gaetano Milano," according to the invitation adorned with gold lettering.

The Grasso murder case is heavily supported by the testimonies of John "Sonny" Castagna and his stepson, Jack "Jackie" Johns, both of whom have started cooperating with investigators. Johns and Castagna, "associates" of the Patriarca family, were also indicted in March alongside Gaetano Milano, Frank Pugliano, and 20 others in New England for engaging in racketeering and conspiring to do so. The police were clueless about the Grasso murder until Sonny Castagna and Jackie Johns agreed to cooperate.

A third informant, who is slated to provide evidence against New York Mafia leader John Gotti later this year, is deemed an expert witness on the inner workings of the Mafia. Philip "Crazy Phil" Leonetti, a former underboss of the Philadelphia mob currently serving a 45-year sentence for racketeering, was summoned as the initial witness in U.S. District Court. Through his cooperation, he only served five years in prison.

Leonetti's uncle, Nicodemo "Little Nicky" Scarfo, sponsored his induction into the organization and elevated him to underboss once he took over as boss. He confessed that at the tender age of 11, his uncle had him act as a decoy while disposing of a dead body, explaining to the young Leonetti that he had brutally stabbed a man in a New Jersey bar with an ice pick for disrespecting him.

Leonetti is anticipated to testify in New York against John Gotti regarding the operations of the Gambino Mafia Family, including a meeting where Gotti boasted about the December 1985 assassination of Gambino boss Paul Castellano.

The investigation has uncovered a highly coveted discovery - the first-ever secretly recorded Mafia initiation ceremony. This significant event, which took place on October 29, 1989, in Medford, saw four new inductees pledge their loyalty by pricking their trigger fingers and taking a solemn blood oath to kill informants and anyone who poses a danger to "This Thing of Ours" or, in Italian, "La Cosa Nostra."

Before the trial's commencement, the prosecution extended an offer to the defendants. The proposed plea deal would have resulted in Gaetano Milano receiving a 15-year sentence, while the rest of the group would have faced a maximum of 6 years. This was a significant reduction from their potential life sentence in prison. The prosecution knew they had a weak case, which relied heavily on the unreliable testimonies of two informants who were known to be liars and violent felons that they didn't trust.

However, the offer stipulated that all defendants must plead guilty. The majority of the group agreed that it was their best option, except for one - Nicholas Bianco. Bianco, who had been identified as the new leader of the Patriarca Crime Family, refused to plead guilty. Despite the risk of facing life in prison for his associates, he held out, unwilling to serve just 2 ½ years in prison. This was the most lenient sentence offered to all defendants.

On May 14, 1991, a heavily guarded John "Sonny" Castagna, acting as an informant, slowly made his way to the witness stand in a crowded courtroom at the U.S. District Court.

For four hours, he testified, dressed in a light gray blazer, an open black shirt, and white cotton pants. He nervously fiddled with his glasses while responding to questions, deliberately avoiding eye contact with his former accomplices. Castagna, who has confessed to racketeering, fraud, conspiracy to commit murder, and weapons charges, could face up to 90 years in prison. In exchange for his cooperation, he has been granted immunity from prosecution for other offenses, including the assassination of Grasso. This shows the high stakes and grave consequences of his actions.

During his testimony, Castagna provided intricate details about the Grasso murder. Castagna stated that

Gaetano Milano was meant to be rewarded for eliminating a troublesome member of the hierarchy in La Cosa Nostra. According to Castagna's testimony, he was to be promoted to captain of organized crime for the Patriarca family in Connecticut, but this promotion has yet to come to fruition.

During his testimony on the seventh day, Castagna disclosed that he served as a backup gunman a decade ago when Joseph Maruca was shot five times. The crime had remained unsolved for years. Over nine days, John "Sonny" Castagna took the stand against eight individuals, providing crucial and impactful evidence.

Over the next three days, John "Jackie" Johns, Castagna's stepson placed in the witness protection program, took the stand in court. Johns revealed that he had crouched behind the back seat during the Grasso hit, anticipating that Americo "Rico" Petrillo would arrive with Grasso. "We thought Rico was coming for some reason," explained Johns, who said he intended to "hold a gun to him and say, 'Hey, you're with us. Fuhgettaboutit.' "

Furthermore, Johns disclosed that Milano had informed him, "They were going to get rid of Billy and some other guys, and he was going to be a capo, and they were going to make some new guys." Castagna also attested that he and his son were to be "made" or inducted into the Mafia as a reward for their involvement.

During the 20th day of the trial, the most damaging piece of evidence, a tape recording, was played for the jury. In this 15-minute conversation, secretly taped before his arrest in August 1990, Louie Pugliano discussed the possibility of Gaetano Milano remaining loyal to the Mafia's code of silence during a mob execution.

However, he also expressed concern: "If he does roll, we're all in trouble unless you want to do something about it."

When Johns presses Louie "Pugs" Pugliano on the recording about Milano potentially "flipping," Pugliano confidently states, "He's going to bury himself. That's all he's going to bury because it's not that way."

Johns began cooperating in July 1990, donning a recording device to capture Louie's words on August 16 in a Ramada Inn parking area in East Windsor. He refuted any allegations of being prompted about what to say or "scripted," adding only that FBI agents told him not to be nervous.

"Nobody told me to say nothing. I was just improvising. There was no guy in the woods with cue cards," Johns said.

On the tape, Johns asked, "Yeah. What do you think about Gaetano, he's fucked?"

"I think he'll be all right," Louie responded. That's my opinion. If he's not, I'll get the vibes over here." Pugliano said he was more concerned with defendant Louis Failla's resolve.

When discussing Milano's resolve, Johns asked, "You think he told them that he shot Billy and he's looking to make a deal?"

"No. Course not," Louis Pugs answered. "You gotta be fucking wacky to do a thing like that."

The fateful destiny that awaited Gaetano Milano was sealed by the loose lips of Louie Pugliano, who disclosed the murder of Billy Grasso. The jurors were locked into this crucial detail during the trial.

During his testimony in U.S. District Court, Jack Johns revealed his fear of reputed Mafia underboss William "The Wild Guy" Grasso and how it motivated him to participate in Grasso's execution.

Johns believed, "Anyone who did any business with him had a shot at gettin' killed. No one knew from moment to moment. I think anyone in this room who had dealings with him was terrified."

He detailed Grasso's reign of terror as La Cosa Nostra's boss in Connecticut and admitted to hiding in a van while Grasso was shot. "I hated him. But if it came down to where I had to be the triggerman, I'd have been the triggerman."

Johns claimed that a conversation with Grasso regarding a vehicle he bought from Frank Colantoni, a friend and Milano's co-defendant, caused him to suspect that Milano's safety was at risk. He expressed his frustration by inquiring, "What are you doin' with Gaetano?" and was angered enough to order Johns to find a telephone booth so he could call Milano.

Johns expressed his hesitance to become a witness, revealing that he had even removed his father from his jail cell when Castagna shared his plans to testify. Castagna had told his stepson, "I gotta way out."

Johns lamented, "I wish we didn't do this. Do you think I feel good about this? You think it's easy over here lookin' at these guys like this."

He also admitted missing his friends and family, stating, "I wish Louie Pugliano wasn't in the van. He's the best guy up here. I feel sick sittin' up here lookin' at him."

He also recounted an incident when Grasso learned that Johns had "made a score" or had earned some money illegally and had failed to share the proceeds with him.

"He said, 'I'm gonna bury you and leave your arm stickin' out so I can go by every day and kick you,'" Johns said, grinning as he recounted the conversation.

Prosecutors played hours of tape-recorded conversations on the 30th day of trial.

A tiny recording device, discreetly placed within the dashboard of Louis Failla's blue Cadillac, continuously collected incriminating evidence about Failla's loan-sharking business for four months in 1989.

"Gaetano stuck his chest out too fast," said John "Fast Jack" Farrell. "Butch is protecting himself. Butchie is with the strength; what the fuck does he need Gaetano for?"

Responds Failla, "Cause Gaetano feels he is going to take over, somebody's going to take over. He's still got high hopes that he's gonna be there. So, he holds all these meetings every day. Gary, Sonny, his kid, everybody, but not fucking with me. Because I told him, I said, fuhgettaboutit."

"He thought he was going to be the fucking capo regime. He's starting to see they fucked him around in Boston. They let him do this and then see you later."

In another conversation with Farrell, Failla said, "I told Milano everything that he did was wrong. He's still doing wrong. Roundin' up these guys every day and eatin' with them and fillin' up their heads with. Fuck. He's livin' under fucking false pretenses. They fucked him, and he won't accept it."

Informant John "Sonny" Castagna complained when testifying, "Gaetano was callin' meetings every day for four months. Springfield, Hartford, Enfield, we were all over. You name it. We were there."

In one excerpt, Louis Failla discusses Milano's dislike for Grasso and its basis.

"He told Gaetano he was going to do business with him there. Now, he made an about-face. He said that anything you get, you have to put it on record. So, with them up there, you won't have no headache. So, anything he promised Gaetano they were going to do, he backed off."

Failla also told his son, Mark, about his loansharking business, in which borrowers paid 3 percent a week or 156 percent a year.

"Got to give Mel another G-note, that's six," Louis Failla said, referring to Melvin Silverstein of Jewett City. "He better know what the fuck he's doin', boy. That's $210 a week of juice he's paying me, Mark." "Juice" is a term used to describe interest on a loan.

As Louis Failla drove to a meeting with the mob's hierarchy, Gaetano Milano coached him on expressing himself if Milano was not designated captain of the Patriarca family's illegal interests in Connecticut.

"Today, they're going to tell us who's who and what's what," Failla said as a microphone on the car dashboard transmitted the words to a nearby surveillance van.

"They're gonna say, listen, this is the way we're gonna do it, and this is the way we've gotta do it."

"Answer to Mattie," Failla speculated, referring to Rhode Island captain Matthew Guglielmetti Jr. "Thank you very much. I'd be very proud to be with you, Mattie. And I'll be loyal and this and that."

"Ah, don't even say that," Milano interjects. "Because if it comes down, see, and this guy wants some ammunition. You're going to take some ammunition away from him."

"Okay, then whata' we say?" Failla asked. "It's the way, that's the way it is," Milano responded.

"That's the way it is, and no disrespect, but it's okay with us," Failla suggested.

"No," Milano answered.

"It's okay with me?" Failla counters.

"Don't even say that," Milano said.

"How do you wanna say it?" Failla asked.

"Why are you bringing somebody from Rhode Island over here to Connecticut when they all wanted this guy here?" Milano suggested, referring to himself.

"How do we say it? We just say, 'Thank you. I'm with you?" Failla asked.

"Don't say anything," Milano answered.

Failla asked, "They put you with Mattie, you got to say something to him. You gotta shake hands with him."

Milano counseled, "Ya shake hands."

"Tell me how to say this now," Failla asked. "Just shake hands and say, okay, Nick, I respect your wishes."

Earlier, Milano hints at how important the decision is to him when he tells Failla and another reputed mob soldier, John Taddei of New Haven, "I think this and that. I'll tell you, it's not the moment I dreamed of. It goes back to the same thing, John, huh? They don't care."

Milano then laments the direction of "This Thing of Ours" or, in Italian, La Cosa Nostra. "They do not care for La Cosa

Nostra. It's La Cosa Mia, but now, instead of just one guy, it's a couple of guys."

After the decision was rendered that all earned money was to be sent to Providence, and after ranking members exacted their tribute, the balance was to be returned.

"I said, 'If that's the way it is, I guess that's the way it is,' " Milano said, explaining his reaction to the news. "And he says, 'Well, are you satisfied?' If it's already decided, that's the way it is. Who am I to question them? I tell ya, I hope I'm not being rude."

Failla also said that when he went to jail for attempting to bribe the East Hartford police chief, Grasso refused to help his family. "I went to the fucking can because of him. The crap game. I kept my fucking mouth shut."

Milano inquired, "He got, he got an end of that crap game?"

Answered Failla, "Got an end? Him, Franky, and Ski. I worked for them."

"Ski" is Francesco "Skyball" Scibelli, a reputed capo regime for the Genovese family in Western Massachusetts. "Franky" is defendant Frank Pugliano.

Failla also talks about his existence when Grasso ruled Connecticut's underworld with an iron fist. "I used to go home nights worried that he'd say, he'd make statements to me, 'I got the fucking hole dug for you already, go get my fucking money. I'll put you on top and this guy on the bottom.

"I was livin' in fucking fear," Failla said.

"Nowhere to turn," Milano empathizes.

"Nobody to turn to, not a fucking soul except Louie Failla," he said, explaining some of the measures he took with weapons. "I had one here, one in my house, one in my garage. I was ready; if I rolled on the ground, I could grab it outta the garage. I was fucking ready for war."

"Grasso cheated on himself all his life," Failla said, launching into a tirade about Grasso's reputation as a tightwad. "I say to him, 'Listen, you want to wear shitty shoes, that's your fucking prerogative. You can wear whatever shoes you want.' " Failla then assumed the role of Grasso in the conversation: " 'Why you, who the fuck do you, why you fucking, I'll pick your fucking tongue out.' All this over a pair of shoes."

Failla continued, "I can remember we went in the fucking store. I wouldn't even wear a pair of shorts out of the fucking store. He bought two pairs of pants and four shirts. I told him, 'No disrespect, I wouldn't even wash my fucking car with that shirt.' Again, assuming Grasso's role, Failla said, 'Why you, why you fucker. And I'm gonna wear when you makin' fun of my shirts and this.' "

As they leave the Mystic meeting, Milano, Failla, and Taddei hear a beeping sound and panic.

"That this car?" Failla asks.

"Stereo, fuck, the radio," Taddei said.

"Is that the radio," Milano asked.

"Shut this door with the radio off," Failla suggests.

"Holy fuck," Milano said.

Taddei asks, "What is that?"

"If this is a fucking bomb, we better get out of this car," Failla yells.

"Get the fuck out," Taddei said. "I'll stay here and get. How the fuck would I know? Whose car is this?"

"Mine," Failla responds.

"You're asking me?" Taddei said.

Failla answered, "You fucker. I never heard a beep, beep, beep. He drove my car. Look what he did."

Milano interjects, "Hey, you know what, Louie? They knew we were comin' alone. They probably got a place to fucking blow it up now."

Failla suggested, "Put the power button off. See the power button; that one there. It's off. Where's it comin' from? Over there? Somethin' somethin', tryin' to tell me somethin'. What do I need fucking air in one of my tires."

Smirking to himself, Gaetano covertly silenced his pager, the origin of the noise.

On the 32nd day of the trial, the recording of Franky Pugliano's conversation with informant Michael Borriello on November 15, 1989, was played. As the sounds of Italian instrumental music filled the Monte Carlo Restaurant and the dinner crowd chattered, Frank Pugliano revealed to the informant, wearing a concealed microphone, that he had no concerns about "stool pigeons."

"You know why I don't worry about that?" Pugliano tells Borriello. "When they got a stool pigeon like Buzzy Callahan, right, and he can put different people he did business with in trouble, right? They're not gonna take a fucking shot. Just throw a guy in the kettle like me. Because if I beat it, they'll be hit."

Days later, Paul "Buzzy" Callahan admitted to being a kingpin of a narcotics distribution network and agreed to become a government informant. His testimony last fall was instrumental in the conviction of 12 individuals involved in his distribution network.

"Well, here's what happens," Pugliano said in hushed tones. "Ninety percent of the stool pigeons, all of them will end up being selective. They got the pin in for somebody, and it's just selective for them." Pugliano said, "I don't believe this guy's squealing on the people you think he is. I believe he's opening up, but not on everybody."

"Franny Soffen called me the day after the pinch and said I don't think he's going to hurt you because he loves your father," Borriello said of Soffen, a bank robber who is serving concurrent life terms for murder.

During the conversation, Borriello also told Pugliano that there is no time limit for prosecutors to bring felony charges, to which Pugliano replied, "The only thing that has no statute is a murder. It said it right in the paper."

Pugliano then shared with Borriello the news that three Mafia captains in Boston, Joseph "J.R." Russo, Robert Carrozza, and Vinnie Ferrara, had been formally charged the day before.

"These guys are big guys?" Borriello asks.

"Biggest," Pugliano responds. "The biggest in Boston today. I mean real, in my opinion, real good guys, too."

As they went to Lombardo's Restaurant in East Boston to pay tribute to Russo's father, two other individuals, Louis Failla and John "Fast Jack" Farrell, discussed the Pugliano family.

"Franky Pugs, he ain't exactly a college graduate, Lou," Farrell starts.

"No," agrees Failla, "he's not too bright. I really talked to Louie Pugs.

Farrell interjects, "Nice guy."

Failla concurs, "Yep, that's what it is. He's a nice guy."

"But he ain't," Farrell said, "He ain't street-wise, and he ain't, he ain't, just overall intelligent guy. Man, if you talked to him about world politics, world politics or somethin'."

Adds Failla, in a reference to Louie Pugliano, "Louie's not so fucking bright either. The father must have been smart to put that restaurant together."

Farrell answers, "The brother. The other brother. The other one. The quiet one," referring to Frederick Pugliano.

Failla adds, "The accountant you don't see."

Farrell said, "Yeah. He put this all together, right? He don't want to know nothin' about mustaches." "Mustaches" or "Mustache Petes" is a term from the 1930s referring to members of organized crime.

Failla and Farrell also engage in fashion critique.

Farrell asks, "What you think Gaetano's gonna wear?"

Responds Failla, "You watch, shoestring necktie, boots. He can't dress. Like Franky Pugs, same fucking light blue suit."

Later, Farrell becomes a bit self-conscious. "I look like a Fed, don't I, Louie?"

"Sure, you do," Failla said.

"Guys don't know me. What the fuck is this guy?" Farrell said.

"Nah," answers Failla, "you're gonna be there. They all know Jack Farrell, my friend. They might think I'm a Fed, too. Boy, that's how they come, right? One Irishman, one Italian. We'd give John Gotti and his fucking crew competition today, us dressin' up."

A Mafia induction ceremony held 20 months ago in suburban Boston was recently brought to light at the mob trial, thanks to the use of an FBI microphone. The recording captured the participants' solemn oaths of silence, obedience, and lifelong allegiance to the secret society. One of the attendees, Boston mobster Angelo "Sonny" Mercurio, a "top echelon" FBI informant living in the federal Witness Protection Program, "was wired up" during the ceremony.

Despite many individuals denying the existence of the Mafia, known by various names such as La Cosa Nostra or "the mob," this organized criminal underworld has been acknowledged as a reality by the majority. Now, with the jury in U.S. District Court listening to 90 minutes of tape recordings, any doubts about the existence of the Mafia have been put to rest.

"Richie, do you got any brothers?" Patriarca "family" consigliere Joseph "J.R." Russo asked of inductee Richard Floramo.

"Yes," answered Floramo haltingly.

"Do you have sons?" Russo asked.

"Yes," answered Floramo.

"If I told you one of them was an informer, a police informer, gonna put somebody in prison, and I told you you must kill them, would you do that for me without hesitation?"

Answered Floramo without hesitating, "He has to go."

The endurance of "This Thing Of Ours," La Cosa Nostra in Italian, spans generations, but mobster Biagio DiGiacomo insisted that its pursuits are noble.

"Everybody fights this thing they call it Cosa Nostra, they call it my, organiza, organization, and this and that, and the Mafia," DiGiacomo said.

"It is Mafia. There was a founded by Mafia, in Sicily. Started Sicily. They all get together because there was a lot of abuse to the family, to the wife, to the children. Until some people, nice people, they got together and they said, 'Let's make an organization over here but let's start to do the right thing. Who makes a mistake, he's gotta pay. You can never get out alive," explained DiGiacomo.

"There's no such thing as resigning, right, Biag," added an unidentified speaker."

DiGiacomo also explained one of the penalties for breaching security.

"It's no hope, no Jesus, no Madonna, nobody can help us if we give up this secret to anybody, any kinds of friends of mine, let's say. This thing cannot be exposed. The son or the wife or the daughter, whoever, we gonna keep it to ourselves."

Russo told the four initiated that day in Medford, "All families are related all over America."

Interjected the family's "boss," Raymond "Junior" Patriarca, "Throughout the world."

Russo continued, "Through a common cause. But it's like cousins. The immediate family likes to keep their business to themselves. You understand?"

Patriarca "opened up the books" or permitted the Boston faction to add members as an accommodation to settle the festering dispute. He also promoted Russo from a captain or capo regime to a consigliere or counselor, a move that the rank and file regarded as intended to placate Russo and two other dissidents, capo regimes Vincent "Vinnie" Ferrara and Russo's half-brother, Robert Carrozza.

"We're here to bring in some new members into our family and, more than that, to start, maybe, a new beginning," said Patriarca.

"Put all that's got started behind us. 'Cause they come into our family to start a new thing with us."

After nearly six weeks of testimony, eight men and four women took 15 days to deliberate and deliver their verdicts. On August 8, 1991, three of the defendants were found guilty of the 1989 murder of William "The Wild Guy" Grasso, the feared underboss of the family in Connecticut, while a fourth was convicted of conspiracy in connection to Grasso's death.

Gaetano Milano's hands clasped together in front of his face as the court clerk announced the verdict. He lowered his head in defeat as he heard the guilty verdicts for the murder charges. His wife, Judith, wept uncontrollably upon hearing the verdict. Meanwhile, other family members of the defendants gasped in shock.

Anthony Pugliano, Franky Pugliano's only son, consoled members of Milano and Petrillo's families after the verdict was announced.

During the sentencing, everyone involved in the case, including the prosecutors, Milano's lawyer, and even his own family, anticipated that he would continue to deny his involvement in Grasso's death and his affiliation with the mob.

"All my life, I've tried to help people," Milano said, beginning a rambling speech racked with sobs. He seemed to be saying he swore allegiance to the Mafia to protect people from evil. "And that was the reason for my association."

"It was like touching a spider web. Once you touched it," he said, "you just couldn't let go."

As Milano pressed on, appearing gaunt and exhausted following his lengthy imprisonment and the grueling four-month trial, he revealed that he ultimately chose to end Grasso's life after becoming convinced that the underboss had plotted his murder.

"I never buried nor helped bury or killed anyone for Mr. Grasso in my entire life," Milano said, referring to Grasso's habit of burying his victims in out-of-the-way places. "But I do take responsibility for Mr. Grasso because it was kill or be killed," Milano said through tears. "I couldn't carry the charade any further."

"Are you telling me that you killed Mr. Grasso?" the judge asked.

"Yes, sir. Yes, I am," Milano answered.

Then, U.S. District Judge Alan Nevas looked at Milano. "Renounce the mafia!'

"I won't," answered Gaetano.

"Renounce it now!" he yelled, this time looking at Gaetano's best friend, Frank Colantoni.

Milano begged for mercy for Patriarca family associate Frank Colantoni Jr., a childhood friend from the Springfield area whom he recruited into the conspiracy to kill Grasso.

Milano glanced at Colantoni, then began to weep as he told U.S. District Judge Nevas, "I wholeheartedly renounce membership in this organization," referring to the reputed Patriarca crime family of La Cosa Nostra. Milano then broke down in sobs but managed to say, "I know I'm losing my wife and my children. I wholeheartedly renounce my membership in this organization. People like William Grasso, all they do is maim or destroy people, make people disappear."

For the first time in New England, a Mafia "soldier" has broken the code of silence by publicly confessing to his involvement in La Cosa Nostra and its criminal activities. This breach of loyalty could result in a death sentence from the Mafia. After renouncing his life as a hitman for the mob and admitting to the murder of William "The Wild Guy" Grasso, Gaetano Milano was given a 33-year prison sentence instead of facing life without parole.

As he was led out of the courtroom, his wife of nineteen years, Judy, cried out, "I love you, Gaetano. I love you, Honey. I'll wait for you." Tears flowed as loved ones hugged and consoled each other while some called out words of encouragement to Milano. Others clapped, showing their support for his bravery.

Louis Failla, who continuously talked into an undercover FBI device cleverly hidden in the dashboard of his Cadillac, provided valuable insight into the inner workings of the Connecticut Mafia. As a result, a dozen members were convicted, and Failla was sentenced to 10 years in prison. He's convicted for being an organizer of crooked card and dice games in Manhattan as well as a leader of a loan-sharking business that operated as part of the Mafia's racketeering enterprise. Moreover, he was found guilty of plotting to murder Luis "Tito" Morales, a prominent figure in Hartford and the father of Failla's 5-year-old grandson, Jason.

Louis Pugliano, an associate of the mafia, will spend the remainder of his life behind bars due to his careless conversations with an informant. His words ultimately led to the demise of Gaetano Milano. Meanwhile, his brother Frank has been sentenced to 12 and a half years in prison for their involvement in the 1989 killing of Mafia underboss William Grasso.

Nicholas Bianco, identified as the new boss of the Patriarca Crime Family, must report to prison to begin serving an 11 1/2-year sentence for interstate travel in aid of racketeering and for sanctioning Failla's loan-sharking operations.

Frank Colantoni Jr. received a 12 1/2-year sentence for his role in Grasso's murder because he, too, admitted involvement in the plot and agreed not to appeal his conviction.

Americo "Rico" Petrillo was sentenced to 6 1/2 years for racketeering and conspiracy. He operated a dice game at the Southend Social Club in Hartford.

Salvatore "Butch" D'Aquila Jr. was sentenced to serve a six-year sentence for helping to bury the body of hotel executive Theodore Bern in Hamden, Connecticut, in August 1986, followed by a nine-year sentence for racketeering and extortion and running sports bookmaking and football pool ticket operations. Judge Nevas said, "People are judged by the company they keep. The friends that you kept, the company you kept, were the scum of the earth. Terrible, terrible people."

Matthew "Good Looking Matty" Guglielmetti Jr., identified as a captain in the Patriarca Family, was given a

57-month sentence after pleading guilty to racketeering in May, shortly after trial commenced.

John "Fast Jack" Farrell pleaded guilty before trial and was sentenced to 33 months for operating crooked card games for the Mafia.

Richard Beedle will serve a four-year sentence for permitting Grasso to dispose of dead bodies by burying them in the dirt floor of his garage.

"Almost every juror in that room had hesitation over believing Sonny Castagna and Jackie Johns," juror William Calhoun said. "You would have to be naive to take all their statements at face value." But Calhoun said the jurors were able to convict the defendants because of government evidence, including hundreds of hours of secretly recorded conversations. Most damning was the conversation between Jackie Johns and Louie Pugliano.

"Without that, the verdicts might have been different," Calhoun said.

Gaetano's defense attorney, F. Mac Buckley, would months later defend heavyweight champion Mike Tyson for raping an 18-year-old contestant in the Miss Black America pageant in his Indianapolis hotel room.

John "Sonny" Castagna and his stepson John "Jackie" Johns admitted to robbing drug dealers, beating people with baseball bats, helping to assassinate mob underboss William "The Wild Guy" Grasso, and burying a mob victim beneath a Hamden garage.

Castagna and Johns were spared prison for their testimony and are now living in the Witness Protection Program.

Chapter 6

Racquetball With Mobsters

Big Al Bruno, convicted of racketeering in 1990 and serving a five-year federal prison sentence, became the center of a contentious issue that some believe negatively affected the long-standing tenure of Hampden County District Attorney Matthew "Matty" Ryan.

Assistant District Attorney Francis Bloom has accused Matty of being too soft on members of the Springfield mob.

For years, there have been rumors surrounding Ryan, who has held his position since 1958, and his alleged close ties with the criminal underworld. Matty Ryan may have interfered in cases involving organized crime figures such as Skyball Scibelli, Baba Scibelli, and Big Al Bruno, possibly dropping charges, lowering potential penalties, or seeking preferential treatment.

Ryan, who campaigned extensively in 1960 for President John F. Kennedy, has been closely linked to the Kennedys for years. U.S. Senator Edward Kennedy said, "Ryan has been a long-time friend of the Kennedys."

Fortune has smiled upon Skyball Scibelli in cases brought from Ryan's office. In 1960, Scibelli was accused of 8 counts of racketeering, yet he managed to evade any jail time while his co-defendant only received a 6-month sentence. Throughout the years, Ryan repeatedly dismissed charges against Scibelli in 1964, on two occasions in 1973, once in the late 1970s, and twice in 1981, showcasing Scibelli's remarkable luck in these matters.

Matty Ryan acknowledged playing racquetball at the Springfield YMCA alongside notorious Mafia leader Adolfo "Big Al" Bruno. He casually dismissed the incident, stating, "I think people know me well enough to know I can play with somebody today and prosecute them the next day."

Despite FBI investigations, Bruno faced two prosecutions in Springfield by federal authorities. However, despite Ryan's reign in the superior and district courts, no case was ever pursued against him. Ryan intervened when Bruno was apprehended in Hampden County on a New York state warrant. He had the underboss of the Genovese Family in Springfield released from the county Hall of Justice lockup and granted personal recognizance.

Attorney William Bennett was Bruno's attorney and recalled how Ryan rushed to the lockup from his third-floor office. Without permission, he barged in and took Bruno out of his cell. As a result, Bruno was swiftly back on the streets.

District Attorney Ryan did not pursue another incident, as stated in transcripts from a state police interview four years ago.

During the interview, while talking to Ryan's office about a loan shark, a car salesman mentioned an encounter with Bruno in which he was threatened with a broken back. The salesman revealed that Bruno and his associates had threatened him because he failed to pay off a $7,000 debt to another car dealer.

Two men approached him, insisting he go with them and assuring him, "Don't worry, Al Bruno wants to see you. He's getting mad now. You've been avoiding him."

Upon meeting Bruno, he was warned, "I should research who I am going to screw before I screw them. Don't you know who you're screwing?" Bruno says. "This is not State Auto Sales; it is us."

The salesman recalled feeling intimidated.

"I don't know what that means, but, well, to me, it meant Mafia because I guess he was in the Mafia, you know, and he gave me a big lecture all the way there that I should know who I'm messing with."

Bloom also mentioned that Ryan expressed "grave concern" over the possibility of Bruno receiving penalties for offenses committed while serving time in federal prison, which resulted in his relocation to a higher-security facility in Texas.

"Ryan called me into the room, closed the door, and started going nuts," Bloom said. Ryan said the action against Bruno in prison "isn't right, it isn't fair."

Bloom voiced concern for his safety and his family following his revelation of events linked to mafia activity.

He revealed that he has made "security arrangements" to secure his and his family's safety due to the menacing threats he has received in recent days.

Bloom submitted a written resignation three days after an incident in which Ryan intervened to have assault charges against Joseph Basile, a reputed up-and-comer in the Springfield underworld, dropped. Basile was on probation for his involvement in a cocaine trafficking ring that stretched from Florida to Massachusetts and had ties to organized crime. Basile happens to be related to Baba Scibelli.

Just 30 minutes before Bloom was scheduled to appear for Basile's arraignment, Ryan appeared before a judge and successfully negotiated an agreement that resulted in the dismissal of the assault and battery charges against Basile. In exchange, Basile paid $15,000 to two women, one of whom had been knocked unconscious in a confrontation with him outside of Pogo's Lounge. This resolution also spared Basile from a mandatory jail sentence for violating his probation.

Following Bruno's arrest under a New York state warrant, Ryan took it upon himself to secure Bruno's release from the courthouse lockup despite the presence of state police who were waiting to transfer him to Albany. This decision also ended up benefiting Baba Scibelli, a 69-year-old high-ranking member of the Mafia, as Ryan chose not to file a detainer against him.

At the same time, he served 18 months of a two-year federal sentence and awaited trial for gaming charges in state court. Scibelli remained in a less secure federal facility without the detainer and enjoyed certain privileges he may have been denied otherwise.

B&D Bakery, co-owned by Al Bruno and Aurelio Daniele, was previously known as The Italian Baking Company and was owned by James Sarnelli. Sarnelli brought charges against Bruno and Daniele, alleging that they had forcefully taken over his business while District Attorney Matty Ryan was prosecuting him for securities fraud. Despite providing substantial evidence of grand theft and extortion against Sarnelli, the district attorney manipulated the legal system until the case was dismissed.

Ryan, who still plays racquetball with Bruno, denied all claims but ultimately retired that year when the FBI launched an investigation into the corruption allegations.

In the small Italian village of Quindici, located an hour's drive from Naples, Italy, two local Camorra families—the Cavas and the Grazianos—have been waging a deadly battle for control of the valley for 30 years.

The feud between these two clans, which started in the 1970s when the clan's leader and town mayor, Fiore Graziano, was murdered at a football game by a member of the Cava family, has turned into a never-ending cycle of vengeance. The vendettas between these two families have spiraled out of control, with the original cause of the conflict long forgotten. What remains is pure hatred and a relentless thirst for revenge.

In the past three decades, 30 deaths have occurred, causing one in four people from both families to be wiped out. The Graziano family was made up of relatives linked to the Springfield mafia, including the Siniscalchi's, Santaniello's, Manzi's, and Scibelli's.

In 1991, a massacre was orchestrated and executed by the Cava clan to eliminate the "new recruits" of the Graziano family. As a result, some members were forced to flee to the United States for safety.

One of the men, Emilio Fusco, arrived in Springfield to meet with his fellow countrymen Antonio Manzi, Felix Tranghese, and the Scibelli brothers.

Emilio began dating his future wife, Jenny Santos, the daughter of Joe Santos, a prominent baker in the South End. Joe is not pleased with Emilio's presence in his daughter's life and seeks advice from Baba Scibelli. During their meeting, Baba and Emilio realize they are both from the village of Quindici and immediately hit it off. Baba is captivated by Emilio's tales of their shared homeland, and their bond grows stronger.

A year later, Baba Scibelli offers Emilio a job working for him as a bookmaker, collector, and personal driver. Emilio accepts the offer and quickly gets to work, driving Baba to meetings with their bosses in New York, such as Mario Gigante, Little Larry Dentico, and Arthur "The Little Guy" Nigro. Baba and Anthony Delevo appreciate having a tough, young associate like Emilio around, especially one who shares their animosity toward Bruno. They see him as a valuable asset in case they ever need him.

In the same year, Skyball and his decade-long right-hand man, Big Al Bruno, become eligible for parole and are released back onto the streets of Springfield in 1991. After being released from his position as a sales manager at Carando Foods due to his imprisonment, Bruno ventures into the restaurant industry, aligning himself with his brother, Frank Bruno, who owns the Casa di Lisa in Agawam and Bruno Pizzerias. Bruno also holds the title of president at B&D Bakery on Main Street and the Cara Mia restaurant on East Columbus Avenue, located in Springfield's South End.

Members of the Organized Crime Unit under the jurisdiction of the state police coined the nickname "PC" for Bruno, shorthand for "piece of the city," which symbolized his involvement in a multitude of legitimate and illegal businesses that he received a share of the profits.

Following his release from a five-year prison stint, Bruno and Jake Nettis were finally charged by State authorities in Hampden County for their alleged involvement in a failed mob execution at Bruno's brother Frank's Agawam farm almost a decade ago.

This came after Sonny Castagna, who had previously joined Team U.S.A, testified against Gaetano Milano in the Grasso murder trial and revealed that he was a backup gunman during the incident ten years prior when Al Bruno and Nettis shot Joseph Maruca five times. Bruno and Nettis were arrested for the attempted murder of Joseph Maruca, a mobster in the Bufalino crime family from Northeast Pennsylvania. At the same time, Anthony Delevo was named as an unindicted co-conspirator in the case.

Nettis' guilty verdict is overturned when a juror retracts their vote, and Bruno is cleared of all charges when the mob informant testifies that he hesitated to pull the trigger. Meanwhile, Nettis is found guilty of conspiring to commit murder and is sentenced to nine to ten years in prison.

After the trial, several journalists were at a local bar in the South End when Al Bruno and his entourage entered and sat across from them. The bartender informed them that Bruno had bought them a round of drinks. A few moments later, one of the reporters approached Bruno, shook his hand, and expressed gratitude for the drinks.

"Thanks, Al," he said, "do you know who I am?"

"No."

"Good," he said and introduced himself.

"Oh," said Bruno, "Why don't you write something good about me?"

"He does so much good for this community," said a friend of Bruno's. "How come you guys never write that?"

"Al, I've heard about some of the good things you've done to help folks out around here. But don't you think that a person like yourself hurts his standing and reputation in the community by being seen playing racquetball with the likes of District Attorney Matty Ryan?

Despite his joke, Al Bruno remained unamused. His bold statement, "I'll play racquetball with anyone!" even had reporters questioning his close relationships with law enforcement officials.

Rex Cunningham is a legendary figure in the gang world of Western Massachusetts. His name is associated with ruthless debt-collection methods, which have earned him a fearsome reputation throughout the East Coast.

Raised in the Springfield mafia, a branch of the notorious Genovese crime family in New York, Cunningham was groomed by his uncle Mario Fiore, a made member. In the 1980s and early 1990s, he was renowned as the most-feared enforcer for the infamous Scibelli brothers, Big Al Bruno and Carmine Mastrototaro of Worcester. Area mobsters agree that he was one of the Crew's most capable men, and many believe that if not for his mixed Irish-Italian heritage, he would have been initiated into the ranks and risen to the top of the Springfield crew.

The FBI planted a bug in Cunningham's headquarters at Dillon's Tavern on Tapley Street in May 1992. They continued to listen in on conversations there until November, and the hidden microphone caught Cunningham in his most boastful moments, providing federal authorities with "an airtight case." The court sanctioned the installation of the microphone following a month-long interception of conversations on two of Cunningham's cell phones.

During one discussion, Cunningham outlined the contrast between Mafia soldiers associated with the Patriarca Family and those linked to the dominant Genovese Family in Greater Springfield. He recounted a fierce "machine war" between Patriarca soldier Gaetano Milano, serving 33 years for murder, and reputed Genovese soldier Albert "Baba" Scibelli. The two were competing for control over bars to install cigarettes, video poker, and amusement machines.

Despite Milano's attempts, Cunningham stood firm in refusing to allow machines in the bars he co-owned with James Santaniello in the late 1980s. He proudly patted himself on the back for remaining loyal to Scibelli.

Thomas Ferris, a licensed electrical contractor, was at Dillion's Tavern in search of Cunningham to collect the debts owed to him by his business associates. He presented

Rex with index cards containing the names, addresses, and amounts of individuals who had outstanding debts to him, "Smash this one, smash that one, smack 'em all," Ferris demanded. "Beat him half to death if you have to. I don't want to lose a ton of money."

The Government recordings captured Cunningham's retelling of an assault on Ron Goulet to Ferris, revealing his tactics for dealing with such problems. Goulet had borrowed $17,000 and was avoiding repayment. Rex had tracked down the debtor to his sister's wake at a funeral home in the South End to assault him.

"I put a guy in the fucking hospital. He set me up to beat me. He got me for $17k. I have been looking for him for two years.

"Oh yeah, well, I got 'em; his sister died, and we sat outside the wake. That's where I got 'em. I went myself because I prefer that. I sat outside the wake. I followed him, a perfect tail. Followed him, and as he got out of the car, I grabbed him and threw him outta the fucking car."

Behind the Gaslight Room on Allen Street, which Cunningham owned, Rex had a "talk" with Goulet.

"When he got out of the car at first, I said to him, 'The bad news is, I said, the bad news is this ain't no meeting like I told you. And I said nobody's here but me, and I'm gonna beat your ass.' Then I smashed him in the face, and he went down, and then three guys came out from behind a dumpster a couple of minutes later with baseball bats and pipes. And I backed off and said, 'One guy at a time, and don't hit him in the head.' He went down pretty quick, and he didn't wake up 'til the next week."

One of the three guys was Cunningham's right-hand man, a tough Irishman named Brian Hoyle.

"I dropped his car keys on his chest. I told him we just beat your ass. And I said I'll call an ambulance for you. Then I took a wrench used to open fire hydrants and smash, smash on his hands. Fucked him up good, and I told him, 'Ya still owe me the money.'

"We left him bleeding all over the place."

Then Rex explained why he gave the guy such a beating.

"You make sure everybody in Springfield knows that you 'tuned somebody up' to deter anyone else who considers reneging on a debt."

Among a collection of nontraditional loans, Cunningham had made at exorbitant high interest rates of up to 300 percent per year, using money provided by well-known mafia members Francesco "Skyball" Scibelli and Adolfo "Big Al" Bruno.

"I get 1 1/2 to 2 percent depending," Cunningham said.

"I like to get 2 percent because I got my uncle Mario Fiore involved, Big Al Bruno involved. You got to give Skyball a piece of the action."

Ferris marveled, "Three and a half a week, that's armed robbery."

Cunningham corrected him, "Well, that's why they call it usury. That's why it's 15 years in the can," Cunningham said.

Cunningham extended loans to at least three individuals and received weekly interest payments of up to 5%, equivalent to an astronomical 260% annually, significantly surpassing the state's legal limit of 20% annually. He claimed that he was obligated to pay his uncle, Mario Fiore, a "made" member of the infamous Genovese crime family; mob caporegime, Francesco "Skyball" Scibelli; and Adolfo "Big Al" Bruno, by providing them with financial tribute.

"I've been doing this for 20 years, and to tell you the truth, I never outsmarted myself. I always think," he said, referring to his willingness to split his profits with members of organized crime. Despite numerous convictions for gaming in Hampden County, Rex Cunningham proudly declared that he had never experienced the closing of a jail cell door during his time as an "earner" for the Mob.

"This is my 23rd year in the business," Cunningham said within range of a microphone secretly installed by state police. "Seven convictions, no jail time. Thank you very much."

On one occasion, Cunningham engaged in a heated discussion about the advantages and disadvantages of running gambling junkets to Puerto Rico. The topic also involved deciding whether to give Bruno or Scibelli an interest. As part of their arrangement, he must share some of his earnings from loan sharking.

On another occasion, he recounted a story about a man who had been apprehended on drug charges in Texas. The man approached Cunningham with the names of four potential informants. Together, they deliberated on methods to determine the true identity of the informant and how to handle the sensitive information.

Brian Hoyle, a bartender at Dillion's Tavern, is found guilty of conspiring to use extortionate means to collect $21,000 in outstanding debts owed to Ferris by customers. In addition, he was involved in beating Ron Goulet while being on parole for a previous federal drug offense.

Consequently, he is sentenced to 12 and a half years behind bars. During his incarceration, he shares a cell with John Gotti Jr., boss of the notorious Gambino Crime family and son of the infamous John Gotti.

Rex Cunningham pleaded guilty to a litany of charges, including racketeering and loan sharking, as well as conspiring to use force to collect a debt and operating an illegal sports betting ring. He acknowledged knowing Frank Scibelli, Adolfo Bruno, and Carmine Mastrototaro but refused to admit the existence of La Cosa Nostra or the Mafia. Despite this, he was still sentenced to 16 and a half years behind bars, with a release date set for 2011. The indictment also named Ronald Goulet, John Gelzinis, Robert Marchetti, and Joseph Marino as victims, who were all given one-year prison terms for their refusal to testify against Cunningham.

Cunningham maintained his innocence in a statement, claiming, "I'm not the terrible person they've presented. I'm not an angel, but I'm not that bad." However, the district attorney quickly pointed out the severity of Cunningham's actions, stating, "If you swing a baseball bat for the mafia, you're going to jail for a long time."

During the summer of 1993, when Patriarca family member Gaetano Milano had begun serving a lengthy thirty-three-year federal prison sentence, "Big Al" Bruno faced a potentially fatal encounter with a loyalist of Milano's.

Vito Ricciardi, the owner of Vito's Barber Shop on Page Boulevard in Springfield, had lent $25,000 to Tony Scotto over several years. At some point in February, Ricciardi witnessed Scotto and Bruno sitting together at a table in La

Fiorentina Pastry Shop in the South End. A week later, Bruno approached Ricciardi inside the pastry shop and requested that they step outside to talk.

Big Al told Ricciardi, "The money the kid owes you is a wash."

Ricciardi said, "Bruno, what do you mean I'm not going to get my money?"

Big Al replied, "That's the way it is."

Ricciardi confronted Scotto, who claimed Bruno told him to pay him $5,000 a month. In response, Ricciardi sought Skyball Scibelli's intervention. However, Scibelli had a single conversation with Bruno, and nothing would be done.

Later that evening, Vito, "The Barber," went to the Mount Carmel Society Social Club, where Big Al Bruno arrived at 12:45 a.m. Ricciardi approached Bruno and requested to talk with him, but he was only met with aggression.

Bruno said, "Who are you to question me?"

Bruno then punched Ricciardi in the left cheek and then punched him in the neck.

Despite Big Al's aggressive response, Ricciardi pulled a .22-caliber pistol out of his right front coat pocket and fired two shots, narrowly missing Bruno. As he left the scene and drove home, Ricciardi couldn't be sure if his shots had hit Bruno.

No charges were ever filed.

Chapter 7

Capable Young Guys

On April 2, 1968, a young boy was born in Springfield, Massachusetts. His name was Anthony Arillotta Jr., but to his father, he was "Bingy." This nickname stuck with him, a reminder of his childhood days spent in his father's store, B&A Fruit and Produce on Bay Street. Tony Sr. had a way of giving nicknames to all the kids who worked in the store, and Bingy was no exception.

The bustling store, established by Anthony's grandfather in 1952, was filled with the sweet smell of fresh produce and lively chatter as customers came and went. Bingy loved being a part of the action, helping his father run the store, and learning the trade from a young age.

And when the wine grapes came in, fuhgettaboutit. When you opened the doors, they were fighting to get in at 8:00 in the morning to purchase Tony Sr.'s top-quality grapes. He was the most prominent wine grape distributor in Western Massachusetts, selling an impressive 30-35 trailer loads of wine grapes every season. Tony Sr. was a dedicated and hardworking individual who had run the store since the 1970s.

The Arillotta family was close to Al Bruno and Anthony Delevo, two soldiers who served under the Scibelli's. Unbeknownst to him, they often held meetings at Tony Sr.'s store in a back room stocked with pasta and olive oil. As a young boy, Arillotta would watch in awe as the New York, Connecticut, and Boston gangsters arrived for these meetings. With his sharp attire and cigar-smoking, Bruno exuded the bold and flashy demeanor of a genuine gangster. Through these encounters, the young Bingy first encountered Big Al Bruno. Even mobsters needed their produce, and Bruno was a regular at the store. He took a particular liking to Bingy and would always notice him. He would also generously tip him whenever he was at the store, often slipping Bingy a $20 bill as he helped load items into his car.

As Bruno browsed through the store, Anthony's father treated him with utmost reverence, like a king. As soon as they walked in, they got the red carpet treatment. His father would pack their boxes with care. However, Anthony's father's demeanor changed when the mob was out of sight. Anthony's father would warn him to steer clear, as these guys aren't going to last.

"Look, they get caught and go to jail," he told him.

To young Bingy, that didn't make sense. His family all say they're not good people, but when they come in, they fawn over them like royalty. Anthony believed that his father may have been a little jealous. There was a sense of resentment, albeit subtle, as his hard-earned money paled compared to the easy wealth these men acquired.

His father was not connected to the mafia, but he was hard-working and enjoyed gambling. He only placed bets on sports and had no involvement in booking games or anything like that. It was common for mobsters to visit his store regularly. Growing up in our neighborhood, it was common knowledge who the wise guys were.

Bingy was constantly causing problems and getting in trouble, and they noticed him at a young age. Former friends recall that Arillotta developed an "obsession" with gangster movies like "Scarface" and Italian mafia movies and books during his youth. They hung around the South End of Springfield, where all the prominent Italian clubs were located, and they were around the wise guys their entire lives. Anthony was not officially working for them or having affiliations like that; he was betting and booking games. His penchant for betting led to his downfall at 16, blowing close to a staggering $70,000, and there were all kinds of sit-downs over that.

Much to his father's disapproval, Anthony fell in love with the street stuff. His father admonished him, saying, "You're not hanging around with these fucking bums; you got to work in life."

However, Anthony had no interest in the tedious grind of a typical workday like his father. He craved quick and easy money. In high school, he abandoned his job stocking spinach at his father's store and instead focused on selling a different type of lucrative "green." This decision proved fruitful as the teenaged Bingy amassed a considerable fortune of approximately $200k selling marijuana.

Anthony Arillotta grew up in the Italian neighborhood of Springfield, Massachusetts, and was constantly exposed to the local leaders of Organized Crime. He soon became affiliated with their illegal activities. By the end of the 1980s, he was actively participating in criminal acts such as assaults and debt collections with other associates and members of the Genovese Family's Springfield crew.

At the age of 21, Arillotta began carrying a 9mm gun because his crew had a beef with another faction of Italians, and they got the better of them. Their friend warned them that they were being targeted, so Arillotta made sure to be prepared if they were ambushed while leaving a restaurant. As a message to the opposing group, he ended up shooting one of their dogs.

In 1990, while driving around with some friends, Arillotta got into a heated dispute with individuals in another car. With the gun in their possession and being stupid, they recklessly fired it out of the vehicle. After the altercation, Arillotta put the weapon away and drove off. However, it wasn't long before he realized they were being followed, and as soon as they parked, the cops approached them with guns drawn. Lying on the ground, they were thoroughly searched, and a firearm was discovered in the car.

During his time on probation, Arillotta was found to be in violation of the terms and was subsequently sentenced to a five-year term in state prison, with a mandatory one-year minimum. The prison rules were clear - any missteps would result in the full five years being served, but good behavior could lead to a parole hearing after just one year. Fortunately for Arillotta, they had somebody on the parole board who was always looking out for Anthony and always had the 2-1 vote to get out. This individual was the future mayor of Springfield, Michael Albano. He wasn't corrupt; he was just a good guy who knew his father.

However, his time in prison didn't straighten him out at all, thinking it was the best thing that happened to him. They're young kids having fun. How can you not? They were playing sports, working out, and even betting games on the streets. Arillotta was known to wager as much as $2,000 per game while behind bars. The prison itself was like a college dorm, eating pizza, Chinese food, and even booze for those who wanted it.

During his time in prison, Anthony gets approached by two made-men, Big Al Bruno and Skip Delevo, who were part of the Genovese crime family's Springfield faction. Al Bruno was considered a distant cousin, as they shared an aunt on his mother's side, so Bruno always referred to Anthony as his cousin. While incarcerated, Anthony received letters from Delevo's wife expressing Anthony Delevo's desire to have him with him. Similarly, Big Al Bruno also wanted Anthony by his side. These men were relatively young at the time, in their forties, and held positions as soldiers within the Genovese family.

The Geas brothers, both from nearby West Springfield, were initially drawn into the Genovese circle when Bingy crossed paths with Ty Geas while serving time in prison. Impressed by Ty's skills, Arillotta liked what he saw, describing Ty Geas as "capable," a mob term of high praise for a potential killer. Along with his brother Fotios "Freddy" Geas, a frequent visitor to the prison, the trio devised big plans for the crimes they would commit together.

Ty was expected to be released in 1991, the same time as Bingy, but as Arillotta was preparing to leave, Ty revealed that he had received an additional four-year sentence, thanks to a vicious beating he'd doled out to a prison guard no less. This setback delayed Arillotta's plans to partner with Ty in their criminal endeavors. Still, it only solidified his confidence in Ty's abilities as a seasoned criminal who could assist in carrying out acts of violence upon his release from prison.

The year 1991 marked the end of the fun. After serving a year, Arillotta was released and returned home. To his surprise, an unexpected guest paid him a visit. Big Al Bruno arrived at his doorstep and warmly hugged Anthony, eager to discuss the matter of the gun.

He questioned, "You were carrying a gun. What do you need a gun for?" Blah, blah, blah. They talked about what Arillotta wanted to do with his life. Did he wish to continue working at his father's produce store? However, the true intention of Bruno's visit was finally revealed.

He proposed, "Why don't you come work for me and be with me?" From now on, Anthony "Bingy" Arillotta was officially on record with the Springfield Crew, reporting to Big Al Bruno as an Associate.

During the early 1990s, Arillotta's criminal activities primarily revolved around three main areas - trafficking narcotics, running a loan shark operation, and participating in illegal gambling. His primary source of income was from distributing marijuana, averaging around 100 pounds per month throughout most of the decade.

While serving time in state prison, Arillotta formed connections with some serious guys and expanded his reach in the marijuana and cocaine trade. Springfield, being approximately an hour's drive from major cities like Providence, Boston, New Haven, and Albany and two hours from New York City, allowed Arillotta to establish his connections and expand his illegal activities quickly. When approached by Bruno, Arillotta was already making significant profits from selling marijuana, which had nothing to do with Bruno. However, being around Bruno was to get involved in sports gambling. Arillotta was a degenerate gambler who bet on the games, but he also booked the games. When Arillotta booked the games, he was his best customer, betting against his own office.

In terms of Arillotta's illegal rackets, his primary source of income was the marijuana trade, which Bruno had no involvement in and wanted no part of. Initially, Big Al was unaware that Arillotta was selling drugs. Later on, he would hear rumors about Arillotta's drug dealing, but he always denied the claims. However, the truth was that Arillotta was indeed selling marijuana, which, in Massachusetts, was considered a misdemeanor if the amount was under 50 pounds. This fact was kept hidden from Bruno and only added to the deceit and danger of their criminal endeavors.

Big Al Bruno was a high-ranking member of the Mafia organization and a "made" man. Being made means you took an oath of silence called Omerta, and you're an official member of the secret Mafia society, La Cosa Nostra. Bruno took it upon himself to mentor his young protege, showing him the ins and outs of the Springfield mafia, also called the Springfield crew. The crew consisted of about six "made" men, each responsible for overseeing a group of associates to assist in running their rackets and making money.

Although not as vast as the Mafia in New York or Chicago, the Springfield mob still had a significant presence in the city, given its size. Under Bruno's tutelage, the new recruit was taught the inner workings of the Mafia's lucrative operations.

Bruno was deeply involved in everything, you name it. During that time, sports gambling was considered illegal in Massachusetts. However, for the mob, such illicit activities presented lucrative business opportunities. Springfield area alone had thousands of betters, with money flowing into the hands of 40 different bookmakers. It was a multimillion-dollar enterprise. And that was just the tip of the iceberg. If one were to break down the total revenue generated by the Springfield rackets, it would leave people's heads spinning. It was unquestionably over a million dollars per week.

Of course, the mob didn't keep detailed financial records, but it was common knowledge that these rackets were significant money-makers. Besides being a money-making machine, Bruno also instilled in Arillotta the importance of keeping people in line. He was a master at this skill, and it was a crucial aspect of being a successful mobster.

Once, a barber made a joke that Bruno found insulting. The actual joke is a bit convoluted, so we won't delve into it, but it's important to note that Bruno was displeased when he found out about it.

So, one day, Bruno took Arillotta aside.

Bruno says, "Take a ride with me."

Arillotta had no idea of what was about to transpire. They drove to the barbershop. Bruno entered, his eyes fixed on the man he was looking for. Suddenly, Bruno unleashed his fury. Boom. Bruno starts breaking his face apart. Boom.

He punched him repeatedly. This all took place during broad daylight. The man's nose was broken, his lips bleeding, and he was knocked to the ground. The beating was so severe that another barber in the shop pleaded with Bruno to stop.

He implored, "Please, Bruno, please, no. Hit him no more, please. He's had enough, Bruno. Please."

The beatings, keeping people in line, the rackets, the money-making. That's how Al Bruno conducted business. And he excelled at it.

Now, the Springfield crew is not independent. They are a faction of the infamous Genovese crime family, one of the five most powerful mafia families in New York. The Genovese family, known as the most renowned, inspired Marlon Brando's character in the iconic film The Godfather.

However, unlike the flashy and flamboyant John Gotti, the Genovese family operates discreetly and secretively, avoiding any attention. They are cunning and strategic, setting them apart from the average mobsters. They are considered the elite within the Mafia, earning them the title of the "Ivy League" of the criminal world.

Fast forward to 1995, Arillotta's gang had achieved great success. Thanks to Bingy's connections from his time in prison, they were operating in Springfield and raking in profits in Connecticut, Albany, Boston, and Pittsfield. Arillotta, alongside Ralphie Santaniello, Albert "The Animal" Calvanese, Lou "The Shoe" Santos, "Villa Joe" Manzi, Anthony Scibelli, and the notorious enforcers Fotios "Freddy" and Ty Geas, were making major moves in Springfield.

The Geas brothers, delinquents since a young age, were intimidating figures with their large, imposing builds and sinister appearances. And the bond between the Geas brothers was unbreakable.

Apart from their frequent time in prison, Freddy and Ty were inseparable. It was rare to see one without the other. While Freddy exuded charm and cracked a big smile, Ty was more reserved and had a haunting emptiness in his eyes.

Arillotta crossed paths with Ty Geas while serving time for the gun possession charge. Upon his release, he established a friendship with Ty's older brother, Freddy. Both were crazy and ballsy, and they had a taste for fighting. During one brawl, Freddy even bashed someone's head with a bar stool, causing their skull to split open, and it looked like spaghetti coming out of his head.

It should be noted that the Geas brothers were not officially part of the Springfield mob, as they were Greek and the mafia was Italian. Regardless, Arillotta trusted them implicitly.

On one of his stints in jail, Ty Geas formed a connection with Gary Westerman, who was serving time for his involvement in the 1988 Florida-Massachusetts cocaine network case. Geas eventually introduced him to his brother, Freddy.

Westerman, who had relocated to Springfield in his late teens, had his first brush with the law at the age of nineteen when he was caught robbing stores at the Eastfield Mall in the city. Accompanied by two accomplices, they entered the mall by scaling the roof and crawling through air conditioning vents. Their loot included jewelry, furs, leather coats, and pharmaceuticals, totaling more than $28,000. He was convicted of robbery in 1973, and this was only the beginning of his frequent visits to state prisons throughout his lifetime.

After serving time for drug trafficking in the early 1990s, Gary Westerman hooked up with Freddy Geas, and they began robbing drug dealers, committing robberies, and selling large quantities of narcotics. At Antonio's Grinders in the South End, Arillotta first encountered Westerman in 1995. He couldn't help but notice the imposing, decent-looking character, clad in a stylish brown leather coat and dress pants, talking with Freddy Geas. Having heard of Arillotta's reputation while behind bars, Westerman expressed his admiration at finally meeting him.

Freddy and Gary's crime spree came to an abrupt halt in 1996 when authorities apprehended them for their involvement in the robbery of a trailer truck from the Yellow Freight terminal in Westfield. The truck, loaded with valuable computers worth $100k, was discovered five days later behind Edwards Super Food Store in East Longmeadow. They cut a chain and padlock to enter the yard, and a set of bolt cutters were found in Freddy's car. West Springfield police successfully caught them trying to offload 16 computers and 22 monitors to a computer business. Further investigation led to the discovery of a storage unit rented by Michael Frateroli, where a significant portion of the stolen goods were recovered. This marked the end of their criminal enterprise.

Freddy was concerned by the possibility of Westerman snitching for a shorter sentence and made it clear to Arillotta that he wanted to kill him.

"Two can keep a secret if one is dead," he declared. Freddy, Louie, and Arillotta had devised a plan to pick up Westerman and offer him the chance to join them in robbing a drug dealer. They knew he would jump at the opportunity for a quick score, and they knew he liked the thrill of the action. Once they had him in their van, Freddy would put a bullet in his head, and then they would dump his body.

A week later, Lou "The Shoe" Santos went to Westerman's apartment to ask him to come along for a robbery while the rest of the gang waited in the van with a gun.

However, Westerman's girlfriend answered the door and informed him that he had gone out, but she didn't know where he went, so Louie left as well. They knew they couldn't whack Westerman after his girlfriend saw Louie's face. They had not anticipated she would be at his place when Louie went to the door. If they had gone through with the murder, she would have been able to identify Louie in a photo line-up.

Less than a year later, in February 1997, Freddy was sentenced to three to five years in prison, while Westerman received four years. As a result, the hit never took place.

In 1996, Bruno and Arillotta had a falling out when Arillotta was arrested for possession of about 40 pounds of marijuana, criminal activity that went against Big Al Bruno's rules.

Arillotta's house was raided, and authorities found not only the marijuana but also some ammunition. Despite Bruno's suspicions that Bingy was involved in the drug trade, it was only after his arrest that Bruno decided to chase

Arillotta away from that life, banishing him from Springfield.

This effectively shelved Arillotta from Springfield and forced him to leave town. With Bruno's control over everything, all the local strip clubs, restaurants, and bars owned by the Springfield Crew or somebody affiliated with them, Anthony's banishment meant he could no longer associate with any of that. As a result, Arillotta spent the next few years earning by traveling between Connecticut, Boston, and New York, staying away from Springfield and the Springfield Crew.

In December of 1996, two of Springfield's top organized crime figures were sentenced to 15 months in federal prison for their involvement in an illicit gambling operation in Connecticut. Skyball Scibelli and Big Al Bruno pleaded guilty to a single felony charge of interstate travel in aid of racketeering.

Scibelli, Bruno, and their counterpart in Worcester, Carlo Mastrototaro, were convicted after a conversation at the Hartford residence of bar owner Anthony Volpe and incriminating phone conversations that were tapped. The trio's visit to Volpe's home in March was to ensure that Scibelli was receiving his share of the profits from an illegal card game held at the Standish Street Club in Hartford. This visit ultimately led to their downfall and subsequent imprisonment.

The day after Bruno and Mastrototaro visited, Volpe called Patrick Guglietta and told him, "Yeah, I got two visitors yesterday. Ah, Bruno and ah Carlo, and Ski sent them down. They want to know if he got a piece of the club."

Scibelli, the reputed caporegime for the Mafia's Genovese Crime Family in Western Massachusetts, and Bruno, a Genovese soldier, are facing their third stint in federal prison. Despite admitting to all accusations in their plea deals, the two men deny any involvement with organized crime.

Assistant U.S. Attorney Peter Jongbloed said, "If Mr. Scibelli were to tell us that after his sentence, he was going to go to North Carolina to be with his children, the government would be very pleased."

This prompted Scibelli to speak up, "I'll be 100 years old before I get through with all these things," Scibelli complained when given two years of supervised release upon being freed. "It's not fair."

Despite the imprisonment of Springfield's top two reputed mobsters due to their recent racketeering convictions, organized crime may be bleeding but not dead. The demand for their illicit services continues to fuel the persistence of gangsters and La Cosa Nostra, making it difficult to stamp them out. Despite decades of prosecution, the mob has proven to be resilient and able to revive itself after defeats.

Although their absence will be felt, they still maintain a stronghold in organized crime. Scibelli and Bruno may be behind bars but can still oversee and direct mob activities. However, with them no longer at the forefront and in control, law enforcement may succeed more in intervening in day-to-day operations. Nevertheless, history has shown that their families and associates will continue visiting them in the facilities and take messages back.

In Western Massachusetts, the Mafia's lucrative crimes, such as bookmaking, sports betting, numbers running, extortion, and loansharking, will continue as lower-ranked members rush to fill the void. Historically, the FBI targeted mobsters from the bottom up, hoping to get them to rat on their bosses, but this approach seldom worked because the little guys had their lives to lose and the government's limited legal power.

However, since the enactment of the powerful RICO statute, Racketeer-Influenced and Corrupt Organizations Act in 1970, law enforcement has shifted its focus to go after the top leaders of the Mafia, including notorious names like Paul Castellano, John Gotti, and Vincent "The Chin" Gigante. Even so, it may be impossible to wipe out the Mafia unless society's demand for illegal services changes. This is evident in the multibillion-dollar illicit sports betting industry, which remains a significant source of profits for the Mafia.

While Big Al served time in prison, Emilio Fusco was "straightened out" in 1997 and became a member of the Genovese Crime Family in Springfield. Albert "Baba" Scibelli sponsored Fusco's membership, and the initiation ceremony was attended by Scibelli, Felix Tranghese, Anthony Delevo, and his uncle, Anthony Torino, another Genovese soldier based in Springfield.

Fusco hated Al Bruno and even wanted to kill him, which Baba Scibelli found amusing but didn't take seriously. Scibelli told him you didn't do that. Bruno was another made member, and he was off-limits. However, this only solidified Fusco's loyalty to Scibelli and Delevo, who saw him as a valuable ally against their rival, Big Al Bruno.

In 1998, Bruno was released from prison, the same time Arillotta's marijuana case came up. The informant they were relying on turned out to be rogue, as he was caught twice selling cocaine and possessing a gun on separate occasions. However, when Arillotta's case was dismissed, the two managed to patch things up. Big Al summoned Bingy to meet him at his Cara Mia restaurant in Springfield's South End. The message was conveyed to Bingy through Arillotta's associate, Lou "The Shoe" Santos, that Bruno wants to see him.

When they meet, Al says, "You want to come back around me and, you know, you want to be with me?" He said, "I'll give you 25 percent of the sports and the loan shark."

Arillotta told him, "I'll do it, but I want 50."

He asked Bingy if he was all done selling the marijuana, and he told Al, "Yup, I'm all done," which he wasn't, but he just told him that so he could come back around Bruno.

Arillotta then resumed work with Bruno on various illegal activities, including, among other things, extortion, loansharking, and the gambling businesses.

At one point, Bruno nominated Arillotta to become a "made" member of the Genovese Family, but that nomination never proceeded further.

Arillotta's connection to the New York Genovese Family started when he began traveling to New York along with Big Al to meet with Arthur "Little Artie" Nigro and Pasquale "Scop" DeLuca, higher-ups in the Genovese Family, who helped oversee the Springfield crew.

Every week, and sometimes twice, Big Al and Bingy would journey to New York to meet with the captains, indulging in lavish meals at upscale restaurants. In the company of these other captains, they perceived Bingy as merely Bruno's nephew, tagging along for the ride. They never knew anything about Arillotta, what he had going on back in Springfield, the rackets, his reputation, or anything like that.

Christmas time with these guys was always like, you could set your watch by it. Al Bruno presented his Christmas tribute in a distinct way to New York.

Big Al would gather a van full of gifts worth $50,000, consisting of top-shelf liquors, Italian delicacies like Carando boxes of cold cuts, soppressata, prosciuttos, and more. Plus, of course, a selection of homemade wines, including cases of Opus high-end cabernets and Italian Barolos. Arillotta's father was a big wine grape distributor, and he had his guys making wine for him, so he would also load up gallons of it. Once the truck was loaded with all the tribute, Bruno requested Arillotta to drive down to the Bronx to deliver the gifts.

During his regular trips to New York, Arillotta began meeting some of the power players within the Genovese family. He came into contact with "made men," captains, the Gigantes, and members of the other five families. One of these guys was known as "Little Artie" Nigro. Initially, Arillotta was not particularly impressed by Nigro, as he was pretty reserved and had a dry personality. He seemed to be someone who carefully considered his words before speaking. However, after completing a Christmas delivery, Arillotta's visits to New York became more frequent, and he developed a close relationship with Artie Nigro.

During this period, Bruno starts beefing to New York that Skyball is not mentally capable of running the organization due to his dementia.

As Skyball Scibelli approached retirement, it was widely assumed on the streets and by local mob observers that Bruno, his longtime associate, would take the reins as leader of the Springfield crew. Bruno saw himself as the natural successor to captain the crew. His strong bond with Genovese acting boss Frank "Farby" Serpico made him the top choice for the promotion.

Amadeo Santaniello had been Bruno's loyal right-hand man for over 25 years. However, their relationship came to a bitter end when Bruno attempted to take control from the Scibelli family. A heated conflict erupted between Big Al and Amadeo, both well-respected guys in Springfield. Their hatred towards each other was well-known.

Despite serving a two-year sentence in federal prison and keeping his mouth shut, Amadeo's loyalty was questioned, and his stripes were pulled. Big Al sought a sit down with Skyball Scibelli to discuss the matter, and it was approved that Amadeo would be placed on the "pay no mind list" for secretly trying to sidle up to Genovese leaders in New York behind Bruno's back. This decision came at a cost, with Big Al being ordered to pay Amadeo a hefty sum of $200k for his interests in their business together. Fearing for his safety, Amadeo quickly fled the state and sought refuge in Florida.

Chapter 8

Groomed in Gangland Circles

Francesco "Skyball" Scibelli, one of the best-known and most colorful figures in the organized crime world of Western Massachusetts since the 1940s, peacefully passed away on June 29, 2000, at 87. He was known for his role as a successful entrepreneur in dining, entertainment, and travel. He owned the Empire Cafe and operated gambling junkets from the local area to Las Vegas for many years. Having been groomed by the long-reigning area Godfather, Salvatore "Big Nose Sam" Cufari, the veteran mafia leader and Skyball Scibelli served as the face of the Genovese syndicate's rackets in Western Massachusetts for decades.

A wake was held for Skyball, and over 1,000 people turned out to pay their final respects. The parking lot was filled with cars, and inside the funeral home, a lengthy queue of mourners slowly made their way to Scibelli's casket adorned with vibrant red roses. Family members stood by the coffin's side, warmly greeting those who came to offer their condolences. The walls were decorated with numerous floral arrangements from friends, some traveling from as far as Florida. "I've never seen a crowd like this," said one man as he waited in line for roughly 15 minutes in the afternoon to approach the casket and the family members.

At the historic brick church on William Street in the heart of Springfield's Italian-dominated South End, limousines could be seen in parking lots and along the curbside as mourners arrived to pay tribute to Scibelli.

In the sweltering church pews, among a congregation that was only half filled, sat state Senator Linda Melconian - the second most powerful Democrat in the Massachusetts Senate, serving as majority leader. Accompanied by her husband, trucking manager Andrew Scibelli, Melconian acknowledged mourners from both sides of the aisle as she took her seat and later exited alone. Agawam City Council member Anthony Bonavita, a Springfield-based lawyer, was also in attendance. Scibelli's nephew, Anthony Scibelli, a lawyer in Springfield, delivered a brief Scripture reading. Among the prominent lawyers present was Vincent Bongiorni, renowned for his defense of notorious organized crime figures, including Adolfo "Big Al" Bruno. These high-profile cases have marked Bongiorni's career, cementing his reputation as a formidable legal advocate.

As Scibelli's coffin, gleaming with a copper hue, was slowly wheeled into and out of the church, mourners, drenched in sweat, whispered prayers and blessings in its wake.

Reverend Carmen Russo, in his eulogy, expressed, "We shared Frank's life, his love, and his friendship," Reverand Carmen Russo said. "That's why the dark hours of the days of death bring a feeling that somehow, along the line, we are forsaken by God. But the death of Frank should not be a feared and frightening event, no accident or tragedy, because he shared his life with us, and we are grateful. We're here to tell our God, 'Thank you for bringing Frank into our lives."

Big Al's journey to a capo's post took longer than expected. By 1998, Anthony "Skip" Delevo and Albert "Baba" Scibelli had climbed to the apex of the local underworld hierarchy.

The 1990s were a relatively uneventful period for the mob in Western Massachusetts, with steady rackets and satisfied leaders. Baba Scibelli, who had taken over from his brother Skyball, quietly amassed millions through illegal poker machines. Baba was getting up there in years, and the Genovese family felt it was his time to retire and make way for new leadership. He began grooming Anthony Delevo, instructing him to make the rounds in the streets since he was never coming around. Delevo, Baba's protégé, was eventually promoted by the New York bosses, beating out Al Bruno, and was anointed as the captain of the Springfield crew.

Anthony Delevo's roots in the Springfield crew can be traced to old-school boss Salvatore "Big Nose Sam" Cufari, who reigned over the city's mafia empire from the end of Prohibition until the 1970s. Upon retirement, Cufari handed over the operations keys to his trusted protege, Francesco "Franky Skyball" Scibelli.

Delevo's involvement as an active member in the Springfield Crew of the Genovese crime family first became public knowledge in 1980. This came to light when police in Connecticut pulled over a car carrying Delevo and two other members of organized crime, along with two shotguns, two handguns, and betting slips. Delevo was charged, received a suspended sentence, and fined $1,000.

Adolfo "Big Al" Bruno and Anthony "Skip" Delevo were both groomed up in the gangland circles of the East Coast under the guidance of the notorious Scibelli brothers. Despite their similar upbringing, they were known rivals, each with a distinct, contrasting style.

Delevo came up under the direct tutelage of the refined Albert "Baba" Scibelli and was known as a more inconspicuous, understated, wise guy with considerably less thirst for the spotlight, preferring to stay close to home in Springfield. His primary focus was his successful concessions business, which catered to sporting events, concerts, and fairs. He also held a piece of the Mardi Gras strip club, the most prominent nude dancing establishment in town, which he co-owned with his wife, Carol, and Jimmy Santaniello.

Renowned for its decades-long presence, the esteemed Mardi Gras strip club boasts of being the premier hot spot in Springfield. As a local ad said, "It's the perfect location for a bachelor party, a birthday bash, or simply a night out with the boys. The Mardi Gras promises an unparalleled and unforgettable experience. Spanning an entire city block, this colossal four-story establishment offers everything you desire to let you have fun, relax and "unwind."

Delevo would discreetly convene with associates at his concessions warehouse in the city's West End section. As the chief of the regional policy lottery loan sharking business, Delevo was known to keep a low profile. As a previous detective specializing in organized crime once stated, "You didn't see this guy driving around in a Cadillac."

One Springfield crew associate said, "Anthony Delevo was more with the Puglianos, Franky, and Lou "Pugs," they were from West Springfield, which is only five miles away from the South End of Springfield. Felix Tranghese and the guys were with the Scibelli's. Anthony Delevo was a serious guy, and he operated lowkey. Anytime you see him, he looks like a farmer; he has jeans, boots, and one of those Italian Scully caps. An animal, though, and his uncle was Anthony Torino, a big figure in that world, too."

But on December 15, 2000, law enforcement agents rousted three generations of suspected mobsters from their beds, taking them into custody for alleged involvement in illegal gambling and loan-sharking activities. This marked the first round of prosecutions in an extensive investigation into organized crime. A total of nine individuals, including Anthony Delevo, whom authorities describe as the "capo," or leader, of a local faction of the Genovese crime family, South End barber Carmine Manzi, his son Giuseppe Manzi, Emilio Fusco's wife, Jenny Santos-Fusco, Todd Illingsworth, Andrew "Turk" Scibelli, and a police dispatcher, Ralph Santaniello, were apprehended and brought before the U.S. District Court. They appeared shackled and disheveled following coordinated early morning raids in five different communities in the Greater Springfield area.

Other targets included reputed mob patriarch Albert "Baba" Scibelli and Emilio Fusco, who loaned money and collected debts for the gambling ring.

The arrests capped a 15-month probe into a sports-betting and loan-sharking ring that prosecutors claim charged up to 400 percent interest rates and made violent threats against deadbeat debtors.

Investigators monitored the ring's activities using wiretaps for more than a year. Prosecutors claim that Emilio Fusco's wife, Jenny, was overheard attempting to convince her mother, Christine Santos, to launder her husband's money through the business accounts of the Italian Bread Co. in Springfield, which Jenny's parents operate.

According to the wiretaps, a meeting took place at a West Springfield restaurant on June 7 between Emilio Fusco and Anthony "Skip" Delevo. This meeting occurred just hours after two homes were raided, and investigators confiscated $13,000 and betting records. Delevo was livid and demanded to know why the records had not been destroyed before the raid.

"What numbers did they get? " Delevo asked, referring to telephone numbers. Delevo was right to worry about security. As he talked, an FBI agent was listening at a nearby table.

The state police had initiated the wiretapping of Carmine Manzi, Albert "Baba" Scibelli, and other reputed members of organized crime throughout Greater Springfield. Scibelli, brother of the late Francesco "Skyball" Scibelli, who was previously identified as the head of the local Genovese crime family, was among those targeted. The wiretaps uncovered a highly sophisticated sports betting operation and loan sharking ring, raking in thousands of dollars weekly from local gamblers.

Additionally, it was alleged that Emilio Fusco, known as the enforcer for the ring, used threats to beat or even kill those who owed money. Fusco was known to have warned deadbeats they would be entombed in cement for failing to make timely payments. The wiretaps revealed discussions between two accused loan sharks, Emilio Fusco and Todd Illingsworth, balancing their dinner schedules with plans to track down and beat a debtor.

"We have to beat him. So, find out where he goes, guy," Fusco said.

"Could be going to what's his name's house tonight," Illingsworth replied."

"Finish your dinner and everything," Fusco said. Let's wait and see if he shows up to pay the debt. If he doesn't show up, I have to beat him up."

Later, Fusco, expressing irritation with another debtor, tells Illingsworth, "What's this guy want to fucking take a shot?"

For a third deadbeat, Fusco had this suggestion, "Hey, scumbag like this guy put him in fucking cement."

The investigation of the mafia presence in Springfield originated 25 miles away in Amherst, where Jeff Kromenhoek and Richard "Chris" Berte initially attempted to launch their own drug business in 1999.

However, their plans took an unexpected turn when they later settled on robbing a well-known UMass ecstasy dealer. This botched robbery revealed a window into the criminal activities of the South End of Springfield, as Berte boasted to his Amherst friends about his ability to find two things necessary to start a drug-dealing ring: friends with guns and relatives with large amounts of cash, including his "Uncle Carmine," the barber.

Later, when Kromenhoek tried to back out of their planned robbery, Berte told him, "Why don't you grow a pair of balls?"

Berte recruited two Springfield men, including one who owed him $50,000 in gambling debts, to dress up as state troopers and stage a phony raid at the drug dealer's apartment. Within hours of the May 3, 1999, robbery, Amherst police began to unravel the case. Within two weeks, police arrested Berte, Kromenhoek, and the others.

In Hampshire Superior Court, Jeff Kromenhoek appeared anxious as he testified. The former University of Massachusetts football player was recounting a hesitant tale of a drug deal involving his friend's "Uncle Carmine" in Springfield. According to Kromenhoek, Uncle Carmine worked in a barbershop. "They had a private backroom where they played cards, gambled, and ran. I don't know what they did out of there."

When questioned by the prosecutor about Uncle Carmine's involvement in bankrolling the drug deal, Kromenhoek's response was, "Absolutely." Despite the drug deal never coming to fruition, Kromenhoek's account in a Northampton courtroom helped launch the most significant crackdown against organized crime in Greater Springfield in the past decade.

In Ft. Lauderdale, Florida, on February 27, 2001, a group of notorious gangsters, including Genovese capo Salvatore "Sammy Meatballs" Aparo and Joseph Zito, gathered for a meal with 90-year-old Albert "Chinky" Facchiano. As they dined, they fondly remembered past family leaders, such as Vincent "The Chin" Gigante, Philip "Benny Squint" Lombardo, and Anthony "Fat Tony" Salerno, who were now deceased.

During the gathering, Big Al Bruno was outspoken in his praise for then-family associate Michael "Cookie" D'Urso, who was not yet a "made" man. Bruno told D'Urso and the others that he "wanted to have him released" from his New York ties and become a "made man" in Bruno's crew. Little did anyone know that D'Urso wore a wire in his $3,000 Rolex watch.

D'Urso, a rising mafia member, managed to survive a bullet to the head in 1994 during a pre-dawn card game at a social club in Williamsburg. The incident, which resulted from a dispute over a gambling debt, claimed the life of his beloved cousin. However, due to the strict code of the mob family, D'Urso could not seek retribution. He was even threatened by the acting boss of the Genovese crime family, Frank "Farby" Serpico, with assassination if he tried to retaliate. This ultimately led D'Urso to wear a hidden recording device in 1998.

Upon his release from a 12-year prison sentence for his involvement in the "Wild Guy" Billy Grasso murder, Frank "Franky Pugs" Pugliano returned to the streets. However, Big Al had Arillotta's crew lag on Pugliano's activities to get his routine down.

Bruno went to New York, seeking permission to kill Pugliano for his unauthorized role in the Grasso murder. As a member of the Springfield crew, Pugliano's actions could have brought heat from the Patriarca family and sparked a dangerous war. In a desperate attempt to get him made by the Patriarca family, Frank enlisted his brother Louie Pugliano to join him on the Grasso hit. Despite Bruno's growing resentment towards Pugliano, New York ultimately denied his request to kill him.

Chapter 9

Propped Up

The Springfield crew represents an outpost of the New York Genovese family. When it comes to important decisions in Springfield, the ultimate authority lies with the New York bosses, who also have the power to select the leader of the Springfield crew. And in 2001, almost ten years after Bruno recruited Arillotta, they were about to choose a new one. With the arrests of Anthony "Skip" Delevo and "Baba" Scibelli in the 2000 racketeering case, Delevo's legal troubles knocked him from the throne. The chosen successor was Alfonse Bruno, and it was a dream come true for Big Al.

The official handoff occurred in the winter of 2001 during a dinner at Bruno's restaurant, Cara Mia, in the South End of Springfield.

Two high-ranking Genovese bosses, Little Artie Nigro and Pat "Scop" Deluca, made the journey from New York to officiate the event. As the meal drew to a close, one New York boss gathered the members of the Springfield crew around Bruno at the end of the long table. Felix Tranghese, Joey Basile, and Anthony "Bingy" Arillotta were all present. With a commanding tone, he directed them, "From now on, you guys listen to Bruno. He's the boss now."

Bruno's body was shaking, not from nervousness but from pure joy. It was clear to anyone watching that this was the best day of his life. One by one, the members of the Springfield crew approached Bruno, grasped his hand, and kissed it as if he were a newly anointed king. He was high on the best drug you could get your hands on—just like Superman.

Bruno's reign as boss was notable for its unremarkable nature, particularly at the outset. It wasn't like the wild, wild west, or anything in the Springfield area. Instead, it operated as a routine, orderly system, with the "made" guys running their rackets. Interestingly, Bruno's leadership style deviated from the expected norm for someone in the highly secretive Genovese crime family. He did not hide from the authorities but rather joked around with them.

Thomas Murphy, a Massachusetts state police officer who worked on the organized crime task force, remembers one day when Bruno pulled up next to him at a traffic light.

Murphy's like, "Hey, Al, how's it going?"

And Bruno says, "Oh, you guys got to leave them bookmakers alone. You got to get them drug dealers."

For the gangsters, these were the good old days of organized crime in Springfield.

The Scibellis and Bruno set their sights on two guys to be inducted into the Springfield crew. Joey Basile and Reno

Ceravallo were proposed to be made under "Baba" Scibelli and Anthony Delevo.

However, when Bruno took control, he added another name to the mix - Anthony Arillotta. This trio was set to become the newest members of the family.

In his new role, Bruno enlisted the help of "Bingy" Arillotta as a go-between for himself, Little Artie, and the bosses of the Patriarca family in Boston and Providence. Arillotta quickly rose through the ranks, politicking in high-powered East Coast mob circles on behalf of Big Al's interests, much like Big Al had done for the Scibelli family in years past. This was a strategic move by Bruno, solidifying his power and expanding his reach.

A couple months after becoming the boss of the Springfield Crew, an FBI agent named "Cliff" Hedges received intel that there has been or currently is a threat against Bruno's life. A confidential informant for the government in the witness protection program had informed the agency that a certain individual, whose name was blacked out from the report, was vying for control of Bruno's rackets in the area. According to the informant, the would-be upstart "wanted to put a 'hit' on Bruno and take over his business," as the two had a long-standing feud.

A week later, on February 12, 2002, Hedges found himself at Red Rose Pizza in Springfield's South End, watching a political fundraising event for then-City Council candidate Luis Garcia. Though his original intention was to rattle some cages at the height of a public corruption probe, Hedges also coincidentally encountered Al Bruno while there. By chance, he had been assigned the task of informing

Bruno about a threat on his life and took the opportunity to do so when he spotted Bruno in the hallway.

"Al, there's been a threat on your life," Hedges started, "and I'm telling you this information because we believe that the threat was real and current."

Bruno advised Agent Hedges that he knew Chris Berte was a "rat" in the Witness Protection Program and wanted to put a hit on him with Carmine Manzi to take over his business.

Bruno acknowledged the information and thanked Hedges for telling him, responding, "I get threats against me all the time."

He nonchalantly shrugged it off but soon became enraged. He engaged in a 45-minute conversation with Agent Hedges in the hallway, with everyone watching them. The talk covered various topics, from asking about family members and Bruno's golf game to discussing an upcoming trip to Florida and Bruno's belief that the FBI wasn't investigating the correct criminals. Bruno questioned Hedges about the ongoing FBI investigation targeting the city and asked why they were not pursuing the Puerto Rican drug dealers in the South End.

"This type of investigation is giving my son Victor some bad press, and now nobody wants to go downtown with the gangs and the recent fights," Bruno told the agent.

"If you guys would turn your heads for a few weeks, we would take care of them," Bruno said.

Then Bruno reminisced about the old days, saying, "Cliff, I can remember when we could leave our doors open and not worry about our women. Not anymore."

Hedges questioned Bruno about Baba Scibelli and Emilio Fusco, an Italian immigrant relatively new to Springfield's organized crime scene. At this point, Bruno volunteered details about Fusco's promotion in the ranks of organized crime.

Bruno tells the agent, "I don't care for Fusco. He was with Carmine Manzi and was "made" while I was in jail."

Bruno became nostalgic, saying, "It's not like the old days, Cliff. He should not have done this while I was away. Fusco is a hothead, and I hear you guys have some bad tapes of him talking a lot of shit. He is too young and needs to learn how to respect people."

As Agent Hedges turned and walked away, he was taken aback by the fact that Bruno was so comfortable enough with him to talk about something like that. However, in the subsequent days, Bruno seemed to dismiss the warning entirely. He showed no signs of altering his routines and continued to walk the streets alone, without any bodyguards.

It was later revealed in a 302 document that the threats had been intercepted during a prison phone conversation. The informant was Richard "Chris" Berte, involved in the botched 1999 home invasion at UMASS, talking on the prison phone to "Fat Frankie" D'Agostino about Carmine "The Barber" Manzi, Bruno's local rival.

During the spring of 2002, Big Al Bruno ruffled the feathers of local mafia wiseguys and club owners by muscling them for increased "rent" to revive illicit revenues choked from a crackdown on organized crime by law enforcement in Western Massachusetts. Following the passing of Skyball Scibelli and Anthony Delevo off the scene due to legal problems, many business owners discontinued their extortion payments.

Bruno informed Pat "Scop" DeLuca, the ranking member of the Cosa Nostra in New York City, that the Springfield faction was not collecting or making enough money due to their internal disorganization and disarray. As a result, Bruno walked away from that meeting with authority from his superiors to strong-arm establishments such as strip clubs, smoke shops, liquor stores, and pizza joints to pay higher "rent" to compensate for the shortfall. The term "rent" has long been used by organized crime members to refer to the money they demand for so-called protection.

According to an affidavit, reputed members of the Genovese faction began making regular trips from New York to this area on weekends following the meeting. They aimed to stake out clubs, estimate head counts, and skim profits from the door. Despite facing initial resistance, Bruno boldly proclaimed to a business owner, "I own this town."

A city patrolman on an extra detail at the Hot Club in Stearns Square reported the first indication of the alleged extortion scheme. Trooper Thomas Daly was permitted to equip Arillotta's Ford Expedition with a recording device and a global positioning system to gather evidence.

In May 2002, a city police officer informed state police that a burly white male, accompanied by Bruno's son, Victor Bruno, had been sneaking into a local establishment just before closing on weekend nights to meet with the manager.

State police then met with Jimmy Santaniello 10 days later, owner of a business in the downtown area known as the Mardi Gras, a confidential informant, and the nephew of Mario Fiore, a made member of the mafia.

Santaniello revealed that Bruno was pressured by the owners of various businesses to pay him money, even though they did not want to. This coercion was being carried out through the use of intimidation tactics associated with organized crime. The businesses implicated in this alleged extortion scheme included the Mardi Gras on Taylor Street, Teddy B's strip club on Worthington Street, two other unnamed strip clubs, and the Red Rose restaurant on Main Street.

Any establishment collecting a cover charge was required to hand over $1 for each customer to Bruno and his fellow visitors from New York. According to Santaniello, Bruno aimed to triple the current $7,000 "tribute" or "rent" collected monthly from businesses in the downtown area.

However, James Fiore, the owner of Cocktails with Bobby Cunningham and brother of notorious mob enforcer Rex Cunningham, refused to pay, resulting in a heated confrontation at Friendly's restaurant on Sumner Avenue. In no uncertain terms, Rex warned Bruno to keep his hands off his brother, alluding to their shared "secrets."

Bruno planned to bring the strip clubs in line and then move on to other businesses in the city by imposing a street tax on everything. He even managed to stop the pending sales of a smoke shop on Main Street and a liquor store on Worthington Street, both owned by loyalists. Bruno was pulling in over 50k per month through these extortions, which he generously shared with his crew. He also sent 6k to New York and distributed 1500 per month to his associates, including Arillotta, Felix Tranghese, Mario Fiore,

Joey Basile, Frank Pugliano in West Springfield, and even Anthony Delevo, who was one of his victims in the shakedowns.

In 2002, "Farby" Serpico passed from a bout with cancer in subsequent months while on trial, leaving a void in the leadership of the family. This led to the promotion of Arthur "Little Artie" Nigro, a member of the Genovese's historic 116th Street crew, headquartered between Harlem and the East Bronx.

At the time, the imprisoned Liborio "Barney" Bellomo was the actual boss of the Genovese family in New York, having been incarcerated since 1997. In a racketeering case sparked by an investigation into the family's 70-year-long control of the annual San Gennaro Festival, federal prosecutors in Manhattan charged Bellomo with murder and extortion. Despite passing three lie detector tests for the murder charge, Bellomo accepted a plea deal in 1997 and received a ten-year sentence for extortion.

Bellomo was nearing his late 30s when he was placed under the legendary New York City Mafia boss Vincent "The Chin" Gigante as acting boss. In 1996, Gigante faced federal charges of murder, labor racketeering, and other charges after a court ruled that he had been faking insanity for three decades to avoid prosecution for his Mafia activities. He was subsequently sentenced to 12 years in prison in December of 1997.

But the drama did not end there. On January 23, 2002, the Chin, along with his son Andrew and fellow gangsters, including Liborio "Barney" Bellomo, were indicted for running lucrative extortion rackets on the waterfronts of

New York, New Jersey, and Miami. Once again, Bellomo agreed to a plea deal, resulting in an additional four-year stretch. Ernie Muscarella was also charged in the case. Muscarella was a member of the "Panel," an administration that included the Genovese Family "messaggero" or messenger Mario "The Shadow" Gigante, Consigliere "Little Larry" Dentico and was led by Acting Boss Matthew "Matty the Horse" Ianniello.

At various points, a myriad of different bosses held the reins. Frank "Farby" Serpico, known as the "Quiet Don" at the time, was among them, along with "Fat Tony" Salerno, who was propped up as the boss, but in reality, it was "The Chin" who called the shots. As a result, you never really knew who their bosses were.

Since Ernie Muscarella was going away for five years and serving house arrest, he wanted Artie to take his place on the panel. Despite objections from the other two panel members, Mario Gigante and Larry Dentico, Ernie pushed for Artie to be there. Although Larry and Mario would not recognize little Artie, Ernie's wishes were clear. They would only accept it if Artie were promoted to street boss or front boss, not just acting in his place. They emphasized that he must be the one "holding the keys." This was a rapid ascent for Artie, going from a soldier to a boss, with only the top echelon aware of the transition.

Everybody thought Pat "Scop" DeLuca would get that spot because he knew everybody, he was a captain, a little bit older, he had been around forever, and he had an excellent reputation. Knowing how close Artie was to DeLuca, he wanted to break the news to him personally instead of having him find out from someone else. With

Ernie Muscarella in prison, Nigro was essentially running the organization. As he settled into his new role as boss, he became increasingly intoxicated with the power. He suddenly had a driver and a bodyguard and was often seen sporting a fedora, signifying his newfound status.

As acting boss, Nigro took a particular interest in the Western Massachusetts branch of the family. His mission was to generate a more substantial revenue stream from the regime and tap Felix Tranghese and others to rev things up. With Nigro at the helm in charge of everything, including Springfield, Big Al Bruno was feeling it.

Big Al faced an issue with Little Artie Nigro, who held a grudge against him for years. This hatred stemmed from Bruno's dismissive behavior towards Artie before he rose to the boss's seat. Despite Al being Farby's guy, Artie couldn't shake off the feeling of being slighted by Big Al's cold shoulder. This strained their working relationship from the very beginning and only worsened with time. As one former close associate of Bruno and the Genovese "Uptown Crew" recalls, "Al kinda brushed Artie off a few times. Al was Farby's guy, but Farby wouldn't be around forever. That attitude he displayed towards Artie back in the day ended up biting him when Artie was on top, so that working relationship was broken from the word go, and it only got worse."

Arillotta recounted the advice passed on to Bruno by other New Yorkers: "You should reach out to these guys in New York more because when you're in trouble, you're going to need them."

Nigro, on the other hand, was persistently pushing Bruno for more tribute, only adding more fuel to the fire.

During Big Al Bruno's time as a boss, he faced many challenges, including opposition from within and hostility in his once-strong relations with New York.

In May 2002, "Big John" Bologna was sent by the Genovese family to oversee the Springfield operation. Bologna was formally introduced to Nigro in 1999 at a social club on 189th Street in the Belmont area of the Bronx by operator Daniel "Uncle Danny" Cilenti.

As soon as there's a new boss, people come out of nowhere and weasel their way into power. One such weasel was John Bologna, who would constantly throw himself at Little Artie, reign him with compliments, and be right up his ass. Bologna even went as far as saying, "He who has the king's ear is the king."

Unfortunately, Bologna's tactics seemed to work. The new boss, Artie Nigro, quickly welcomed Bologna into his inner circle. Bologna now held the position of Nigro's right-hand man and was given the task of being the Springfield representative, visiting the city every weekend.

However, this didn't sit well with Arillotta.

His first instinct was that the guy was no good. In his mid-60s, the man sported a big gut, a giant boiler. He would often wear loud, floral-patterned shirts. His appearance included a beard, dark sunglasses, and a portly build, giving off a sleazy vibe.

Arillotta first met John Bologna in New York in late 2001. Capo Pat "Scop" Deluca had Big John around him and put him with Arillotta and Joey Basile to collect a debt in New Haven, Connecticut. It was $37,000 from a guy who had a scrap metal yard.

From then on, he assumed the role of a liaison, a messenger, connecting Al Bruno of Springfield with "Scop" Deluca of New York, and it proved to be the worst possible scenario for the guys in Springfield. Initially, his duties involved collecting a debt from someone nearby, relaying messages that couldn't be discussed over the phone, and eventually, just monitoring the Springfield mafia and seeing how Al Bruno was running the show.

Whenever Bologna came to town, Arillotta was always stuck with the responsibility of showing him a good time. He came up with a crew, and Big John and Bingy had fun when they went out. For Arillotta, it was just another night out. And that's how it all began.

Bologna started coming to Springfield on Friday nights to stay at the Sheraton downtown. As he started seeing what was happening in the area, he couldn't help but notice the iron grip Arillotta held in the area. Bologna's seeing everything from his big crew and numerous businesses to the strip clubs, restaurants, and social clubs. Armed with this newfound information, he brought that information back down to the captains and bosses in New York, who soon started recognizing Arillotta even more. The Geas brothers once dazzled the out-of-towner by ruthlessly beating several people to a pulp outside a downtown Springfield bar in 2002.

He saw Freddy and Ty fighting and beating people, and he liked it. He told Arillotta, "Keep them close."

One spot quickly became Bologna's favorite, as his obsession with women was demented and knew no bounds. Whenever he looked at the Mardi Gras strip club, he lit up like a child in a candy store. Even when the clock struck

11:00, and the club was enveloped in darkness, he could be found there, donning sunglasses and puffing on a massive cigar. His behavior was simply outrageous.

But after a few visits, Bologna's purpose for being at the Mardi Gras changed. Rather than seeking entertainment, he posted up right by the front door, carefully counting the number of customers entering the club. He was clocking the place for several weeks, meticulously tracking how much money the club made off the door each night. It was clear that the club was raking in a substantial amount of money, as Bologna eagerly reported to his boss, Artie Nigro.

He carefully poisoned Artie's head. The Springfield crew had gold up there, and he had his sights set on redirecting everything from Springfield to New York solely for Artie's gain. John often reminded Artie, "If you're the boss and Springfield's a faction, well, this all belongs to you."

Big John was a master manipulator, always playing both sides and exploiting any opportunity that benefited him the most. He wanted Little Artie to squeeze more money out of Springfield so he could have more himself. Bologna, eager to impress his rising boss, sought to please him by suggesting ways to increase their profits. In the cutthroat world of the mafia, loyalty is earned by making him money, and Bologna understood this well. Thus, he presented his boss with a suggestion.

"It's like paradise up there. We gotta get some of this money coming back to New York, and they need to be taxed."

This entailed forcing them to pay a monthly tribute to the boss of the Genovese crime family. Artie Nigro, the boss, agreed. The Springfield rackets belonged to him, and thus, they should be paid tribute. As a result, he directed John Bologna to extort more of Springfield's businesses. This extended to not just the Mardi Gras but all businesses linked to the mob in the city, including one of Arillotta's partners, Steve Marshall.

So, John Bologna sees Steve and wants to shake him down. He asks, "Who's that?"

"That's my partner in Club Blue in Hartford," Arillotta tells him.

"Tell him to give you 500 a week."

"I'm not telling him to give me 500 a week; he's my friend."

"You got no friends. All your friends are down in New York."

John Bologna was always seen sporting dark glasses with gold rims, indoors or outdoors, during the day or at night. He often traveled with Timothy Sampson, a towering figure with a rough and intimidating appearance. The shakedown crew, which usually included Arillotta, racketeer Felix Tranghese, and drug dealer Joey Basile, would bounce around Greater Springfield, with police closely tailing their movements.

They regularly stopped at Master's Cigar Shop in West Springfield, Coconut's on Dickinson Street, La Fiorentina, an Italian pastry shop on Main Street in the city's South End, Zonin's meat market on Winthrop Street, and Our Lady of Mount Carmel Society Social Club.

Bologna and Sampson regularly ended up at the Mardis Gras, much to the displeasure of gangster Anthony "Skip" Delevo, a "hidden partner" in the strip club. The two men's presence at the club on weekends displayed the Cosa

138 | P a g e

Nostra's influence in New York and a deliberate attempt by Big Al Bruno to humiliate Delevo, who had once surpassed him for the top spot as boss. Delevo, a "made man," had his men taken away from him by Bologna and Sampson, who were determined to shake down his business partner. This was a disrespectful move, as Delevo had put in work, killed people, and been a soldier his whole life, only to have his legitimate business interests undermined by the duo's efforts to take Springfield and siphon it where it was going to New York.

Before long, news of Bologna had even reached the ears of law enforcement. The few sources they had, the alarm bells went off. The amount of extortion payments skyrocketed, with some of Bologna's extortion victims also being police informants. His name was on everyone's lips, causing quite a stir.

Despite Anthony Delevo's strong dislike towards Bruno, he was not the only one holding a grudge. Bruno's stepped-up collections were alienating former allies. Many people who have had longstanding familial or personal ties with members of the organized crime world are outraged by Bruno's attempts to extort money from them. This has resulted in extremely hard feelings among many life-long supporters.

On June 28, 2002, a high-level boss from New York arranged a trip to celebrate the grand opening of a new liquor store on Main Street in the South End. The boss, Pasquale "Pat" Deluca, also known as "Scop," had a notorious past as a convicted drug dealer. However, after the liquor store's opening, he was set to hold a different kind of meeting. He would also hear grievances concerning Bruno's extortionate activities.

Later that night, the police tailed Deluca, Bruno, and retired wiseguy Baba Scibelli to Cara Mia, a restaurant owned by Bruno on East Columbus Avenue. The trio spent several hours that night and the following discussing matters. During this time, state police documented 32 meetings between the New York members and organized crime figures in Western Massachusetts from June 2 to August 22.

Chapter 10

How Can You Protect Me

As the summer of 2002 approached its end, tensions simmered between Arillotta and Bruno. Arillotta's top two enforcers and close friends, Ty and Freddy Geas, had begun to clash with Big Al. The once-student, now rival, Arillotta, was quickly surpassing his teacher, Bruno, in power and popularity within the mob. Amid this turmoil, Arillotta and Big Al's relationship was rapidly deteriorating. The streets were a battleground, and the fate of the Springfield mob hung in the balance.

The situation reached a boiling point when Big Al and Ty Geas got into a heated argument outside a cigar bar in Springfield, triggered by a Rolex watch-sale-gone-bad deal. Arillotta had to physically intervene and break up the altercation between the two men. The root of the conflict was a fight between Freddy Geas and Bruno's son over a supposedly fake Rolex. The Geas' uncle, who ran a jewelry shop, The Diamond Gold Connection in West Springfield, was the center of the dispute.

While having dinner at Amherst's Pinocchio's restaurant, Arillotta, Ty Geas, and a friend, AJ, received a call from Bruno, summoning them to the Mount Carmel Social Club in Springfield. As they arrived, they were greeted by the sight of a luxurious stretch limo as Bruno and his friends were out celebrating. However, the festive mood quickly turned sour when an intoxicated Bruno stormed from the club and began berating Anthony for his association with Freddy Geas.

"Your friend Freddy is a piece of shit," not realizing Ty Geas is sitting in the seat next to him.

Ty tells him, "Don't talk about my brother like that."

Big Al responded, "You know, your brother's a fucking prick."

In a moment of anger, Bruno starts slapping Ty across the face, which etiquette dictates you sit there and take it. However, Ty refuses to accept the abuse and stops the slap. Al becomes upset that Bingy and a couple of the other guys around aren't more on his side in reprimanding Ty for putting his hands on Al, and it just creates more division.

The real violence that was popping off that summer wasn't even about Bruno. It demonstrated the climate, though, and set a tone.

Then, John Bologna, the unwanted visitor from New York, was doing things behind the Springfield boss's back. Despite being Bruno's city, he was causing a stir and agitating Big Al.

The tension between the two men reached a boiling point over the Mardi Gras strip club. While the club was already paying a small tribute of $500 per week to Bruno, Bologna set his sights on diverting the payments to New York and doubling the amount. However, Bruno wasn't having it. To settle things, Bruno and Arillotta arranged a meeting with the club's owner, Jimmy Santaniello. Bruno made it clear that he was the boss of Springfield and that any demands from Bologna should be ignored. However, the owner was skeptical of Bruno's claims.

"Well, how can you protect me? When John Bologna comes up and he says I have to pay him $1,500 a week, who do I listen to?"

Then Bruno turned to Arillotta and said, "Tell him who the boss is and tell him who to listen to."

With Bruno standing right next to him, what's Arillotta going to say?

"Bruno's the boss. Yes, Listen to Bruno."

On the weekends, Bologna would bring Arillotta back to Mardi Gras and tell the owner the opposite.

"Listen, I'm direct with the boss down in New York, and the New York boss told me you pay $1,500 a week. Tell him, Anthony. Tell him. Tell him who."

So, Arillotta says, "He's with the boss down in New York." He's stuck between his boss Bruno and New York.

Ultimately, the Mardi Gras owner was forced to make a more significant tribute, beginning with a $100,000 restitution installment for backpay and a $ 2,500-a-week payment from that point forward. However, this amount was eventually negotiated down to a mere $1,000. This arrangement was highly irritating to Bologna. Bruno stood in his way, and he made his feelings known to Artie Nigro.

John Bologna was spewing venom: Bruno did this, Bruno did that. Bruno is making a ton of money.

"He should be giving it to you, Artie."

That's what started souring Artie against Bruno.

This was the catalyst for Artie Nigro's plan to undermine Bruno and reassert his dominance. He devised a scheme to weaken Bruno by poaching his underlings and convincing them to shift their loyalty away from Bruno and over to him.

Arillotta was his first target in this scheme.

As time passed, Bingy started getting closer to Artie, regularly traveling to New York to meet directly with the Genovese boss.

Arillotta, a big earner and quick to pull a trigger or throw a haymaker, had earned the trust and admiration of Nigro and the other brass in New York City. He leveraged this influence to his advantage when he returned to Springfield. Anthony's stock skyrocketed in New York; you could hear the whispers from the Bronx and Manhattan that they loved the kid. He already had a big head, and his ego inflated even further, so Al lost his grip on him. New York's allure proved too strong for Anthony, who was seduced away from Big Al.

Soon after, State troopers obtained a court order to install a bug and GPS tracking system in Arillotta's SUV to investigate allegations of extortion involving Arillotta, Bologna, and others.

However, after the devices were put in place, visits from New York suddenly halted. Authorities suspected a possible leak, although they could never prove it. Following weeks of regular trips to Springfield, Bologna abruptly stopped coming. This behavior change coincided with local officials contacting authorities in New York to inquire about Bologna. It was revealed that Bologna was only traveling as far as Hartford, Connecticut, due to his awareness of the ongoing investigation in Massachusetts, which the police had tipped off about him.

Adding to the trouble, Arillotta no longer utilized his SUV and instead exchanged vehicles with his sister-in-law for her Mitsubishi. Annoyed with his actions, state troopers texted him, taunting him, "Hey Bingy, pick up your skirt and quit driving a girl's car," hoping to provoke him to drive the bugged SUV.

In January 2003, things began going downhill fast as a stolen shipment of cigarettes in South Florida caught Big Al's fury and occupied much of his attention. Nigro and Bruno began butting heads due to a beef over a $250,000 scam run on Bruno by one of Nigro's Florida lieutenants. Nigro's refusal to get Big Al proper reparations only added fuel to the fire, resulting in constant clashes between the two.

Bruno had a big deal going with Carmen Bonavita and a few other guys. The deal would be a billion-dollar deal, the biggest one ever; they're all going eat, their bellies get full, and care for everyone. However, they needed political help. The Genovese mob's Florida capo, Ray Ruggiero, comes in on the deal through Artie and says he's got the Governor out of Maryland, Robert Ehrlich, Jr., that they can pay off for $250,000.

Despite Bruno coming up with the 250k, he never saw the cigarettes or the money again.

Little Artie traveled to Florida to conduct a sit-down between Bruno and Ruggiero. The meeting was held in a warehouse located in Boca Raton, and Lil Artie ultimately ruled that Big Al was out of luck. Nigro, in his ruling, ordered that Ruggiero didn't have to repay any money and instead had to write a letter to an insurance company to protect Ruggiero and his crew from a potential fraud accusation related to a failed tobacco deal. To add insult to injury, Little Artie directed South Florida gangster Mitchell Weissman to inform Bruno that he was no longer permitted to put "money on the street" and was blackballed from the Sunshine State.

Mitchell Weissman, a 59-year-old associate of the Genovese crime family from South Florida, crossed paths with Nigro in 2001 and quickly became involved in running a loan-sharking operation for the New York-based crime boss. Weissman had been acquainted with Bruno for many years and believed that Nigro had intervened in a past dispute within the Genovese organization, potentially saving Bruno's life.

Big Al was later heard complaining about the edict strictly forbidden in organized crime. At the time, Bruno was unaware that Artie was the boss and was heard saying, "This guy robbed me, Ray; he's a brother, a 'made' man, a captain in our family." Artie pushes him to the side, and Bruno asks, "How can a brother rob me of 250k?" It is uncommon for someone to challenge a decision made by a boss in the mafia. Because he's the boss, and that's the way it is.

Ray Ruggiero convinced Bruno to hand over a quarter million dollars, believing they were investing in bootlegged Marlboro cigarettes to be sold in China. Ray and Artie split the money and swindled Bruno. The situation in Florida was not about fair or not fair or scam or no scam, but rather Artie letting Al know who's in charge and that he could do whatever the fuck he wanted to do no matter what.

Bruno's downfall began with the cigarette export deal he partnered with fellow mobsters. This was only the beginning of a series of incidents that would undermine Big Al's authority, often in subtle and passive-aggressive ways that he was completely oblivious to. This same treatment also trickled up to Massachusetts, as Arillotta worked to weaken Big Al's power there.

As the days passed, he was losing touch with the streets. His bosses in New York, top protege Anthony Arillotta, and former right-hand man Felix Tranghese all turned on him under his very nose. Tranghese was sponsored for membership into the Genovese crime family by Big Al Bruno in a 1982 initiation ceremony carried out by the legendary Franky Skyball Scibelli in the basement of a restaurant in Springfield's South End. Interestingly, Tranghese was Scibelli's cousin.

In March 2003, John Cody, a freelance bookmaker and loan shark, was in a precarious predicament. Unbeknownst to him, the Massachusetts State Police had wiretapped his cellphone, and he received an urgent call from an old friend.

In a recorded conversation on March 20, 2003, Cody's friend, Reno Ceravolo, can be heard urgently pleading to meet him as soon as possible.

"I got to see you ASAP, very, very, very urgent!" Ceravolo exclaims. "It's, ah, some kind of problem, buddy."

"Oh, yeah?" Cody responds, pretending to be nonchalant.

"Yup," Ceravolo stresses, "I got called down somewhere at 10 o'clock last night."

Investigators obtained recordings of a conversation while investigating an illegal offshore gambling ring in which Cody from the Feeding Hills area of Agawam was involved. The investigation uncovered a successful offshore sports-betting organization that connected local gamblers to a clearinghouse in Costa Rica and revealed a potential mutiny under Bruno.

It was discovered that Arillotta and Cody had partnered to take betting action and provide high-interest loans to Cody's associates. This caused a stir when Bruno found out, thanks to a panicky debtor who protested to a longtime Bruno friend, thus outing the loans.

Later in the conversation, Ceravolo says, "You're probably going to be a little shocked when you hear it when it's one of your guys like, he ah, said something to somebody, you know?"

Two individuals who owe money to Cody complained to Bruno's buddy, Tim Hourihan, about drowning in so-called juice, or outrageous interest, on past loans. During a trip to Florida, Hourihan informs Bruno of the situation, who, under customary mob profit-sharing standards, is due a percentage by way of his position and knows nothing of the loan.

It was a problem for Cody, Ceravolo, and anyone with enough mob savvy. That same evening in 2003, Bruno summoned Ceravolo to his Italian restaurant, the Cara Mia, on Columbus Avenue.

Bruno was furious.

The wiretap transcripts revealed a debt record bearing Cody's name, and Ceravolo was charged with conveying Bruno's anger to Cody. Cody contended he was solely collecting on Arillotta's behalf and knew nothing of cutting Bruno out.

Ceravolo's initial call on March 20 triggered a flurry of phone calls and hastily arranged meetings within the next day.

"I think you fucked me real good, my friend. I just got a call. I don't know what you did to me. But, uh, I don't appreciate it," Cody accuses debtor Matthew Dowd based on his suspicions.

During the barrage of recorded cryptic phone conversations set off by Ceravolo's initial call, it became evident that Arillotta was not sharing the expected profits with Big Al.

"The little kid there," Cody said to Ceravolo, using Arillotta's nickname, "doesn't go to him. Mr. Brown," Bruno's nickname, "seems to think nothing's coming his way. Because there's a lot of stuff going the other kid's way, but that kid's got to step up to the plate."

In brief, Cody is arguing to Ceravolo that Arillotta must stop hoarding profits.

In light of the repercussions of the rogue loans, Cody urges Arillotta to tell Bruno that he is not withholding profits. The three plan to meet at Zonin's Meats on Winthrop Street on March 21, 2003, to discuss the issue. Arillotta heads inside to tell Bruno while Cody waits outside. When Cody later talks with Ceravolo about the meeting, he voices suspicions regarding Arillotta's decision to go in alone.

"The little kid doesn't want me anywhere near Mr. Brown, 'cause I went down there, and he goes, 'no, no, no,' he don't want to talk to you. He don't want me near the fucking guy, for some reason," Cody tells Ceravolo.

"Yeh, that's gotta put a little, uh, light bulb up there, no?" Ceravolo responds.

Additionally, in the same conversation, Cody reveals that Arillotta has advised him that he is no longer aligned with Bruno.

He told me he was not with him. He said, "I got a better out' than Mr. Brown."

And I said, "Oh geez," Cody reports.

Towards the end of their discussion, Ceravolo shares some of the most profound guidance in their exchange.

"The thing is, John, you don't want to get caught up in the fucking middle of some kind of fucking uh, battle going on, you know?"

Over the years, Bruno was a go-between for the Springfield crew's dealings with the Patriarcas in Boston. Speculation arose in late 2002 and early 2003 regarding a potential beef between Bruno and the Patriarcas, stemming from bad blood developing between Big Al and the Providence faction of the Patriarca crime family.

During this time, a close associate of Bruno's in Connecticut, Joe Mazzotta, began getting muscled by the Patriarca crime family's Providence branch to pay tribute for a bar he owned in Cromwell, Connecticut.

In March of 2003, someone left a severed pig's head on the front steps of Cocktails on the Green, where low-level rackets were being conducted and allegedly no street tax, or at least not enough, was being shared.

Less than a month later, Joe Mazzotta was gunned down at his desk at his office in Mazzotta Brothers Equipment

Rentals in Middletown, Connecticut. Although it was a Saturday and the business was closed, Mazzotta knew his killers and willingly let them in. To this day, no one has been arrested or charged for his murder.

One theory is that Connecticut Genovese mob associate Joe Mazzotta was killed on the orders of Western Massachusetts capo Big Al Bruno.

According to sources, Mazzotta had shown disrespect towards Bruno. Mazzotta was familiar with Bruno through his dad Sal and Uncle Seb, a pair of Connecticut contractors and equipment-rental kings. They paid protection money to Big Al and the Genovese crime family in Springfield. However, when Joe began assuming more responsibility, he threatened to reduce the flow of money going to Massachusetts. He even attempted to cut off Bruno's tribute from his and his family's businesses. Additionally, his dad, Sal Mazzotta, was famously acquitted of drug trafficking charges in a high-profile trial in 1990. He hired a bodyguard in the days after his son's slaying.

This occurred while Big Al was organizing a group of young soldiers in Connecticut to expand their territory and encroach upon the turf of the Patriarca crime family in New England. Bruno created a list of potential candidates to be "made" in Connecticut, which was sent to New York for approval. It remains unclear if any of the proposed men got their buttons.

A second theory is that Mazzotta was murdered on the orders of the Patriarcas after Bruno failed to get Nigro and the bosses in New York to go to bat for him with the Patriarcas in the dispute, attempting to protect Mazzotta from a Patriarca shakedown. If this theory holds, it would suggest that Bruno's inability to secure a sit-down meeting, which would have been his second failure in as many months, was a clear indication to all members of the East Coast mob that Big Al's influence was declining and in serious jeopardy.

Big Al appeared at Joe Mazzotta's wake and funeral in Connecticut just as he began losing control of his crew back in Massachusetts. Big Al was trying to expand into Connecticut against Nigro's wishes, causing further friction, as well as growing dissent within his ranks in Springfield.

Bruno faced a series of troubles, lacking the juice to protect his own guy. He was drinking more, and there was something off in his behavior. New York sent a guy to Springfield to assert control, ensuring people knew they were keeping tabs on Big Al. This demonstrated what New York thought of Bruno and their desire to keep a close eye on him. While nobody would have predicted what would happen to him, it was evident that he was slipping, and there was incoming fire from all directions as problems continued to arise everywhere.

Chapter 11

Piece of Work

In May of 2003, the connection between Anthony "Bingy" Arillotta and "Little Artie" Nigro and "Big John" Bologna grew stronger each day. Bingy was drawn into their inner circle, becoming increasingly involved in their activities. Bingy reveled in the thrill of being part of their world, with the adrenaline pumping through his veins as he worked alongside his new associates.

One day, as Arillotta and Nigro cruised through the Bronx, they searched for "made" man Anthony DiFranco. They were looking to greet him with a lead pipe. DiFranco had shown disrespect towards Nigro in front of another capo. Although they could not find him that day, it exemplified the flavor of their partnership.

This was how Nigro operated in the Genovese family, using physical attacks to assert dominance. This was how one got a reputation in the Genovese family. The actual beating was carried out later by Little Artie, Big John Bologna, and Steve "DD" Alfisi, solidifying their loyalty and fearlessness.

Big Al Bruno had "proposed" Anthony Arillotta, Joey Basile, and Reno Ceravolo for membership in the Genovese Family in Springfield. However, Nigro wanted Arillotta "direct with him." To solidify this, Nigro had Arillotta drive down to New York without explanation. It wasn't until he arrived that he learned the purpose of the trip. Nigro's right-hand man, John Bologna, had a message for him - Artie wanted him to carry out a "piece of work." In other words, to do something violent. Bingy was then handed a piece of paper with a name on it: just a name, no address. As Anthony read the name, it sounded like Dabadoo.

At the time, Arillotta remained unaware that the individual in question was Frank Dadabo. This man was a 65-year-old shop steward in the Cement Masons union in New York City, a union that was under the thumb of Artie Nigro and the Genovese family. Despite an argument over his failures to service workers he was supposed to help as a shop steward, Nigro and Dadabo were once close friends. They often dined at restaurants, attended shows, and frequented Rao's, a popular East Harlem eatery favored by wise guys, politicians, and celebrities. In turn, Nigro would hook Dadabo up with union jobs.

However, in 2003, their relationship became strained due to a falling out over concert tickets. When Dadabo heard about the Tony Bennett concert, he ordered tickets through the wife of a union buddy. However, he changed his mind when this same pal double-crossed him by not supporting his candidacy for a union post. When Dadabo told Nigro that he wasn't going to the concert, he said, "Don't worry about it," and Dadabo got his money back for the four tickets he had bought.

In the end, Nigro went to the concert without Dadabo and then lied to him about it. When Dadabo eventually discovered the truth, he was consumed with rage. However, he knew better than to confront a powerful mob boss. Instead, Dadabo played it passive-aggressively, decided he "didn't want to be bothered no more," and shunned the Genovese mobster. Nigro would ask to see him, but Dadabo wouldn't respond. He even stopped going to Nigro for union work. Instead, he reached out to a "made" member of the Lucchese Family he had known for 40 years for protection from Artie, further infuriating him. He hadn't seen or spoken to Nigro in seven or eight months.

For Artie Nigro, that was an insult too great to ignore. So, he asked Anthony Arillotta to do a "piece of work."

Agreeing with the plan, Arillotta met with Nigro and Bologna in the Bronx. They then drove him to an apartment where a guy lived. They pointed out that the man left his apartment every morning at around 6:00 a.m., allowing Arillotta to get the job done. At first, Nigro and Bologna did not specify precisely what they wanted Arillotta to do to this man. Arillotta asked, "What do you want to do with this guy?" It was then revealed, "Kill him."

Anthony refrained from asking any questions, an act that would be deemed unacceptable. You would never do that. You don't ask questions because only rats ask questions. Despite his unwavering loyalty, Anthony's allegiance was being put to the test. He found himself caught between two powerful bosses - Artie Nigro, head of the New York

Genovese family, and Al Bruno, the boss of the Springfield Crew.

In the world of Cosa Nostra, murdering at the request of one's boss is seen as the ultimate act of loyalty. It demonstrates a willingness to kill because your leader gave you an order. And once the deed is done, an unspoken bond is formed among those involved, a forbidden bell that cannot be unrung. Therefore, when Artie Nigro tasked Anthony Arillotta with a "piece of work," he was genuinely putting his loyalty to the test. More importantly, if Anthony proved his loyalty to the New York boss, it would weaken his allegiance to Big Al Bruno in Springfield. This "piece of work" was unlike any other Anthony had completed. He had never killed anyone, but he displayed no unease or hesitation.

Growing up, it was not uncommon for Anthony to encounter situations where violence was considered acceptable. It was not unusual if someone instructed him to do something violent. Throughout his entire life, he had a tendency towards aggression. This also allowed Joey Basile, Reno Ceravolo, and Anthony Arillotta of the Springfield Crew to be inducted into the organization and become "made" members.

However, when the time came to carry out the hit on Dadabo, Joey and Reno were nowhere to be found. Joey confided in Anthony, who then informed John Bologna that he wanted to be taken off the list and no longer wanted to get "made." This was a risky move, as it could have resulted in severe consequences. He could have gotten killed over being on a list and refusing to go on a hit when the boss told you to.

Consequently, rumors began to fly that Big John Bologna may have been an informant. Joey Basile's brother, who had a friend whose brother was a state trooper, warned him about the potential trouble he was putting himself in. This could have been the reason for his decision to no longer be on the hit list. Unfortunately, he failed to share this crucial information with anyone else, including Arillotta. Reno Ceravolo, who had a full-time job in construction, struggled with the time and logistics required for planning and traveling between Massachusetts and New York City, causing him to be pulled off the job.

This wasn't a one-person job that Arillotta could do by himself. For the hit to be executed with precision, it called for two shooters and a driver. So, he needed two more people right away. Knowing exactly who to turn to, he enlisted the help of brothers Ty and Fotios "Freddy" Geas to carry out the job.

As soon as he asked them, there was no hesitation. They responded with, "Sure, no problem." The Geas brothers, being Greek, were unable to be inducted into the Italian mafia. However, they didn't care about that, and none cared about it. Despite this, they always pushed Bingy, "Oh yeah, get your button," and eagerly began devising a plan to make it happen.

Their first order of business was to conduct a dry run. They wanted to see what Frank Dadabo looked like when he left his apartment and what car he walked to.

Early one morning, they made the journey from Springfield to New York, which usually took two and a half hours if they followed the speed limit. Their destination was Frank Dadabo's apartment building, which Arillotta was already familiar with. He knew where Dadabo parked his car and where he lived, and he always left his apartment at six o'clock in the morning. Without having even posted up yet, they happened to be driving by at the exact time, and there he was - an Italian-looking guy who matched the description of their intended target. Excitedly, Arillotta pointed him out, exclaiming, "That's him right there!" It was a perfect opportunity, and if they had their guns with them at that moment, you couldn't have asked for a better chance. With this encounter, they'd seen Dadabo's face, confirmed his car, and observed his morning routine. Now fully prepared, Arillotta and the Geas brothers returned to Springfield to finalize their plan for the hit.

The next day, they came back to New York City. They opted to use a pair of handguns with silencers they got from Nigro, to avoid the neighbors hearing them. This decision was risky, as guys with their criminal records would have gotten 20 years if they had been pulled over on the way down. To further conceal their actions, they adorned thick rubber gloves to prevent leaving any incriminating fingerprints behind.

The car was parked directly on the street where he typically comes out, and Arillotta instructs the Geas brothers to discreetly conceal their firearms beneath the car, just in case some cop pulls up and asks, "What are you guys doing?" The time was approximately 5:30 AM. To explain their presence, they concocted a story about meeting some girls who had instructed them to meet them on the street. The inside of the car was "clean," just in case they got pulled out. However, on this occasion, he did come out of the house. They waited there for the entire day, until seven in the evening, but he never emerged. Now, they faced the arduous task of driving back to Springfield.

They decided to return two days later, on May 19, 2003. Arillotta instructed Freddy to go down and get a hotel room with the guns while he and Ty would drive down the next day in a separate vehicle. The meticulous preparation was crucial. They had to steal a car equipped with a secondary set of plates affixed with magnets, and they needed a designated location to dispose of the gloves and guns immediately after their operation. They aimed to strip off all incriminating evidence and discard it into a nearby marsh off a bridge.

The busy street of New York City's Bronx neighborhood was lined with towering apartment buildings on one side. Across from them, an underpass was surrounded by wild brush and trees. The three post up. Freddy, the getaway driver, parked his car down the block while Anthony and Ty sat on a bench diagonally from where the target had come out of the house. As they were sitting there, the two friends were busting each other's balls. The guns were hidden in a nearby wooded area, and as Ty went to take a piss, Anthony couldn't resist busting his balls.

"What are you doing? You just pissed where we're going to kill a guy, and you left your DNA all over the fucking crime scene." he bantered. The intended crime scene was still 150 feet from their parked car.

"That's where we were going to shoot him!"

Ty was like, "Are you serious?"

He was only busting his balls, and they were laughing. They didn't notice that the guy was already halfway across the street. He exited his apartment and walked across the street to get into his car. The mood shifted. "There he is, let's go," Arillotta said with a serious tone, signaling the start of their plan.

They jumped up, went to the spot, retrieved the firearms, and swiftly walked down the sidewalk. As they got into the street, Frank Dadabo was opening his car door. By the time he settled behind the steering wheel, Ty was right beside him, firing his gun and shattering the window. Arillotta headed to the other side and began firing into the vehicle.

Ultimately, they ran out of bullets, and crimson blood covered his body. He lay motionless as Freddy arrived on the scene. Upon seeing him, even Freddy recognized his lifeless state - his head tilted back, mouth open. "Oh, yeah, he's definitely dead." A total of nine bullets had pierced him before the perpetrators hastily fled, abandoning their guns in a marsh a few blocks away. They shred their gloves and toss the pieces out the car window as they sped back up the highway.

Upon their return to Springfield, the two shooters were faced with one final task - disposing of any remaining evidence. Worried about potential gun residue on their hands, they had heard that vinegar could be effective. However, another suggestion had also caught their attention - using your piss to eliminate any traces of the gun residue. Thus, when they arrived back home, they proceeded to piss on their hands and discard their clothing.

There was no moment of sorrow or remorse. It was just another ordinary day, except it carried a heavier weight this time. However, the downside was that it occurred in New York, followed by a lengthy drive back home. For Arillotta, the grueling long commute was the most unbearable part of the day, not the act of mercilessly filling a guy with bullets and leaving him for dead. Even for mobsters, this act is cold-blooded.

The following morning, Arillotta searched the New York newspapers to see if they had published any reports about the shooting. If someone were murdered on the street, it would surely make the headlines, especially if it was believed to be a mob-related hit. However, to their surprise, the papers did not mention the incident.

It was later revealed that the reason for the lack of coverage was that everyone assumed Dadabo had been killed. However, against all odds, Dadabo miraculously survived the brutal attack. Despite being shot multiple times in the chest, catching bullets in the neck and the head, he managed to escape with his life. The bullets had shattered the car windows, but they had missed his vital organs, allowing him to live to tell the tale.

As bullets rained down on Frank Dadabo, he remained resolute in the face of danger. Despite being shot repeatedly, he was sure he was not going to die, telling himself, "He's shooting me. Sooner or later, they're going to stop." And he just felt that he could take it. When he got into the car, he pulled his jacket over his head and sat up a little bit because he didn't want them to shoot him in the head. They just kept shooting him, and all the shots were on the side of him.

When the shooters drove off, he desperately tried to call for help. He reached for his cell phone to call his wife, but his bloody hand caused it to slip onto the floor, leaving him unable to make the call.

Summoning the last of his strength, Dadabo managed to pry open his car door. He walked across the street carefully and called out to his wife through the window. After opening it, she asked, "What's the matter?"

Struggling to speak, he gasped, "Call 911. I've been shot." With a sense of urgency, Dadabo's wife rushed to the phone and dialed for an ambulance. When it finally arrived, her husband was unconscious. The next day, he woke up in the hospital to find a New York police officer sitting by his bedside, waiting to take his statement. However, Dadabo adamantly refused to speak about the shooting. With no eyewitnesses, the cops had little to go on, and the incident was ultimately labeled as unsolved by the NYPD.

After a few days, Arillotta returned to New York and was walking with Nigro. He said the guy's still alive. Nigro asked him if he used the guns he gave him, the one's with the silencers.

Arillotta confirmed, "Yeah."

Nigro then asked, "Did you leave anything there? Did you pick up the bullet casings?"

Anthony thought to himself, "How are we going to pick up the bullet casings," but he said, "Yeah, I got rid of the guns."

Nigro was satisfied, but he wanted to offer some advice to Arillotta. He remarked, "Yeah, you got to get better at headshots."

Was Nigro joking, or was he serious? The guy was sitting in his car, and every shot was from his chest up.

Anthony couldn't help but think, "Well, you should get better at giving me better guns."

However, Artie's tone was simply sarcastic. He was pleased and quite impressed. Dadabo was out of the picture.

This was the first time Arillotta had shot someone, but there was no recognition or praise for his actions. After going to New York and shooting a guy they believed to be dead, they returned to Springfield expecting to get a name for doing something like that on the streets. However, they could not tell anybody. No one's gonna know about this, so they're not gonna get a name for that because they shot some guy they don't even know in New York.

Anthony couldn't help but feel that if the victim had been someone who had done something to him in his area and killed him, he would have felt more satisfaction in taking their life. But in this case, he didn't even know the guy they had killed. It wasn't that he felt remorse; he simply had no connection to the victim, and their actions were solely to gain recognition and status within the mob.

"Yeah, I mean, I didn't feel anything," Anthony recalled.

Little did he know this one act would have a domino effect, straining his loyalty to his boss, Big Al Bruno, and causing chaos within the Springfield crew.

Just weeks later, in June 2003, a dozen defendants pleaded guilty after being indicted two years prior for their involvement in a sports betting and loan-sharking operation that dated back to 1994. Among those were two of the region's reputed organized crime leaders, Anthony "Skip" Delevo and Albert "Baba" Scibelli. These two and their co-defendants, who acknowledged their positions at the top of the criminal hierarchy, could have faced lengthy prison sentences if they had been found guilty by a jury.

Amid a slow and deliberate demeanor, Anthony Delevo growled out admissions of guilt for one count of racketeering conspiracy and one count of money laundering. As part of the agreement, he could face a maximum of five years behind bars. Delevo admitted to running an illegal street lottery. The government's case against him was strengthened by wiretaps and a crucial meeting held by Delevo, where he openly discussed the ongoing investigation with three other defendants. The meeting took place in 2000 at a West Springfield restaurant, and an FBI agent covertly overheard the conversation at a nearby booth.

Scibelli entered a guilty plea for one count of extortion and now faces a potential two-year prison sentence. The admission was made regarding his involvement in extorting money to pay off a gambling debt.

In addition, Todd Illingsworth, a former city employee who had previously been indicted in 2000 and 2001 for racketeering and drug-related charges, also entered a guilty plea. Illingsworth pleaded guilty to four charges, including racketeering conspiracy and conspiracy to distribute marijuana.

In 1999 and 2000, state police wiretaps captured Emilio Fusco threatening gambling debtors. As a result, Fusco pleaded guilty to one count of racketeering conspiracy and one count of money laundering. In exchange for his plea, federal charges against his wife, Jenny Santos-Fusco, were dismissed.

Additionally, the remaining defendants, including Vincent Canavan, Franco DeCaro, Andrew Scibelli, Robert Gossman, Michael Tancrati, Anthony Grasso, and Antonio Esposito, all pleaded guilty to one count of participating in an illegal gambling ring.

South End barber Carmine Manzi, his son Giuseppe "Little Joe" Manzi, and Ralph Santaniello are facing trial in September.

Big Al Bruno was not among the defendants.

Just days before the highly anticipated plea agreement, Giuseppe "Little Joe" Manzi was prosecuted in state court for a separate incident where he beat a man with a golf club outside a local bar. The attack was triggered when the victim, Eduardo Parilla, innocently wished a stranger "Happy birthday" around 2 in the morning in the Hot Club's parking lot on Stearns Square. Manzi reacted by beating Parilla after a brief exchange of words. The first blow knocked Parilla unconscious, but Manzi continued to beat and kick him relentlessly.

A broken golf club was discovered near Parilla lying on the concrete. His facial bones were fractured, and his jaw was broken. During questioning at the scene, Manzi provided false information, including a phony address, Social Security number, and alias known as Anthony Victor. Manzi drove off in an SUV that morning but was later apprehended on a warrant after Parilla and two witnesses identified him from a lineup of police mug shots.

Chapter 12

A Better Out

Nigro wanted total control over the Springfield rackets. He craved the power to demand tribute from the city's businesses as he saw fit. But with Al Bruno standing in his way, Nigro's grip on the underworld was weak at best. Enter Arillotta, a man who had proven his unwavering loyalty to Nigro, while Bruno remained completely oblivious.

The first step was to secure Arillotta's spot in the inner circle, to make him a "made" man within the ranks of La Cosa Nostra.

In the mafia, where murder for one's boss is the highest form of devotion, being made is the ultimate reward. It is the key to a new world of privilege and protection. No one, not even the most daring rival, would dare lay a finger on a "made" man without the boss's blessing. Arillotta could potentially level the playing field by sitting with bosses and captains.

As Nigro saw it, having Arillotta in his corner would supply him with an inside man in Springfield, allowing him to take over the city's lucrative criminal rackets. So, on an August morning in 2003, Arillotta was instructed by John Bologna to meet on Arthur Avenue in the Bronx at a Nebraska Steakhouse in the heart of Little Italy.

Donning a pair of black dress pants, a matching shirt, and polished shoes, Anthony completed his outfit with a platinum Rolex adorned with diamonds around the dial that was given to him as a gift by his boss, Artie Nigro. Opting to borrow his mother's ordinary Nissan Maxima instead of his flashy black Ford Expedition, he started on a two-hour journey to New York City.

As Arillotta arrived, he found the restaurant closed, but the door was unlocked. He immediately recognized the four men seated at the table, all capos, street bosses in the family he soon joined. They hugged or shook hands and kissed on the cheek. A cup of espresso was offered, which he sipped while awaiting the arrival of three more men. And so, the time had come.

An unfamiliar man said, "Anthony, put your jewelry, phone, beeper, or anything like that in this ashtray over here."

Arillotta and the other three initiates followed suit, removing their personal items and setting them on the table. Their phones were retrieved from their jackets and added to the pile. Arillotta removed his watch and the golden crucifix from around his neck.

Afterward, the man offered this advice: "Whatever you do when you get in there, make sure you tell them you don't know why you're there."

Finally, the man led the group to a black Cadillac Fleetwood parked outside the steakhouse. The trip was brief, spanning only a few city blocks. The Cadillac stopped in front of a weathered apartment building in the Bronx, where the men, some in suits and others in slacks and shirts, walked up a narrow set of concrete stairs to the third floor. Inside, the apartment resembled a private social club, with low lighting and old wooden tables and chairs. It reminded Arillotta of an underground gambling hall from the 1920s. One of the captains, Stevie Alfisi, instructed him to change into a white bathrobe in the small bathroom down the hallway.

They were extremely cautious about who they were bringing into the family, ensuring that no guys were wearing a wire or anything like that. He was then led into a back room where Pat Deluca and two other captains were waiting. Standing alongside them was a familiar face, someone Arillotta knew well. Arthur Nigro, the current acting boss of the Genovese family, was dressed in a sleek grey suit and a crisp button-up shirt.

"Do you know why you're here?" Nigro asked Arillotta.

"No. I don't know why I'm here," he said. He was well aware of the responses expected of him. It was an age-old script.

"We are part of a secret, honored society. It's exclusive, and the reason you're here today is because we'd like you to be part of this brotherhood of ours. Is that something you would want to be part of?"

"Yes," replied Arillotta.

"If your wife was giving birth to your child and the boss called for you, would you leave her bedside and come?"

This resonated particularly strongly with Arillotta. His daughter would be born the next day.

"Yes," he said.

On the small wooden table beside Nigro there was a .38 revolver and a marble-handled knife with a six-inch blade.

"You see this gun and knife," Nigro asked him. "Would you use the knife that's on this table to kill someone if your bosses asked you to do it?"

"Yes," said Arillotta.

"If your brother did something to harm a member of our family, and we asked you to take this gun and kill him, would you do that?"

"Yes."

He asked Arillotta to point to his trigger finger, and Nigro took the knife and made a small incision. A bead of blood appeared. Nigro took a small piece of cloth, wiped the blood away, and placed the cloth in the palm of Arillotta's hand. He then struck a match, lit the corner of the cotton, and Arillotta tossed the burning linen from one hand to the other.

"Non romperò mai questo giuramento," Nigro said, then asked Arillotta to repeat in English: "I will never break this oath. If I do, it'll be death on me. I will be destroyed like this cloth in my hand."

That's when Pat Deluca got up from the table, kissed him on both cheeks, and shook his hand. "Hello, friend, you're one of us now," he said. It's a 10-minute process, very quick, and you're part of the mafia with them, part of that family.

Then Nigro said something that isn't typically part of the ceremony. He goes, "You're direct with me," meaning Arillotta no longer reported to Big Al Bruno in Springfield. That was very, very big. That never happens. A boss never has somebody report directly to him. It's always an underboss. They are always insulated. But because he was from Massachusetts and Bingy was his guy, he was going to report directly to him.

A scene reminiscent of Goodfellas or an image straight out of the history of American crime was unfolding in the present-day USA. Arillotta had just been "made" and inducted into the Genovese crime family, the largest and most powerful of New York's notorious Italian-American mafia families. The contemporary mob looked a hell of a lot like the old mob. Bingy had come a long way from simply carrying groceries for Al Bruno at his father's produce store.

Upon gaining acceptance into the Genovese family, Arillotta was cautious about openly revealing his new status to other captains and avoiding unwanted heat. The goal was to remain low-key and avoid drawing the attention of law enforcement. As a "made" man, he would have a target on his back and be the crew's leader, so he had all the power in the area. He got "made" directly with the boss in New York; that alone puts him as the target.

However, wiretap recordings later revealed Arillotta telling his friends that "he was with Artie and no longer answered to Bruno."

Anthony told people, "I have a better out, but we have Bruno operating on a parallel track."

It was a momentous power shift in the history of the Mafia in Greater Western Mass. Such a phenomenon had never been seen before. That night, he attended a baptism at Roma's Restaurant in Southwick, accompanied by Baba Scibelli, Emilio Fusco, Big Al Bruno, Felix Tranghese, and Mario Fiore. His hand still bore the scars of a burnt card, leaving a black mark. No one was aware of what had transpired earlier that day.

The next day, while his wife was in labor with their daughter at the hospital, he revealed the news to his father. However, the reaction he received was not what he had anticipated. His father had always hoped for a different life for him.

As part of his induction, Arillotta swore an oath to the Genovese Family, prioritizing them over his own family, and vowed never to cooperate with law enforcement. As Nigro was the one who made him in the Bronx, Arillotta's chain of command technically went directly to Nigro rather than his current boss, Big Al Bruno, the Springfield Capo. This gave him considerable "clout" within the realm of organized crime.

As Anthony Arillotta's relationship with Artie Nigro, the boss in New York, grew stronger, Emilio Fusco likely perceived that Arillotta was gaining power. While Fusco may not have respected Arillotta, he appeared to have respect for power. Fusco, himself, was a recent Italian immigrant.

Upon his arrival in the early 1990s, his English skills were relatively poor, which often caused Arillotta's crew to make fun of him when they talked about him. They would talk like he talked and burst into laughter. Fusco, on the other hand, would suck up to Arillotta and show him all kinds of respect, even taking him to dinners and picking up the tab, just really smoothing him over.

However, behind this façade, Fusco was no fan of Arillotta. He hated Bingy, who was known as a big money maker. Everyone hates guys that make a lot of money. And Fusco didn't hide his disdain. He constantly beefed with Arillotta, even attempting to get him killed at least half a dozen times. As expected, this only fueled Arillotta's deep-seated hatred towards him.

One day, while Arillotta was at the YMCA, Fusco made a beef on him again.

In a fit of rage, Arillotta slammed his fist against the locker and declared, "One day, I'm going to kill this fucking grease ball. I'm going to kill this fuck."

After a few days, Arillotta gets called to the house of Jake Nettis, a brutal killer and enforcer for Bruno. Taking no risks, he brings Freddy Geas along.

Nettis demands to know why Arillotta continues to defy Bruno's orders to stay away from Emilio Fusco, a fellow made member whom he despises.

"He's the boss. You do what he says," Jake orders him.

Arillotta acknowledges Bruno's authority but contacts New York boss, Little Artie Nigro, shortly after the confrontation. Nigro tells him to do whatever you want up there. Little Artie then reaches out to Capo Larry Dentico, a former cellmate of Nettis, to straighten out the issue.

Dentico's message to Jake Nettis was loud and clear.

"When you see "Bingy," you treat that young kid the same way you would treat me."

This revelation made the Springfield Crew fully aware of Anthony Arillotta's significance in New York and his position in Springfield. Upon receiving word from Nettis, Bruno cautioned his son Victor and Lou "The Shoe" Santos not to fuck up around Bingy.

Now, with Arillotta being made, Nigro's plan to take over Springfield was almost complete. However, the lingering obstacle of Big Al Bruno still stood in his way.

During their dinners at a steakhouse in the Bronx, Nigro expressed his frustration to Arillotta that Bruno was not "kicking enough revenue upstairs" although he had his hand in everything. Nigro also complained about how Bruno was constantly reaching out to New York regarding the failed cigarette agreement and his excessive drinking, which made him appear sloppy at times.

Furthermore, Nigro was upset that he was allowing Lou "The Shoe" Santos, a known informant, to hang around him.

So, they had no choice but to demote Bruno, breaking him down from a captain to a mere soldier. Their ultimate goal was to get this other guy, Felix Tranghese, and put him up as a captain.

This vicious plan was fueled by their insatiable greed and desire to gain complete control over the prosperous city of Springfield. Before Artie became the boss, everything ran smoothly. The area was unbelievable. Guys used to come in from Boston, New York, and other parts of the country and want to move to the area because they got treated so well. However, once Artie took over, he had his guy, John Bologna, and everything changed. Their selfish ambitions drove them to try to take the area for themselves.

Interestingly, despite being the boss, Nigro lacked the power to demote Bruno without the involvement of a governing council. This "panel," comprised of three high-ranking members representing different factions within the Genovese crime family, operates in secrecy. Who's on the governing council and where they meet is unknown to most members. As such, big decisions, such as demoting a captain, must be put to a vote, which takes time. To avoid arousing suspicion from Bruno, Nigro advised Arillotta not to tell anyone he'd been made.

They didn't trust Bruno.

Bruno was never put on the shelf, yet he felt something was wrong and was scared. He knew he was losing power, and it was happening now. When Bruno ascended to the position of Springfield's leader, he frequently spoke with Artie Nigro and Pat DeLuca, the captain who was present at Arillotta's initiation ceremony. However, both mobsters were now giving Bruno the cold shoulder.

Pat and Artie told Arillotta, "Listen, Bruno's been trying to reach out to us."

Then they gave Arillotta a message. They said, "Tell Bruno, stop reaching out to anybody in New York, that when we're ready, we'll call for him."

A few days later, Arillotta chose a strange time to deliver that message. One night, while attending a bachelor party, Bruno stormed in and began to scold Bingy. Bruno was furious that Arillotta continued associating with Emilio Fusco and demanded it stop.

Big Al says, "Didn't I tell you to stop hanging around with Emilio?"

Arillotta responded, "Bruno, what's the big deal? The kid's a "made" guy.

"I told you, it doesn't matter. I don't want you hanging around with him. You keep defying me."

Then Arillotta pulled a power move.

"Hey, I got a message for you," Bingy tells him.

"From who?" Al asks.

"From Pat and Artie."

Anthony has never seen Big Al so rattled. He was stuttering, and his wheels were turning. He was trying to figure things out.

"Why did you go down there? Why'd they call you?"

Then Arillotta gave Bruno the message.

"They said that you've been reaching out to people. Stop reaching out to them, that they'll call you when they're ready to see you."

Big Al Bruno just kept going over.

"Why did they call you? What did they say? How exactly did they say it?"

And finally, the light bulb moment.

And then he looked at Bingy, pointed to his chest, and said, "You got your button?"

"Bruno, I didn't get anything," he responded.

Again, Big Al pointed and rubbed his fingers together at his chest.

He says, "You got it."

During the sizzling and tumultuous summer of 2003, Anthony "Bingy" Arillotta emerged as the new leader of Springfield's mob crew. This power shift came as other senior made members, including the once-dominant Big Al Bruno, were pushed to the sidelines by Nigro. As tensions grew between Bruno and his superiors in the Bronx and the rank-and-file within his small crew, Arillotta rose through the ranks, quickly gaining favor with the leaders in the Big Apple. Big Al Bruno began to lose his grip on Springfield's mob crew and failed to realize the deadly consequences of every move and misstep he made; his hold on power became increasingly fragile.

During this period, Arillotta was waging war against a former business partner turned adversary, which kept both the Springfield police and FBI working overtime as they tried to contain the growing tension. Arillotta's loyal crew of tough mobsters, barroom fighters, and young gangsters was regularly on the local bar and club scene every night.

They were highly concerned and heavily invested in Arillotta's ongoing war with the independent Manzi crew rather than in Bruno's drama in New York.

Carmine "Carm the Barber" Manzi, the patriarch of the Manzi crew, was a devoted follower of the Scibelli brothers. He staunchly refused to come under the rule of Big Al Bruno and kickup tribute to anyone other than the Scibellis. This caused tension between Bruno and Carm the Barber, with Bruno claiming that the nearly one million dollars in cash found in a federal raid on Carm's residence should have been taxed and shared with him as the new boss.

At one point, Carm the Barber's nephew, Giuseppe "Villa Joe" Manzi, was Arillotta's partner in the drug trade. However, their relationship soured in the summer of '03 during the larger Springfield mob beef, leading to their feud that reached a boiling point in August.

Springfield was viewed as a minor player in the Mafia world for years compared to larger cities like Providence and Boston. However, crime was still thriving in the area at that time. After Arillotta joined the Genovese Family, tensions rose within Springfield's organized crime circles.

Arillotta's crew, including the Geas brothers Freddy and Ty, found themselves in multiple conflicts with Guiseppe Manzi and his faction, who were also involved in narcotics. The situation reached a boiling point in late August of 2003 when a violent confrontation, complete with gunshots, erupted outside the Civic Pub in Springfield, Massachusetts.

It was the evening of August 29, 2003, when Brandon Croteau, a member of the Arillotta crew, was bartending at Tilly's Bar in Springfield. Suddenly, "Villa" Joe Manzi and his entourage of seven men walked in, causing a stir. One of his associates threw a bottle at Croteau, causing a commotion. In response, Croteau quickly contacted Ty Geas, who happened to be with Arillotta and a crew of fifteen guys at the nearby Café Manhattan. They immediately rushed to Tilly's, but the Manzi crew had just left.

Later that night, Arillotta, the Geas brothers, Croteau, and three carloads of associates found the Manzi crew at the Civic Pub owned by Carm the Barber's son, Giuseppe "Little Joe" Manzi.

The Manzi crew, anticipating their arrival, stood outside, ready for a confrontation. Chaos erupted as Arillotta and his crew unleashed a barrage of weapons - guns, knives, ice picks, golf clubs, and baseball bats; every weapon available was being used. Amidst the chaos, Arillotta was yelling to Freddy Geas to shoot them or give him the gun, who responded by emptying its contents into the crowd.

In the crossfire, two patrons of the Civic Pub were injured - one with a bullet in the foot and the other slightly grazed in the head. The scene was one of utter violence and mayhem.

Arillotta and Ty Geas were stopped by Springfield Police down the street just a few minutes after leaving the bar. Fortunately, Freddy was not in the car, having taken off running with the gun. While lying in the street on their stomachs, the guy who was shot in the foot came to identify them but said he didn't recognize them.

The next evening, on August 30, an unidentified gunman sprayed Anthony Arillotta's home on Chalmers Street. The drive-by shooting, which occurred in the early hours, involved 20 rounds of ammunition and took place while Anthony's wife and two young daughters were inside the house.

The bullets shattered the windows, and one even became lodged in the sofa. Additionally, the Bingy's SUV parked in the driveway was riddled with bullet holes. Irene, Anthony's wife, quickly fled with her children through the back door. When questioned by the police, the Arillottas stated that they did not know who fired the shots. Meanwhile, Anthony himself was in Hartford at a nightclub.

Nobody was hurt, but that didn't stop Arillotta from instantly blaming Villa Joe Manzi. They identified a car parked up the street just before the attack in front of Bruno's girlfriend's house. There was concern that her house may have also been a target.

Arillotta, the Geas Brothers, Emilio Fusco, and others sought revenge, even though Artie Nigro advised Arillotta to let the dispute cool down. The Geas brothers offered Frankie Roche $10,000 and then $25,000 to eliminate Giuseppe Manzi, a rival restaurateur whom Ty Geas believed was poaching their marijuana customers. They also suspected two other guys of actually carrying out the shooting at Arillotta's house. Freddy and Ty Geas suggested Roche use an AK-47 and carry out the murder in a busy intersection in downtown Springfield.

Bruno informed Arillotta that he didn't have permission to kill. In response, Arillotta told Bruno he didn't need permission, hinting at his recent making in New York and saying he would do it regardless.

Antonio "Tony" Manzi, Carmine's brother in Quindici, Italy, ordered the shooting of Arillotta's house.

The night prior, they had beat up "Fat Franky" D'Agostino with a club at his son's Villa Joe's bar, the Civic Pub. Being old school, Tony believed the younger crew was becoming too fearless. In Italy, the way to send a message was through a violent display of shooting up someone's home.

Years earlier, the elder Manzi brothers were jailed, but Tony was deported upon his release because he was not a US citizen. It was widely believed that Al Bruno used his connection with District Attorney Matty Ryan to have his rival removed from the country.

Under the orders of Arillotta, "Villa" Joe Manzi narrowly escaped multiple attempts on his life. One such instance was when his idling Mercedes was riddled with machine gun fire from a passing vehicle while he waited at a stoplight in the South End, but he managed to avoid being hit. At another time, they had a kid waiting at the back door of his restaurant, waiting for him to come out to ambush. Another time, Freddy Geas tried to shoot him at his restaurant, Villa Napoletano, in East Longmeadow, but there were too many customers and cameras in the building.

After Bruno became boss, he granted Felix Tranghese a second opportunity to work with him despite knowing that Felix was a liar and could not be trusted. Bruno had previously shelved him in the 90s. However, it was the final straw when Big Al discovered that Felix was going behind his back and meeting with Boston boss Carmen "The Big Cheese" DeNunzio. Bruno instructed Arillotta to find a place for Felix's body and had a ditch dug for his disposal.

Arillotta had a prime spot in mind: his friend's backyard in the neighboring town of Agawam. It was considered the ultimate spot, with an abandoned house next door that provided complete privacy once you got off the road. Once you pulled in, nobody could see you. It was a ghost town from five to eleven every night, giving them a few hours to dig up the hole. And that was precisely what they did - digging a deep hole, measuring over 8 feet, for hours.

However, Bruno was unaware that Little Artie had risen in the ranks and was now a boss. He planned to appoint Felix as the capo in Springfield. Despite Bruno's insistence, Little Artie declined his request to kill Tranghese.

Meanwhile, in September of 2003, Arillotta became entangled in a plot to kill someone else, Lou "The Shoe" Santos, a bookie based in Greater Springfield.

Santos had been a longtime associate and friend of Arillotta for two decades, and they had previously engaged in drug dealings together. Moreover, Santos had a close relationship with Big Al Bruno. However, "Baba" Scibelli's sources within the courthouse had confirmed that Santos had been cooperating with law enforcement. As a result, although Bruno wanted to "keep Santos close," Nigro ordered Arillotta to kill him to send a clear message to Big Al that he was willing to kill his men.

Since the 1980s, Arillotta and Louis Santos had been friends. However, not once did he say a single word in an attempt to spare this guy.

"That's the life. That's the Mafia life," Arillotta calmly remarked.

Arillotta recruited the Geas brothers, who brought in Frankie Roche. Roche and Ty Geas staked out Santos' physical therapy office on Main Street in Springfield, devising a plan to take him out in the parking lot as he left for his car. However, that never happened because the crew became consumed with planning to kill Manzi, whom they considered a more aggressive thorn in their sides.

"He's a headache. He's gotta go. We've had enough of him. We gotta kill him," the Geas brothers said, expressing their disdain for Manzi.

"Freddy asked if I would kill him, and I said yes," recounted Roche.

These unsuccessful murder attempts only fueled the Geas brothers' determination to establish their "strength" in the criminal world.

Ultimately, the plan to murder Manzi was scrapped in favor of a new target - Adolfo "Big Al" Bruno.

Chapter 13

This Piece of Paper

In September 2003, Emilio Fusco became the second person to receive a prison sentence following a long-term probe into racketeering in Greater Springfield. He will only spend a brief period behind bars before transitioning to a "shock incarceration" program, modeled after a boot camp, and then to community confinement, totaling less than three years.

Ever since he was indicted along with 14 others by a grand jury on racketeering charges more than two years ago, the Italian immigrant has consistently been depicted by state police and federal prosecutors as a leading figure in the local mafia hierarchy.

However, at his sentencing, Fusco's defense attorney argued that his client was simply an unlucky gambler who aspired to a supervisory role within the organization to stop losing money.

"We're looking at a straightforward gambling case," stated Anthony Cardinale, the mob lawyer representing Fusco who previously defended notorious mob bosses John Gotti, Fat Tony Salerno, Cadillac Frank Salemme, and Carmen "The Big Cheese" DiNunzio.

Three years ago, Fusco was caught on state police wiretaps discussing a gambling debtor who had fallen behind on payments. In the conversation, he threatened to bury the debtor in cement, but Fusco's lawyer has continuously argued that it was only "puffing."

"This guy was a pivotal character in this investigation. To say that a mere gambler works his way up through the ranks is not how this works," remarked Lieutenant Timothy Alben, head of the Massachusetts State Police organized crime unit in Springfield, following the sentencing hearing.

Cardinale refuted the government's claim that Fusco, one of the 15 defendants involved in a global plea agreement, was a "made man" in the New York Genovese crime family.

While awaiting sentencing, Fusco reviewed his pre-sentencing report, commonly known as the "PSR." Federal probation officers prepare this standard document for every criminal sentencing in federal court. According to a memo from Assistant U.S. Attorney Karen Goodwin to the probation officer in charge of compiling the report, Richard Rinaldi, this information was provided in response to Fusco's argument that he had no ties to organized crime. The detailed summary serves as a crucial piece of evidence in determining the severity of Fusco's sentence.

Goodwin wrote, "The defendant argues that all references to his role in the Genovese Crime Family of La Cosa Nostra should be deleted from the Presentence Report because he had no association with La Cosa Nostra and was not a made member. Those objections are not well-founded."

Goodwin claimed that the government recorded Fusco engaging in illegal business with other members of the Genovese family. Furthermore, a cooperating witness, Richard Berte, would have testified that Fusco's co-defendant, Carmine Manzi, informed Berte that Fusco had "earned his button."

New York's Michael "Cookie" Durso, who was also cooperating with authorities, secretly recorded Al Bruno on a wire, Goodwin stated. Goodwin also mentioned that in 2001, Al Bruno informed Durso that there were seven Genovese made members in Springfield. Goodwin's report revealed that Bruno disclosed that one of the newly inducted members, Emilio Fusco, had gotten "the skipper," Anthony Delevo, arrested.

Assistant U.S. Attorney Goodwin's report included the FBI 302 intelligence report, which Springfield FBI agent Cliff Hedges wrote up after an impromptu conversation with Bruno in the hallway of the Red Rose Pizzeria during the winter of 2002.

"Al Bruno confirmed that Emilio Fusco had been 'made' while Bruno was in jail," the prosecutor wrote and provided details from other recorded conversations that solidified Fusco's "dominant role" in illegal gambling and loan-sharking activities in Western Massachusetts.

Al Bruno badmouthed Emilio Fusco, a member of the Springfield mafia, to an FBI agent. He expressed disappointment over Fusco's induction into the Genovese family by Baba Scibelli while Bruno was away, serving a brief prison sentence. Although Bruno was not an informant, his loose lips to a long-time acquaintance in law enforcement were used to create a 302 report, typically reserved for Confidential Informants and potential witnesses. The unredacted release of this report in Fusco's case file put Big Al even further in the crosshairs of his enemies.

Fusco was infuriated by this revelation until his lawyer, Cardinale, clarified that it did not mean Bruno was a "rat." Cardinale assured him that if Bruno were formally cooperating with the government, it would not have been revealed in such a way. However, including the 302 report resulted in Fusco receiving an additional year in his sentence, proving his involvement in a criminal organization.

As he served his time for this conviction, Emilio Fusco solidified his ties with the New York mob bosses by stepping into a fight to help Genovese capo Ernest Muscarella against an inmate at the federal prison in Fort Dix, where they were both incarcerated at the time. This act further showed Fusco's loyalty and reputation within the criminal world.

Big Al Bruno was losing his grip on the streets, as his bosses in New York, trusted protege Anthony Arillotta and former right-hand man Felix Tranghese were all turning against him right under his very nose. Not only that, but Bruno was also gradually losing favor with Nigro and other influential figures throughout 2003 due to various reasons.

Seizing the opportunity, the young and ambitious Arillotta took advantage of the friction, cozying up to Nigro and fueling the rebellion in his stomping grounds of New

York while also igniting the flames of discontent in Springfield. Meanwhile, the more experienced and established Tranghese saw an opportunity to replace Bruno as the capo of the Springfield crew and saw Bruno's troubles in New York as a personal advantage.

However, the decision to whack Bruno was made when Emilio Fusco, a member of the Genovese Family and facing charges for racketeering and loan-sharking, disclosed that Bruno had shared confidential information with an FBI agent. Fusco, originally from Bracigliano - a small town in Southern Italy located an hour away from Naples, had no personal vendetta against Bruno, unlike the old-world conflict between their neighboring towns, Quindici and Bracigliano, in the heart of the Campania region.

Big Al upset the Genovese family in the Bronx by bad-mouthing his bosses and claims of skimming off the top of tribute payments being sent to New York. Additionally, a 302 document from the FBI detailing a conversation between Bruno and an agent in the hallway of the Red Rose Pizzeria further added to the hostility. Bruno may have gotten a bit too friendly with the FBI, as he ranted to an agent he was familiar with about the state of the mob in Springfield.

Emilio Fusco urgently contacted Arillotta, insisting on seeing him right away. "It's very important," he said, rattled and angry.

Later, the two met at a Friendly's restaurant, where Fusco handed Arillotta a document.

"You're not going to believe what this guy Bruno did. I just found out he ratted me out. He's a rat," Fusco complained.

As Arillotta examined the paper, he exclaimed, "Wow, that's not good. Bruno made a bad move by talking to the FBI agent."

Infuriated, the two men began waving "the paper," the FBI brief recounting Bruno's loose lips around the Greater Springfield underworld. Fusco was livid and sought to make a beef against Bruno. He implored higher-ups in the mob to sanction a hit on Bruno, as he had confirmed to an FBI agent that Fusco was a "made man."

The leak sparked outrage within Springfield's underworld, prompting Felix Tranghese to contact John Bologna. Tranghese, a veteran bookie and numbers guy, was a go-between between the notorious "Springfield Crew" and their superiors in New York when doubts arose about Bruno's loyalty.

Mobster Felix Tranghese, present at Fusco's induction ceremony, brought a single-page death order to New York due to Fusco's fear of violating his bail conditions by traveling outside of Massachusetts. Felix journeyed nearly 200 miles south to reach John Bologna in Port Chester, New York, who acted as the Springfield crew's connection to Nigro. Before returning to Springfield, he handed the document to Big John to await further orders. John Bologna was in his glory - it was like a beautiful gift.

Previously, it was just to break him and take him down, but now he had the opportunity to get Bruno killed, and Artie would have no choice.

A few days later, Bologna reached out, and Tranghese made the trip to Port Chester again. Bologna met him there and drove him to meet Nigro in the East Tremont section of the Bronx. As Big John stood off to the side, Artie returned the paper to Tranghese. He informed Felix that he "would have to sit down with somebody else, other people, and explain that paper to 'em." Tranghese noticed that the " pertinent paragraph " had been highlighted upon its return.

A few days passed, and John again contacted Tranghese, informing him that he would bring him to another meeting. Felix joined John, and they headed to the Nebraska Steakhouse in the Bronx, where they were met by Nigro and a group of Genovese wise guys known as the "Panel." Tranghese, Artie, and the other gentlemen, including Mario "The Shadow" Gigante and "Little Larry" Dentico, gathered around the table. Following a script outlined by "The Little Guy" Artie Nigro during his previous trip to New York, Felix spoke up and presented a document.

He said, "I have this piece of paper, and we're concerned about it. I think it affects everybody here at the table. I think it has to be dealt with." Felix handed the paper to Artie. He passed it around.

Then, the panel went and talked alone. There is no greater sin in the mob world than speaking to law enforcement. It's a violation of Omerta's oath. A few minutes later, Nigro returned and told Tranghese he would get back to him.

Several days later, upon receiving instructions from Bologna once again, Tranghese met with Nigro at the Nebraska Steakhouse. This time, The Little Guy was flying solo. They exited the restaurant and walked in front of a laundromat in the Bronx, where Nigro frequently held covert meetings with his underlings. Artie conveyed to Tranghese that he should go back to Springfield to take care of Bruno and that it would be better if the body weren't found.

The order to carry out Bruno's assassination was officially delivered.

Upon returning to Springfield, Felix joined Arillotta and Emilio Fusco.

Arillotta inquired, " What happened?"

"They want us to kill him," Tranghese disclosed.

However, Felix was unaware that Anthony had been made months ago and was now direct with Genovese boss Artie Nigro. As a result, he doesn't tell Arillotta what to do. The order to assassinate Bruno was assigned to Tranghese.

The air was tense at Arillotta's baby daughter's christening in Southwick, Massachusetts. Despite the order from the boss Artie Nigro, Bruno had yet to be taken care of. Tranghese broke the tense silence with a joke.

"Does anyone have a gun? We can just do it here," he said with a sly grin.

The men chuckled nervously, but their laughter reflected an underlying unease. As the christening ceremony went on, the tension only seemed to grow.

On October 18, 2003, a federal judge sentenced 83-year-old vending company owner Baba Scibelli to pay a $250,000 fine and serve four years of probation, including one year of home detention. However, this decision was criticized by a top state police investigator, as it frustrated the organized crime unit, which was hoping for a harsher punishment for Scibelli and other defendants involved in a gambling and loan-sharking ring in Greater Springfield. By using his wealth to pay the hefty fine, Scibelli protected himself from serving time in prison.

"I would say he is buying his way out of incarceration," Alben said. He said Scibelli was young and healthy enough to supervise a betting ring and share the profits. "That was his choice; nobody forced him into it," Alben said.

However, the lenient punishment was handed down for a more significant and costly reason. Baba Scibelli, the dapper vending machine magnate, admitted as part of his plea that he is a made member of the "Springfield Crew" of the Genovese crime family based in New York. This breach of the sacred code of silence, known as Omerta, resulted in his immediate banishment from the streets and "shelved," being stripped of all his illegal rackets by Arillotta. This revelation holds significance for the general public, who have always questioned the legitimacy of the mob's presence in Springfield. Still, it confirms that the Cosa Nostra is the real deal.

As his 2-year-old daughter played in the hallway outside the courtroom, Giuseppe "Little Joe" Manzi received a 36-month federal prison sentence on October 30, 2003, for his involvement in a gambling and loansharking operation.

A few days later, his father, Carmine "The Barber" Manzi, was given a 3 1/2 year prison sentence for running a gambling and loansharking ring. Judge Ponsor directed Manzi to surrender over $750,000 seized from Tony's Famous Barbershop on Main Street. According to prosecutors, the money represented Manzi's cut from the profits of a regional gambling and loansharking operation that was under the control of the Genovese crime family based in New York City. After making a request, Ponsor concurred and recommended that Manzi serve his sentence alongside his son at the federal correctional center in Ft. Devens.

The last hold-out in a 16-defendant racketeering case brought by federal prosecutors in 2001 pleaded guilty to one count of conducting an illegal gambling business.

Ralph Santaniello, son of Amadeo Santaniello, was sentenced to five years and a $250,000 fine.

Michael O'Reilly, head of the FBI's Springfield office, also urged anyone owing money to local bookies or loan sharks to contact the FBI.

"Before you think about refinancing your homes to pay off debts, call us," O'Reilly said.

Chapter 14

On Top of Old Smokey

Anthony Arillotta's wife's younger sister, Sandra, lived for the thrill of partying and indulging in drugs like ecstasy and cocaine. Despite her parents' disapproval, Sandra began a serious relationship with Gary Westerman when he was released in 2002. Her parents were worried about her safety and the influence Gary could have on her. They feared that Sandra's reckless behavior would only escalate with Gary by her side. However, Sandra was too blinded by her love for him to see the warning signs. Her parents could only watch helplessly as their daughter spiraled out of control.

Freddy Geas had been released a year earlier and joined Westerman, resuming their street criminal activities. It was all about making money. Westerman was known for his street smarts and knack for pulling off heists.

However, Freddy didn't like or trust Westerman, and none of the crew did. He was a snake in the grass, and they knew they would eventually have to cut his head off.

"We knew we had a hole dug," Arillotta said, "Ty was amped up about no one getting killed. Freddy gets amped up. He gets me amped up."

"We're about nothin', we're weak. No one's dyin'," Ty Geas said.

Just two days later, Gary Westerman suddenly vanished.

A local organized crime investigator received an unusual call. The man contacted state police Lt. Timothy Alben in the late hours of November 6. According to Alben, the caller implied that Westerman, whose rap sheet stretched from his teens to drug and robbery convictions later in life, may be a victim of foul play, Alben said.

"Do I think he's somewhere safe? I would think not, given that no one has heard from him in well over a week," Alben remarked, revealing that the caller provided a specific lead on what could have happened to Westerman, yet he declined to disclose further details.

Before law enforcement knew of any trouble, an unidentified person contacted Alben's unlisted phone number, sparking the initial inquiries into Westerman's whereabouts. Despite Alben's focus on organized crime, he affirmed that there is no known connection between Westerman and current mob investigations. This short call triggered subsequent efforts to contact friends and family to verify Westerman's absence. Alben noted that no missing person's report had been filed before the call.

Westerman's late-model BMW was abandoned at a McDonald's restaurant in West Springfield; his keys were recovered less than a mile away at a supermarket. State police Lt. Peter Higgins of the Hampden County Crime Prevention and Control Unit, who is leading the investigation, said Westerman's disappearance was being treated as a missing persons case, not a murder.

A friend of Westerman, who wished to remain anonymous, saw him "happy and relaxed on a downtown street just hours before he went missing." The friend shared that Westerman talked about his recent marriage to a woman who was almost 30 years old, his junior, and the daughter of Italian immigrants who own a specialty market in the city's South End neighborhood.

Giuseppe "Joe" Zonin, the proprietor of Zonin's Market, revealed that he had never met Westerman, even though he had wed his 20-year-old daughter at a Florida ceremony several weeks ago.

Zonin said, "I never knew she had any type of boyfriend. Parents are always the last to know," he added, noting that his daughter is "hysterical" over Gary's disappearance.

Alben theorized that the unidentified informant could have ties to a prior organized crime investigation. Only a select few individuals know his department's existence, which is discreetly located within the lower level of the Registry of Motor Vehicles on Liberty Street.

"People don't generally know where to find me unless they've had some dealings with me before," Alben said.

Westerman's lengthy rap sheet also includes a 1989 conviction for cocaine trafficking that netted a 10-year sentence - though he served less than that - and a charge of theft from a building when he was 16 years old.

Westerman was incarcerated in a Concord state prison in 1997 after being found guilty of stealing a truck loaded with $100,000 worth of computers and other items. He was given a 3-5 year sentence for the offense and was released in May 2002. His accomplice in the 1996 truck theft, Freddy Geas, was also convicted and served time for the crime in 1997. He was released from a minimum security facility in Shirley in September 2001. Westerman maintained a strong connection with members of the Geas family.

According to Arillotta, Freddy reached out for his assistance in a plan to kill Westerman for fear that Westerman would cooperate against him.

"I mean, that guy, he was gonna get killed like three different times," Arillotta said.

Arillotta, Lou "The Shoe" Santos, and Geas made arrangements to have Santos lure Westerman into a van, where Arillotta and Fotios Geas lay in wait, ready for Geas to fire the fatal shot.

"We were going to kill him in 1996. Freddy had a case with him, and then when we went to go kill him, my friend Lou "The Shoe" Santos knocked on the door; his girlfriend was there, so we had to call it off," Arillotta said.

In 2002, Arillotta devised another scheme to kill Westerman after he refused to end his relationship with Arillotta's sister-in-law, who was 30 years younger than him—seeking the assistance of Freddy Geas and Michael DeCaro, who would invite Westerman to a dinner where Arillotta and DeCaro would carry out a drive-by shooting. However, the two arrived at the designated location late, thwarting their plans again.

Arillotta says, "Gary starts dating my wife's sister. She was on drugs, and she was a mess at the time. Gary was selling drugs, giving her drugs. He was 30 years older than her, and I told him, 'Gary, find another girl, stay away from her.' Then my mother-in-law and father-in-law, immigrants from Italy who speak broken English, own a specialty store with Italian meats and olive oils; the sausage was their specialty; they have the best sausage in the area, and they're busting my balls. 'This guy's 30 years older than my daughter. What are you gonna do about it?' 'This guy's giving her drugs. What are you gonna do about it?' I said, 'I'm gonna talk to him.'

"Now, at the time, my car had a listening device in it. I was driving an Expedition, and the Feds put a bug in it; they were listening to me, and I pulled up to him at a strip club, and I said, 'Gary,' it's on tape; I said, 'Gary, will you stop, go get another girlfriend.' And it's got him saying on tape, 'I'm gonna, I'm gonna, I'm gonna.'

"So, I went to my mother-in-law's store. That place was a hangout for me; it was where I met people, and there was a nice room upstairs. It was in the Italian South End of Springfield; the Italian club was across the street, and the Italian coffee shop was a nice spot. So, when I used to go there, Joe, my father-in-law, busted my balls; he says, 'He won't stop dating my daughter; what does that say about you? He's got no respect for you.' They're basically asking me to hurt the guy.

"My friend Michael DeCaro was in the store that day, and I said, 'Michael, do me a favor, drive me, I'm going to shoot this kid tonight.' So, we set it up. I had Freddy take him to dinner, and Michael and I waited outside. I said,

'Freddy, beep me when you're 10 minutes away from eating. When you're walking out the door, I'll pull up, I'll get out, and I'll shoot Gary.'

"So, we did all that, he beeps me, and we got ready. It was a big restaurant. Gary drove a Porsche, and the Porsche was parked in the parking lots over there, so we figured they had to walk this way for sure. What happens is that the walk is short, and they get into the Porsche, so by the time we pulled up, they were in the car. I would have had to shoot in the car and maybe hit Freddy at the same time, so we had to call that one off.

"Eventually, my mother-in-law welcomes him back. They go out to dinner, so they start dating and end up getting married. So, I just washed my hands with the whole situation. I didn't want the guy around me, that close to me, being with me, but they ended up getting married."

Anthony Arillotta, Fotios "Freddy" Geas, Ty Geas, and Emilio Fusco suspected Gary Westerman of cooperating with law enforcement.

On November 4, 2003, Freddy and Ty Geas decided to murder Westerman later that day, convinced of his betrayal. They enlisted Arillotta's help, who then contacted Emilio Fusco to test his newfound loyalty and respect.

Later that day, Arillotta went to see Fusco, who was having dinner with his girlfriend at a restaurant. He came off the table, met Bingy, and Arillotta said, "Hey, we're going to clip Westerman tonight. You want to go?"

Fusco says, "Yeah, when?"

"Right now, tonight."

He finished up with the girl there. They had a cognac, and then he jumped up, and they left.

The four men planned to murder Westerman at the home of a man named Joseph Iellamo, a marijuana dealer whom Arillotta knew.

So, they set out to kill Westerman that night, the Geas' luring him to the home in Agawam where they knew the elderly resident, a friend, was not home, with a promise of a "score," cash, and marijuana they could rob inside. They picked Westerman up at a grocery store and headed to the home on Springfield Street.

Arillotta and Fusco arrived at Iellamo's garage and patiently waited for the arrival of the Geas brothers and Westerman. They proceeded to the garage, each taking a shovel and concealing themselves. After a half hour, the Geas brothers and Westerman pulled up in an SUV. Arillotta and Fusco quickly ducked down, wary of the windows and not wanting to be seen by Westerman. Positioned near a door, they stayed low with their shovels at the ready. The sound of the truck's arrival and doors opening and closing filled the air, followed by the distinct sound of footsteps. The brothers then guided Westerman around the house, out of sight.

The shouting caught their attention, and they heard cries of "Ouch! Ouch!" However, it was not immediately evident that Westerman had been shot, as the gunshots had not been heard. It was later discovered that Ty Geas had used a .22 caliber handgun with a silencer to shoot at Westerman, but the bullets did not prove fatal. It turned out that the silencer was faulty, slowed down the bullets, resulting in them bouncing off Westerman's head instead of penetrating his skull.

The two onlookers quickly ran out of the garage and saw the brothers dragging Westerman across the grass, who appeared to be unconscious, towards a nearby wooded area. However, to their surprise, Westerman suddenly started "moving spastically" again.

As Fusco witnessed Westerman's survival and the Geas' struggle with him, he immediately sprang into action. Emilio swiftly maneuvered past Ty Geas, wielding a shovel he had been carrying over his head, and mercilessly bashed it into Gary Westerman's head with brute force. Fusco repeated the act more than a dozen times while Arillotta hurried back to retrieve his shovel and bludgeoned Westerman from behind.

After rendering Westerman unconscious, the four of them each grabbed a piece of him and proceeded to drag him towards the hole. This 8-foot ditch in the nearby woods had been dug earlier on Bruno's orders in a twist of fate. Bruno considered having Tranghese killed while the two were at odds. The ditch had previously been marked with the names of many gangsters, but now it served as Westerman's makeshift grave.

Arillotta ordered Freddy to shoot him and ensure that he was dead. He pulled out a gun and blasted Westerman five inches from his head to finish him off. Unlike before, the bullet did not ricochet.

Freddy searched Westerman's pockets, snatched his prized Rolex, and broke his phone in two before tossing it into the hole. Then Ty dragged him by his ankles into the concealed hole, and the four proceeded to fill it up with dirt, concealing it once again with cardboard and leaves. As they got ready to depart, they stowed the shovels in the back of their SUV and climbed in, speeding away without looking back.

Everything was done.

After tossing the shovels from a bridge, they headed to the grocery store for white vinegar to remove the gun residue from their hands. However, they never returned to the scene and cleaned up the evidence.

Later on, Anthony Arillotta and Emilio Fusco shared a toast to celebrate their merciless murder of a police informant, followed by an embrace to signify their newfound bond.

"It was like a gesture that we had just accomplished something. We were like brothers," recalled Arillotta.

Westerman's killers agreed they'd never speak about the murder, yet shortly after, they gathered at Morton's Steakhouse in Hartford, Connecticut, to commemorate their deed. Arillotta owned a sleek white Cadillac at the time, with Ty sitting in the back and Freddy in the driver's seat. They all understood the rule of never discussing anything in Freddy's car. Now that the heat is on, everyone knows they were the last to see Gary alive.

As they drove past the scene of the murder, Freddy couldn't help but start singing, "On top of Old Smokey all covered in blood," before bursting into laughter. Arillotta's not one of those paranoid guys, but he shook his head and turned up the music.

He caught a glimpse of Ty in the rearview mirror, also shaking his head and gesturing with his hand in disbelief, like, "What the fuck is he doing?"

According to court documents, Westerman was an informant for the Massachusetts State Police. However, the agency eventually terminated their relationship with him when he got caught up in a check fraud scheme.

Several months later, Westerman contacted state police again with an offer to inform on his fellow mobsters. In 2003, Westerman repeatedly disclosed to law enforcement that Anthony Arillotta, Fotios Geas, and Ty Geas were "making moves" and seeking authorization from members of organized crime in New York to "retire" Al Bruno.

"That's the ditch where Gary Westerman ended up. That was his grave, but the original ditch they were asked to dig was for Felix," Arillotta said.

It's been suggested that Arillotta was jealous of Westerman's marriage to his sister-in-law, as Arillotta had engaged in sexual relations with his wife's sister on two separate occasions during a period of separation from his wife.

Less than a week later, on November 9, 2003, Frankie Roche had a beef with Bruno that was completely unrelated to the low-key gangland feud Bruno was involved in with the Genovese family. Roche became heavily intoxicated and was tearing up area bars and restaurants, all of which were under the protection of the Springfield crew. Roche had a reputation for being a nasty drunk and a violent guy. When he drank, he didn't have a casual beer like most people but instead opted for straight vodka, which was a dangerous combination with his aggressive nature.

Michael DeCaro and Frankie Roche were playing a game of pool at Emo's Place, a dive bar co-owned by convicted drug trafficker Emiliano Gonzalez. The establishment, located in a rundown area of Springfield, was known for its seedy atmosphere. While Roche was shooting pool with a couple of guys, one of them said something that Roche inferred was disrespectful, and a verbal exchange quickly escalated into a heated argument.

The guy's refusal to stop smiling at him only further enraged Roche, who savagely beat the man, flooding a section of floor with blood as a dozen horrified onlookers, including DeCaro, who stood by laughing, watched. Eventually, the bar manager intervened and forced DeCaro and Roche to leave.

Later, a female witness told the police, "I have never seen a beating like that in my life. I thought the guy was going to kill him."

About a half-hour later, DeCaro, Roche, and Branden Croteau returned to Emo's Place, with Roche carrying a baseball bat. Upon arrival, Roche demanded to see the manager, and when informed he was not in, he proceeded to trash the whole place. Mirrors, bottles of booze, a video poker machine, fixtures, and glassware were all casualties in this chaotic scene, which resembled the aftermath of a nuclear war.

Although Emo's was known as a dive bar, it was unlike any other. It was under the protection of the mob, making it untouchable. When the owner discovered what had happened, he immediately ran to Al Bruno and told him what had happened. Bruno wasted no time ordering Emilio Fusco to track down the troublemaker, Roche.

Bruno said to Emilio Fusco, "I want this kid, Roche. Get me this kid, Roche."

He was determined to get answers and receive some form of reimbursement for all the chaos caused.

Later that evening, Roche and DeCaro were found at the State Street tavern, just an hour after Roche wreaked havoc at Emo's. Bruno and Emilio Fusco, a notorious loan shark soon to serve a three-year prison sentence, approached them. The bar owners were upset about damaging their lottery equipment and other supplies and called Bruno to mediate the situation.

Al Bruno put the word on the street that he expected $4,300 in compensation for the bar's damage. He ordered Frankie Roche to make reparations with the owner, but Roche was extremely defiant. Bruno spoke with Mike DeCaro in front of a bar in the South End and urged him to talk to Roche and get the money for the bar's damage.

On November 21, 2003, an unnamed informant, wearing a wire around the city while under investigation for real estate fraud, caught a telling conversation on tape. He recorded Al Bruno and Michael DeCaro discussing Roche.

"He's got ten guns on him," a transcript shows DeCaro told Bruno.

"And you got twenty-five. Fuck him up. Don't take a licking. There's nothing to it. He can shoot, but our barrel can shoot, too," Bruno said.

On November 22, 2003, Roche grew increasingly agitated by DeCaro's constant pestering about Bruno squeezing him over the Emo's bar vandalism. Fed up with the situation, Roche gave DeCaro a beating, feeling that Bruno had always held power over him due to the death of DeCaro's father, Victor, in 1972.

After the altercation, Freddy Geas called Roche to question his actions, asking, "What did you do to DeCaro?"

This further fueled his anger.

Now infuriated by DeCaro's call to Geas about the punch, Roche stormed to the nearby State Street Tavern to confront him. With a .45-caliber gun in hand, Roche made a public threat to shoot DeCaro, placing the gun to his head and announcing that he planned to kill Bruno as well.

Just twenty-four hours later, Frankie Roche would once again draw his gun on another target, this time unleashing its full fury.

Chapter 15

It's Been Green Lighted

According to a former member of the Springfield Crew, "There was nothing Big Al Bruno could do at this point, in Springfield or out in New York where Artie and Genovese brain trust was. He was living on borrowed time and didn't even know it."

Felix Tranghese was given the order to kill Bruno, but he wasn't capable of killing and lacked the crew around him to carry out the hit on a boss. To remedy this, he enlisted the help of Anthony Arillotta, who was already preoccupied with trying to kill the Manzis and some other guys. As a result, Tranghese isn't getting much done on his own to whack Bruno.

After several weeks, Bruno was still alive, and Little Artie summoned Arillotta to New York. During the meeting, Artie asked Arillotta if he knew what was happening.

Arillotta isn't even supposed to know about the planned hit on Bruno. When questioned, Anthony feigned ignorance and acted as if it was the first time he had heard about it. Felix wasn't supposed to tell anyone about the plan to kill Bruno. The code of silence in the Mafia dictates that when you get told to kill someone, you only speak of it to your crew that you're going to kill with, or if you're going alone, you don't tell anyone. But Felix knew he needed Arillotta's help to carry out the hit successfully, so he pulled him into it by telling him.

Little Artie Nigro implored Arillotta to get his guys, the Geas brothers, to aid Felix Tranghese with the murder and also directed him to utilize Emilio Fusco.

"Help them plan it, help them set it up or whatever, but don't get your hands dirty. Don't get involved directly," Anthony was told.

Upon his return to Springfield, Arillotta told Freddy and Ty Geas their new orders. Together, with Felix Tranghese and Emilio Fusco, they discussed numerous plans for eliminating Bruno. Their primary goal was to devise ways to kill Bruno quietly and make the body disappear by luring him to a secluded location.

A plan was created to lure Big Al Bruno into a vehicle, where they would shoot him in the back of the head. The intention was to then drive the car, along with Bruno's dead body, to a scrapyard owned by Emilio Fusco's friend. The car would be crushed and shipped overseas, ensuring that Big Al Bruno would never be seen again.

However, Bruno was always accompanied by his best friend Fitzy, making it difficult for them to carry out their plan. Bruno had a gut feeling that something was up and refused to go anywhere alone with them. Despite their numerous attempts to kill him, Bruno proved to be a difficult target, ducking proposed trips to New York and dinner parties during which where he was meant to be murdered.

Despite not being involved in the direct planning or giving the order itself in the Bruno assassination, Bologna knew the order had been given full well. When Arillotta and Felix Tranghese were slow to carry out Nigro's order, he told them to "do what they had been told to do" in carrying out the murder.

Consequently, Arillotta delegated the task of farming out the contract to Freddy Geas. It turned out that Geas had a close friend from his time in state prison who was a perfect fit for the job. Geas recruited his former cellmate, the loose-cannon Frankie Roche, to be the triggerman and kill Bruno "cowboy style." Geas saw Roche as a crash dummy, someone he could manipulate into doing something crazy. Just a week prior, Freddy had used Roche to baseball bat some lawyer he had an issue with.

Freddy and Ty Geas approached him and held their meeting in the parking lot of the Basketball Hall of Fame located in the heart of downtown Springfield. Freddy made an offer to provide a gun and a sum of $10,000 to kill Big Al Bruno and get out of town. According to Freddy, the order came from Anthony Arillotta, Bruno's trusted right-hand man. Frankie Roche saw Arillotta, also known as "The Little Guy," as a key organized crime member and his ticket to easy money.

However, the situation was more significant than it seemed. Arillotta was simply the messenger in this dangerous game. This one wasn't going to be on hold. This one came from up top, New York. It's been green-lighted. Nothing is going to stop this one. It's got to be done. It can't be messed up.

On the night before his 58th birthday, November 23, 2003, Adolfo "Big Al" Bruno gathered with his family for dinner. Afterward, he hopped into his Chevy Suburban and visited the Society of Our Lady of Mount Carmel Club. Once there, he joined in a few rounds of briscola, his favorite card game.

Little did he know Emilio Fusco had placed a call to Freddy Geas, who promptly informed Roche of Bruno's location.

"Al's down at the Mount Carmel playing cards."

Roche sprang into action without hesitation, his body tense with anticipation as he prepared to carry out his sinister plan. The scene was set, the pieces in place, and Bruno was completely unaware of the danger looming outside the club's doors.

Earlier that day, Emilio Fusco discreetly stashed a .45-caliber firearm, carefully wrapped in rags and stored in a plastic bag, under a dumpster behind Family Pizza in Springfield. Later, Freddy retrieved the weapon and an extra ammunition clip from beneath the dumpster and promptly delivered it to Frankie Roche.

Brandon Croteau drove Roche in an unregistered vehicle to the Italian social club to await Bruno's appearance. He then positioned himself around the corner, waiting for Roche to complete the mission. Brandon knew that Roche was up to something illegal, but little did he know that

Roche's ultimate plan was to assassinate Big Al Bruno, the boss of the Springfield crew.

Roche had stalked Bruno to the Our Lady of Mount Carmel Society club and concealed himself behind a vending machine, patiently waiting for Bruno to exit his weekly Sunday card game.

In the dimly lit parking lot, Roche waited for about a half-hour, but what felt like an eternity until he finally heard Bruno's voice piercing through the silence. It was filled with anger and frustration, yelling like he was upset about something. As Frankie emerged from the darkness, he noticed Bruno's Z-71 Chevy Suburban interior lights flickering.

Roche attempted to time it when he would get to his car, but as he emerged, he noticed Big Al already entering his truck.

With a shout, Roche exclaimed, "Hey, Al!"

At first, Big Al was unaware of who was calling out to him. "What's up, buddy?" Bruno replied.

"I heard you were looking for me," Roche responded, alluding to a recent beef over a bar brawl between the two brewing for days.

First, Roche fired a single shot into Bruno's chest.

With Big Al collapsing against the car, Roche relentlessly pulled the trigger, closing the distance between them. Standing over the dying crime boss, he pointed a shot at his nuts before delivering the sixth and final bullet to his head.

After the shooting, Brandon Croteau drove Roche to ditch the gun in a dumpster at a shopping center, followed by a visit to American International College to discard the dark fleece jacket, jeans, and battered Red Sox hat he had been wearing into a trash can on campus. Subsequently, they retrieved Roche's vehicle, where he paid Croteau for assisting him with some of the money he received from Geas to help him get out of town after the shooting.

During the chaos, the audacious and larger-than-life Big Al Bruno was gunned down in the parking lot of his social club after his weekly card game.

Bruno was accompanied only by one of his right-hand men and closest friends, Frank "The Shark" Depergola, who was entering the passenger side of Bruno's vehicle when the deafening sound of gunfire erupted. In a frantic escape, Roche disappeared into the darkness while Depergola cradled Bruno's lifeless body in his arms.

A police detective named Maurice Kearney heard the dispatcher's voice over the radio.

"We have a shooting down on Winthrop Street. We need an ambulance fast because the guy is in tough shape."

Homicide detective Thomas Malidi also heard the dispatch.

"Al Bruno just took about eight to the body at the Italian club on Winthrop Street."

Kearney and Malidi raced over. Al Bruno was still there on the ground. He wasn't moving.

Another officer rolled Bruno onto his back and started doing chest compressions to try to revive him. He then made eye contact with Detective Kearney, looked right at him, and shook his head.

"Ah, he's dead. He's gone."

They ripped his shirt off. You could see the holes in his chest. Blood was coming out of him from just about everywhere. He was lying back flat when he still had the cigar in his hand.

Joe Signorelli, a friend of Al Bruno's, departed 30 minutes earlier, briefly stopping by Bruno's table on the way out. He last said to Joe, "I'll see you tomorrow."

Anthony Arillotta's aunt heard about the shooting on the police scanner and called his house. When Anthony's mother answered, she informed her she just heard on the radio that Big Al Bruno had just been murdered. Bingy had taken precautions to secure an alibi, as his mother, wife, and children were all present with him at the time of the murder.

Upon learning the news from his mother, Anthony couldn't help but feel a little saddened. His mother grew up with Al, and his father had also been close friends. Growing up in an Italian community, he was a known guy, respected, and looked up to by many, including Anthony.

His father stares at him sternly and questions, "And you want to be a criminal?"

According to Arillotta, "New York should have never killed Big Al. They should have gotten Felix Tranghese propped up and gone to Bruno and said, 'Give us a percent of all your legitimate businesses around the country,' as New York now can't get any of that money."

On the night of the murder, the sole witness was Frank Depergola, a friend of the Springfield boss and mob associate. While Bruno was shot six times by the gunman, for some reason, he left Depergola alone.

That same night, Springfield police detective Maurice Kearney interrogated Depergola, hoping to gather information about the shooter. He probed, asking if Depergola got a look at the shooter.

"Did you hear his voice? Did you know who the shooter was?"

But Depergola's response was the typical reaction of a mobster.

"I don't know who it was. I don't know what happened."

Mobsters were averse to speaking with law enforcement, and Kearney was met with resistance. But he persisted, pointing out the suspicious circumstances of Depergola's presence with Bruno before the shooting.

He asked, "You walk out with Bruno, and then the guy gets shot. How do you think that's going to look?"

Depergola's response remained unchanged.

"I didn't have nothing to do with nothing. I don't know what happened. I don't know who the guy was. Just came up, shot him, and ran away."

After being taken to the police station, Depergola was interrogated further. Despite their persistence, he eventually admitted to seeing the shooter, although he didn't get a good look. All he could recall was a 6-foot-tall individual wearing a dark-colored hoodie.

"I couldn't see him."

This vague information did not offer much help, as plenty of men fit this description. However, Detective Thomas Malidi from the homicide unit had a gut feeling that Depergola knew more than he was letting on.

He claimed to have no idea who the guy was, which we suspect to be a lie. However, I believe he did know, as he persistently asked for Victor that night.

"I want to talk to Victor. I want to talk to Victor."

Victor, being Victor Bruno, is the son of Al Bruno. The police were perplexed. Why was Depergola so insistent on speaking with Bruno's son? Did he know something he wasn't telling the cops? Did he recognize the shooter? Well, within a few days, these questions were answered.

After news of the shooting made headlines all over the East Coast, Big Al's son wrote a letter to the editor of The Republican.

"Once again, I find myself defined by my father's criminal record and purported misdeeds," Victor Bruno wrote. "Let me make myself clear: I love my father. He has been a good father to me. But I have never done any business with him. Period."

It was an odd statement to make after his father was assassinated in the streets. To distance himself from him so quickly.

Shortly after that, one of the Springfield detectives received intel from Frankie Depergola, who passed it along to Victor. This information was then relayed to one of the officers by Victor, revealing that Frankie Roche was the kid who shot his father.

Their focus then turned to locating Frankie Roche, described as a 6ft tall individual often seen in hoodies. The investigators were eager to find him and inquire about his involvement in Al Bruno's murder. Did you kill Al Bruno? Did you work alone? Or were you put up to it by someone else? The entire case could be altered if they could get Frankie Roche to answer these questions.

There was an eyewitness to the murder who claimed he had no idea who the guy was, but we suspect this to be a lie. If we can unravel this mystery, it may lead to cooperation and reveal new insights into the workings of the Springfield mob.

Upon hearing Roche's name, I had very little knowledge about him. Authorities in Westfield, a Springfield suburb, were asked, "What do you remember about Frankie Roche?"

The police captain responded, "I'll tell you what I remember about Frankie Roche. Fast. He was fast." Known for his ability to evade law enforcement, Roche would often outrun them, rarely getting caught.

According to Thomas Murphy, a former Massachusetts state police officer who used to monitor Roche's previous hangouts, Roche's rap sheet was as thick as a phone book. At the young age of 17, Roach was arrested for stealing a car. Two years later, he was taken into custody for assault with a deadly weapon, robbery, and another car theft. He was subsequently sentenced to prison. In 1993, Roche managed to escape from prison and proceeded to steal not one but two cars. However, he was apprehended just seven days later. In 2000, Roche was arrested again for breaking into a liquor store.

When questioned about his motive, Roche stated, "Because they were closed."

Murphy reveals that when Roche drank, he tended to become belligerent.

But did Roche possess enough defiance to haul off and kill Al Bruno, a mob boss, over a bar fight? Officer Murphy expressed doubt, as it seemed unlikely that this Roche kid just decided to go hunt down Big Al on his own.

"It didn't sit well with us."

On November 29, 2003, hundreds gathered outside Forastiere Family Funeral Home, stretching down Locust Street. Among them were influential and affluent individuals, patiently waiting under the watchful eyes and telephoto lenses of mob investigators across New England. The crowd continued to grow for over two hours, just a short distance from where Bruno was fatally shot. Those in attendance included Anthony Arillotta, Emilio Fusco, Felix Tranghese, and the Geas brothers, Freddy and Ty.

Victor Bruno, a prominent downtown restaurateur and unquestionably the most high-profile among the five sons of Al Bruno, spoke of his father. "My father lived life intensely. His greatest joy was being around people. He was an honorable man, a man of principle."

Less than a day after Bruno was gunned down, Anthony Delevo, the former boss of the Springfield crew, was sentenced to three years in federal prison for his involvement in racketeering and money laundering. This investigation has resulted in 15 indictments. In addition to his prison sentence, Delevo was fined $100,000 and placed on probation for 5 1/2 years after his release from jail.

The mafia's downfall of its old-school bosses and the absence of clear successors may leave it vulnerable to a lack of direction and anarchy.

On the eve of his 58th birthday, Bruno was killed, leaving behind a legacy of dominance in Greater Springfield's criminal underworld alongside his predecessor, Anthony Delevo. These two were dominating forces for two decades, along with the notorious Francesco "Skyball" Scibelli and his younger brother, Albert "Baba" Scibelli. In the year 2000, the elder Scibelli, known as "Franky Skyball," died at the age of 87, while "Baba," now 83, was recently placed on one year of home confinement after pleading guilty to extortion.

The brutal gangland-style slaying of Bruno has sparked speculation as to who will seize control of the city's illicit rackets. Theories range from established members of organized crime to lesser-known associates and successors of the previous regime.

Police have refrained from labeling the shooting as a Mafia hit and have avoided making assumptions about potential changes in organized crime leadership. Among those previously recognized as top lieutenants is entrepreneur Felix Tranghese, who owned Mulino's and was incarcerated for racketeering in the mid-1980s.

In addition to the veteran mobsters who were casualties of the recent crackdown, rising stars who held significant influence over local gambling and loansharking rings were also sentenced in the same investigation. Giuseppe "Little Joe" Manzi, alongside Emilio Fusco, an Italian immigrant who arrived in the city in the 1990s, received a three-year sentence. These two individuals brought youth to the aging leadership of the local mafia.

As Bruno's murder left a void in Springfield, Arillotta saw an opportunity to claim it as his own. However, the repercussions of Bruno's death could not be ignored, and the infamous code of silence within the mob would soon begin to falter.

The only solution to unraveling the enigma was to locate Frankie Roche. If Roche were not acting alone, another faction would be eager to pursue him—a small entity known as the Federal Bureau of Investigation. Their primary objective is to dismantle organized crime, so if this was a mob-related hit, it could be a big deal.

This golden opportunity did not escape the attention of Brian Warren, an FBI special agent stationed in the Springfield office.

"If we could work up the ladder on a mob hit, and people are looking at the death penalty, mandatory life, we might get people to cooperate and talk to us. If we can crack this, we will get cooperation and open the doors into the Springfield mob."

Warren requested that the investigators from three agencies sign a document affirming they wouldn't share information outside of their small circle. This tight-knit group formed their unique alliance, bound by their code of secrecy. With their signatures now in place, they could openly discuss and exchange vital information, focusing on their primary suspect, Frankie Roche.

It didn't take long for the investigators to make a breakthrough, as they received a tip about a phone being used by Roche. The Springfield team then issued a subpoena for the phone records, and their expert analyst immediately began his work. According to the phone records, Roche fled the city after the murder and took refuge in a friend's apartment in Tampa, Florida.

However, the investigators faced a hurdle in obtaining a warrant for his arrest, as the evidence linking him to Bruno's murder was not strong enough. To overcome this, they devised a workaround by charging Roche with a parole violation, as he had fled while on parole, and also for vandalizing Emo's bar. As a result, the Massachusetts District Attorney issued an arrest warrant based on these charges, while the federal government also issued their own warrant.

"We can attach what's called an unlawful flight to avoid prosecution. And that allowed us to go and search and look and try to assist in locating and arrest Frankie Roche."

Chapter 16

All Street Money is Mine

Western Massachusetts is at a crossroads as organized crime faces a major disruption. Following the murder of one top leader and another bound for prison, the future of this criminal network is uncertain. Despite a relatively peaceful decade, the local Genovese faction has recently experienced chaos, resulting from frequent law enforcement crackdowns and the murder of Adolfo Bruno outside a social club in the South End.

Mob investigators ultimately label Anthony "Bingy" Arillotta as Bruno's successor. He ruthlessly climbs the ranks of the Springfield Crew, a faction of the Genovese crime family from New York City, seizing control of the region's illegal rackets with a brutal and cold-blooded focus. Freddy Geas and his brother Ty Geas assist their close friend Anthony Arillotta in taking over the Genovese crew in Springfield.

Still, due to their Greek heritage, they are never formally inducted into the family.

Throughout his adult years, Anthony Arillotta was deeply involved in a wide range of crimes, many of which were characterized by extreme violence. He posed a constant threat to the city of Springfield, using violence, intimidation, and his connections to organized crime to terrorize the city and line his pockets with money from his various criminal activities. He had fully dedicated himself to a career as a professional criminal and mobster and was quite skilled at it.

During his time, Arillotta had extensive connections across the Northeast, ranging from the Patriarca family in Rhode Island to the Angiulos in Boston and the Gambinos and Bonannos in New York. His network also included figures such as Billy "Wild Guy" Grasso and Whitey Tropiano in New Haven, as well as Whitey Bulger's Winter Hill Gang. As the leader of the Springfield crew, Arillotta enjoyed luxuries such as beautiful women, power, and millions in cash. However, this power and riches eventually came at a cost.

After Bruno was killed in November 2003, Amadeo Santaniello began to send feelers out about his return. Eventually, he returned to town and resumed his former role as an associate of the Springfield crew. Big Al and Amedeo were once close friends, but their relationship soured, and Bruno banished him from the city in the late 1990s. Despite never being officially inducted into the mafia, Arillotta welcomed him back as an active associate. The older Santaniello pleaded with Arillotta constantly to promote both himself and his son, Ralphie Santaniello, even going as far as to visit Anthony's father's produce store to make his case to his longtime friend, Tony Arillotta.

"Bingy, we'll do anything you ask."

Arillotta stated plainly, "If you guys want to get your buttons, you need to use the gun."

However, this never came to pass. They were incapable and never became made members of the Springfield faction of the Genovese family.

The younger Ralphie Santaniello worked with Albert "The Animal" Calvanese, the most highly-feared collector in Bingy's crew, as a loan shark. As far as Victor Bruno, Big Al's son, Arillotta gave him a message from Nigro.

"All legal business is yours. All street money is now New York's."

Just three days after Bruno was killed outside the social club in the South End, state police apprehended Anthony Arillotta at the Springfield YMCA. Arillotta stands accused of running a loan-sharking operation and supervising an illegal gambling ring that raked in as much as $150,000 per week through various local offices and a toll-free betting line based in Costa Rica.

During their investigation, state police placed listening devices in Arillotta's SUV and planted a tracking device, revealing that the father of two did not hold a legitimate job. It is alleged that the crime boss colluded with eight other individuals, including state court officer Charles Catjakis, the son of State Representative Athan "Soco" Catjakis, and John Cote.

The muscle behind the operation was John Cote, a construction worker who wore a Red Sox team jacket, handcuffs, and leg chains in court.

"This is the one who did the threatening. As you can see, he's a big man," said the prosecutor, who described Cote as a debt collector.

After, Arillotta was released on bail and placed under a strict curfew from 6 p.m. to 6 a.m. This marked the beginning of 24/7 surveillance on him. Before Bruno's murder, there was a lot of other violence that happened, and Arillotta's name frequently surfaced in law enforcement circles.

On one occasion, while driving in a car together, Victor Bruno was startled by an unexpected phone call from an unknown friend. His complexion drained of color as he was informed that the same individuals responsible for Westerman's death had also murdered his father. Overwhelmed with nausea, he wants to throw up. He's sitting next to Arillotta and the Geas brothers, all of whom were believed to be Gary's killers. Without uttering a single word, Victor urgently tells them to pull over and let him out of the car.

Michael DeCaro and Brandon Croteau are charged in connection with a bar fight that erupted two weeks before Bruno's murder. DeCaro, the grandson of the late organized crime boss Skyball Scibelli, is the son of Victor DeCaro, who went missing in May 1972. Frankie Roche fled the area and is now considered a fugitive.

Roche, a towering figure at 6 feet and 4 inches, with a formidable weight of 205 pounds, adorned with sinister tattoos, disappeared months ago. According to a transcript from a grand jury, the alleged beating victim has chosen not to file charges, fearing potential retaliation.

In response, the police released three mug shots of Roche and warned the public against approaching or attempting to apprehend him. Police descriptions of Roche reveal a menacing ex-convict with tattoos covering his body, including a depiction of the grim reaper on his chest, "Built for War" emblazoned on his upper left arm, "World Get Over Me" inked on his upper right arm, and "God" etched onto his abdomen.

DeCaro is eventually acquitted in connection to the altercation at the bar, which allegedly sparked Roche and Bruno's rivalry. The charges against Croteau are dropped following a key witness retracting her statements about the brawl at Emo's Place.

One month after Bruno's murder, reports began to circulate, fingering Roche as the likely killer. Nigro told Arillotta that Roche should be whacked in a public place.

He told him, "Take out Roche, chop off his hands, and leave them on his body to send a message that he was slain for killing Bruno."

The obvious implication here is that Little Artie Nigro was furious over Bruno's death and sought vengeance. Nigro's order was to "deflect the heat off us," creating the illusion to the cops that "we weren't behind the hit on Bruno; the mob was not behind it."

Roche was on the lam, his whereabouts a mystery to all.

Under the leadership of Arillotta, the Geas brothers from West Springfield, along with Emilio Fusco, became the muscle on the streets, instilling fear in the hearts of established gangsters. They took control of the streets, demanding higher "tribute" payments from local business owners and gambling debtors that had traditionally been paid to Bruno.

"Bingy" continued to traffic marijuana, participate in loansharking and extortion activities, and run an illegal sports betting operation. However, once Arillotta assumed control, the younger, more formidable, and intimidating regime rose to power. Arillotta also intended to establish his own vending company and install his machines in establishments that already housed machines from other mobsters.

At Nigro's request, Arillotta increased the shakedowns of associates involved in the vending machine industry in Springfield. The lucrative Joker Poker machines yielded an average of $2,500 per week at each location, with some earning less and others as much as 10k. The primary targets were S&M Vending, owned by Baba Scibelli and his son-in-law Michael Cimmino, and C&S Vending, owned by brothers Carlo and Genaro Sarno.

First, they made their way to see James "Jimmy" Santaniello. Jimmy, the nephew of aging area mafioso Mario Fiore, had previously admitted to being a low-level bookmaker and current owner of the Mardi Gras strip club in Springfield and several other businesses. Additionally, he held a stake in the mobbed-up world of vending machines, video poker, and slot machines.

Felix Tranghese demanded a monthly payment of $3,000 and even went as far as threatening to "poke out his eyes" if Santaniello refused to pay. Worcester crime boss Carlo Mastrototaro and Franky Pugliano of West Springfield also wanted to bring Santaniello under their protection and demanded a weekly tribute of $500. During a conversation with Arillotta, Jimmy Santaniello revealed that he was paying a hefty amount of 4 to 6k every month to Baba Scibelli and Michael Cimmino's S&M Vending for their cut of profits from the Joker Pokers in his bars.

Eventually, Arillotta emerged as the victor in the battle for control over Santaniello, squeezing him for a straight tribute of $3,000 per month, which Santaniello reluctantly accepted.

Next, they visited C&S Vending, where they met with the Sarno brothers, Carlo and Genaro.

Following Bruno's murder, the Sarnos were paying mobster Felix Tranghese $800 monthly, considering it a "cost of doing business." Felix Tranghese and Jimmy Santaniello's uncle, Mario Fiore, believed they were entitled to it. But in May 2004, Fusco and the Geas brothers came knocking, demanding half of their weekly profits.

However, they unknowingly disclosed their plans to a State Police informant, Emiliano "Emo" Gonzales, who was wearing a body wire during their meeting at the White Hut restaurant in West Springfield. Arillotta was caught on tape requesting $4,000 to $6,000 in weekly profits from the Sarnos.

The captured conversations contained mocking allusions to aging mobsters Felix Tranghese and Mario Fiore, portraying them as insignificant characters trying to offer Sarno's protection. Freddy Geas scoffed, "And then you got these old timers that think they wrote the fucking book on being sharp, and they're fucking stupid. You know?"

During another recorded meeting on the same day, Arillotta made threats of taking sledgehammers to Sarno's's machines and having 15 guys "run them over 85 times" with a car if the police intervened. He then asserted, "Those vending machines, those are ours. If we want, we'll take every single one of them. Felix ain't stopping us, and Mario Fiore ain't stopping us. But we don't want to do that. We're being fucking gentlemen about it this, but we don't have to be."

According to a recorded conversation, Emo Gonzales, an ex-convict who worked for the Sarnos, revealed to Arillotta that two other men, Reno Ceravalo and Anthony Basile, had already approached the cousins with a demand for "monthly envelopes full of cash" for Tranghese in exchange for protection.

The Sarnos were well aware that they were dealing with a different and more dangerous group of criminals, which instilled a sense of fear for their well-being—resorting to carrying a gun.

Later, Arillotta declares, "It's the hard way or the nice easy way, OK? We are in the machine business. So, we're going into spots."

Arillotta reveals plans to install 10 of their slot machines in prime locations throughout the city. He knows they have 50 locations, so he demands 10 of them, or else "we'll come in and take the whole thing."

The informant, Emo Gonzales, was so spooked by Freddy Geas that he instantly cut ties with law enforcement. Gonzales, who is reportedly facing a state prison sentence for drug charges, hastily fled the country.

Next, Arillotta turned his attention to S&M Vending. He proposed purchasing the vending company, but they refused.

Anthony Arillotta and Joey Basile held a two-hour sit down with Michael Cimmino, a prominent real estate developer and restaurateur, at his Hampden House restaurant. Cimmino's father-in-law, Shelved Mobster Baba Scibelli, was at the meeting. Arillotta, now the crew's new boss, took S&M Vending for himself in a forced sale conceded to by Cimmino. Jimmy Santaniello would be co-owner of the vending company with Arillotta, kicking $12k up to Arillotta monthly. Baba Scibelli was rendered powerless.

According to Cimmino, he had no intention of standing in the way of Arillotta's efforts to dominate the vending machine business in the area. This was about the remnants of S&M vending, a company dismantled mainly by a crackdown on illegal poker machines by the state police in 2001. Given the individuals he is dealing with, it is the wisest decision for himself and his family. For years, Scibelli had held a tight grip on the lucrative business of supplying illegally rigged poker machines to bars and restaurants. Cimmino, who S&M employed, had previously pleaded guilty to a felony gambling charge in connection with the 2001 sting.

Despite feeling a "pit in his stomach," he handed over his business to Arillotta. However, his wife, the daughter of former crime boss Baba Scibelli, strongly disagreed and accused him of being "a coward and a joke of a man." Overcome with emotion, he tearfully pleaded with Arillotta at his home, desperately hoping to retain some ownership of the business. Arillotta agreed to jointly run 20 locations, splitting 7-10k a week in a gesture of compromise.

Lastly, Arillotta started his own business alongside his partner, Steve Magnolia. As a former employee of the Sarnos, Steve was well-versed in their top-performing locations. The brothers had a whiteboard showing their 50 locations and how much each brought in. Arillotta and Magnolia strategically took the six most profitable sites, splitting a weekly profit of 5-7k.

Down in New York, Arillotta and his crew were not as effective.

Despite the Genovese crime family's longstanding reputation for power, influence, and sophistication, they were outmatched by the small but formidable Colombo family when it came to shaking down the owners of the Hustler strip club in New York. Acting on orders from Lil Artie Nigro, Arillotta and his crew attempted to squeeze $12,000 per week from Michael and Tony Grant of Hartford, who had recently purchased the club and were taking down a whopping $300,000 each week.

The first humiliation for the Genovese family was when Nigro dispatched a crew of twelve men to intimidate the brothers at the Hustler, hoping to pave the way for Bingy and his associates to extort them. However, the gangster's efforts were fruitless, and they forked over $500 for drinks at the club. Later, when Arillotta and the Geas sat down with Michael Grant and demanded $12,000 per week, the Patriarca family approached Arillotta and offered some advice. They warned Bingy's crew that the Grants were "weak" and would "give us up" to the FBI if they were extorted and advised them to back off.

Nigro disregarded the advice, maintaining that the rival gangsters were merely trying to move in on the Grants themselves. Nigro commanded, "Keep going forward." However, a week later, the wiseguys quickly bailed after the Grants informed Arillotta that the FBI had visited them and presented them with an FBI agent's business card as evidence.

Larry Flynt, the founder of The Hustler, also joined the battle, vowing to feature an exposé in his magazine every month about the mob's extortion of his clubs if they didn't back off. Despite this, the club remained an inviting target. Eventually, the Genovese family learned that the Colombos entered the picture years earlier, who had been under the guidance of their underboss, John "Sonny" Franzese, for years. While the Genovese family had failed, the Colombo's persisted and extorted approximately $150,000 from the Hustler and Penthouse clubs.

Later on, in June of 2004, Springfield Police Sergent John Delaney witnessed Ty Geas level with a punch Hippodrome nightclub owner Steven Stein outside his club. Despite Stein's refusal to press charges, Delaney secured a criminal complaint against Ty Geas based on his testimony. According to Delaney, Geas believed he had been waiting too long for a drink. "He sucker-punched him right in the jaw for no good reason," Delaney said. "The minute I put the cuffs on him, it was all, 'Do you know who I am? Do you know what I've done to people in jail?'"

Eventually, Ty Geas pleaded guilty to that charge and spent a year in jail.

A year has passed since the murder of Adolfo "Big Al" Bruno, who was ruthlessly gunned down outside of his weekly Sunday night poker game. Despite the efforts of local law enforcement, no charges have been brought forth, and the late mob boss's burial site remains unmarked by a headstone.

Instead, a simple yet poignant hand-carved wooden cross was placed at the site, and a spent cigar was placed in the earth surrounding it. A fresh bouquet of red roses, a single pink bloom, a flowering cabbage, and a tasteful silk arrangement. As a final touch, a photo of Big Al Bruno was affixed to the top, accompanied by smiley face stickers on either side.

Under the leadership of Arillotta, who had recently gained significant power as the Greater Springfield Mafia Capo, Ralphie Santaniello provided valuable assistance in the areas of accounting, strategy, and debt collection. He generously offered his parents' house on Converse Street in Longmeadow as a meeting place for sit-downs. However, unbeknownst to them, the state police had planted multiple listening devices in the house, capturing their discussions for several months. The recordings revealed details of the crew talking about who was placing which bets, who owed what money, and who was behind on their debts. In one particular segment, Santaniello and Arillotta were heard devising a plan to approach a debtor who owed more than $21,000.

"Grab him and say look, either come up with the money or get out of business," Arillotta says.

"I'll say I'm not going to play games," replies Santaniello.

"Say, pay ah, fifteen hundred a month. He pays us, we'll leave ya alone. Otherwise, we're going to send people into ya. You might come home; someone's grabbing ya like that."

Santaniello instructed his co-defendant, Richie Valentini, a former mailman, to "slap him." As a result, the pair forcefully hijacked the debtor's car and title and proceeded to sell it at auction.

The affidavits submitted to extend the warrants for surveillance revealed additional details about Valentini and Santaniello's drug addiction. They were reportedly dependent on both "prescription and non-prescription drugs," and their phone conversations included references to drugs that needed to be "cooked." Despite being under constant surveillance, the two men took measures to stay ahead of the police by purchasing new "burner phones" using fake identities. However, investigators intercepted their phone conversations 24 hours a day, seven days a week.

The police picked up fragments of their complicated accounting practices through multiple extended warrants to intercept their phone conversations, including one on March 22, 2005;

Richie Valentini, "I mean, so, you know. Nicky's going to give you a call, right?"

Ralph Santaniello, "Who?"

"Nicky is."

"Nicky, who?"

"Little Nicky."

"Oh."

"Nicky used to be like clockwork every Monday," laughing.

"Okay, uhm, now, Timmy's fucking one fifteen, and ah, Gugle's is what, two forty, right. So, we'll shoot down and grab it."

"Yeah."

"Should be on the piece of paper this week, fuckin' Richie, you know, we should start organizing the money in order. Fuck yeah, hell, we got Granby two weeks; he is all set. Anthony, I don't see. Pauly Calcasola, you see him?"

"I called him, but he didn't call me back."

"Well, we'll get that. So, we'll just put it on owed. Okay, Umberto, Pauly C, Pat, we see and Mark, that's (unintelligible), Mike, I see him, (unintelligible), did Louie, he didn't (unintelligible), Mike I see, Danny I see, Dino gave me four weeks, Anthony still owes Rico, we're all set, T owes two hundred. Dog owes, ah, two hundred. Mark it down (unintelligible)."

Valentini: Okay, the five?

"Yeah, he gave me ah, eight, I'll take it out of mine, (unintelligible), you know what I mean? So, we got to deduct (unintelligible), so the total, okay Richie's (unintelligible), two thousand two dollars, that's what you get Richie for the thing, okay? So, one-fifty plus ninety is what? Two forty?"

"Two forty."

"Two forty, you get Jimmy's Stellato's?"

"Jimmy Stellato, I called him. He didn't call me back."

"So, okay, so Jimmy's Stellato's, we'll get him too. We'll just add it to you, our figure. Okay, that equals, okay, three ninety divided by three. Is one thirty got to come off each of our figures, okay? All right, Richie?"

"Yup."

Santaniello pleaded guilty and was sentenced to two years in jail, followed by probation. As part of his probation, a judge mandated that he speak to local high school students about the dangers of gambling. Although his mother was also charged in the illegal betting ring, she was given probation.

Legal problems hampered Arillotta during his entire seven-year reign as boss.

Anthony Arillotta, along with many others, was arrested on March 8, 2005, at his home for participating in a sports betting operation that raked in over $2,000 per day. One month later, he faced a second set of charges in Hampden Superior Court for loan-sharking and separate gaming offenses. The possibility of Arillotta cooperating with prosecutors against his co-defendants was a topic of discussion, eliciting smirks from his lawyer, Attorney Bongiorni. The FBI has identified Arillotta as "an important figure" in local organized crime circles.

"Mr. Arillotta could know something about 15 or 20 cases I have in state court," defense attorney Bongiorni said. "I don't see it being a remote possibility here."

Although Arillotta claimed to be in the business of selling produce, a state prosecutor revealed that he was the boss of a loansharking and gaming ring that grossed $500,000 a month. According to a federal prosecutor, closed circuit television planted by FBI agents in a pizza shop in Westfield captured now-deceased gangster Adolfo Big Al Bruno providing access to an illicit sports-betting line in 2001.

The pizza shop owner, known only by the code name "Mushroom," was revealed in court documents as Leone Daniele, a confidential informant in a separate loansharking case. According to Assistant U.S. Attorney Ariane Vuono, Daniele made scores of illegal bets at the FBI's direction. Another source claims that Daniele was paid over $114,000 from the FBI, including relocation expenses and other fees.

The exact date when he was placed on the federal payroll remains unknown.

According to a statement from Sergeant Michael Imelio of the Massachusetts State Police, investigators have identified Anthony Arillotta as the current ranking organized crime boss in the Springfield area. Recently seized gambling records from the home of Louis Naioleari, Arillotta's co-defendant in the federal case involving illegal gambling, revealed that Naioleari's office received approximately $2.7 million in bets within four months in 2002. Further evidence from another residence showed that the same office accepted over $375,000 in sports wagers during 25 days in 2001.

According to one former employee who handled phone calls at the office, "They had an 800 number that went to Costa Rica. That was a good method. You would pay, depending on how many guys you have, anywhere from 12 to $25 a guy per week to take bets. It was 1500-$2000 a week, and they would take all the action, the best lines you could. How are you gonna rob them? You don't know 'em. They're in Costa Rica, these people. So, at the end of the week, Friday or Sunday night, they would send the sheet with all the figures. And they were never wrong because in Costa Rica they got a bunch of people getting hardly anything to correct it. Given that, it was a great method."

That same month, in April of 2005, Ty Geas was arrested following a violent brawl in the "champagne room" on the second level of the Mardi Gras Gentleman's Club. Some witnesses claimed that Geas knocked out another patron at the Mardi Gras with a single punch. However, others provided conflicting accounts, with some stating that Geas hit the man twice, the second time with a glass and that the man had announced he was "packing heat" before the fight. Security manager Kevin Drainville said he rushed upstairs from the lap dance area to intervene just before 2 a.m.

"Mr. Geas began to walk away, and the other man said he was going to find out who Mr. Geas was and put him six feet under," said the heavily tattooed bouncer. Geas punched the man, sparking a brawl among dozens of patrons. Geas was arrested and charged with assault and battery with a dangerous weapon.

Former local mob boss Anthony Delevo was expected to be released from federal prison in August 2006. However, his three-year prison term turned into a life sentence when he passed away in April 2005 at a nearby hospital. Delevo, a prominent figure in the local Springfield crew, was serving time for racketeering conspiracy and money laundering. Delevo maintained a discreet lifestyle and did not frequent the usual meeting spots of organized crime members and associates.

Two months later, Brandon Croteau sells drugs to an undercover state police trooper during months of surveillance and is charged with drug trafficking. He ultimately pleads guilty and receives a 10-year state prison sentence.

Anthony Arillotta started serving a 3 to 3 1/2 year sentence in state prison on December 1, 2005, after admitting to managing a gambling operation and engaging in loan-sharking. Federal authorities charged him with money laundering, interstate commerce, and illegal sports betting. In February of 2005, he was released on bail but was later indicted again in April for running an illegal gambling enterprise. As a result, he faced three separate cases, all involving racketeering. Eventually, Bingy pleaded guilty and was sentenced to 29 months in federal prison and an additional 3 to 3 1/2 years in state prison for his crime involvement.

Arillotta recalls, "The money that was involved was in the multi-millions. I had three cases going on and pled guilty to a two million dollar sports gambling operation, hundreds of thousands on the street numbers business, and out of three cases, I got only three to three and a half years on a plea deal. I had the greatest lawyer in my area behind me, but I got three to three and a half in the state and 29 months in the feds."

David "Chicky" Cecchetelli was sentenced to eight months in prison after admitting his participation in the gambling ring operated by Arillotta. Chicky accepted bets over the phone at Arillotta's office, which prosecutors claimed was connected to organized crime.

During his incarceration, Arillotta continued to receive extorted money and had his people on the street working on his behalf to collect it and distribute it as before. Meanwhile, Emilio Fusco assumed control over several Genovese family rackets in Springfield and, with Arillotta's approval, halted the flow of money from those rackets to the New York bosses.

Arillotta also employed his lawyer, Dan Kelly, to pick up money from the Madi Gras on his behalf and deliver it to his crew and his wife and children at home. Kelly was also used as a messenger to deliver notes to other inmates during their visits, ultimately reaching Arillotta and allowing him to maintain his grip on his street empire from behind bars.

Following Arillotta's incarceration, Big John Bologna attempted to persuade Frank Pugliano to assume the role of boss. However, Pugliano refused the offer as his brother Louie was in the process of appealing his conviction and did not wish to jeopardize his chances. Consequently, Franky Pugs was called down to New York by Lil Artie Nigro and shelved in 2005.

Chapter 17

Dominoes Begin to Topple

After a two-year, multistate manhunt conducted by various federal and local law enforcement agencies, Frankie Roche was indicted by the Hampden County District Attorney's Office on December 12, 2005, for the killing of mob boss Adolfo "Big Al" Bruno.

The prevailing theory at the time was that Roche had murdered Bruno out of fear that Bruno was coming after him to seek retribution for damages Roche had caused to a bar several weeks prior.

Sixteen months prior, Federal agents descended on a residence in Tampa, Florida, on August 20, 2004, with a fugitive warrant, having traced the whereabouts of Frankie Roche across multiple states. After a judge signed off on those warrants, they were ready to strike. The collaboration between the FBI and the local police paid off. The police contacted the FBI office in Tampa and provided them with the necessary information, granting them legal powers to go out and conduct a fugitive investigation.

But the arrest didn't go as planned.

While handcuffed and lying face down on the floor in the lobby area of this home, and without any form of resisting arrest, a member of the SWAT team fired a round into the tattooed back of Roche. The SWAT member, when he was rolling his rifle over his shoulder to attempt to handcuff him, there was an accidental discharge. The bullet pierced through Roche's stomach area, inflicting severe, life-threatening, and permanent injuries.

According to Springfield homicide detective Thomas Malidi, "Everyone was scared he would die. The whole case is kind of over. I mean, dead men tell no tales. He got shot right in the back, and he bled. He bled quite a bit. The FBI says there was no blood left in him when the ambulance got there."

When the news broke, Malidi received a call from the district attorney. He says, "You're going down to Florida right now. Pack your bags. Just go. I already got a flight for you." Ninety minutes later, Malidi and his partner were on a plane down to Florida. When they arrived, their first stop was Roche's hospital room.

"He was handcuffed to the bed. We went in and we talked to him. He was hurt. He was under heavy medication and all, but he could talk to us." They told Roche they had a warrant for his arrest for malicious damage to Emo's bar.

Malidi says, "He kind of smiled at us. He looked at us. He goes, 'I might not be too bright, but I know one thing. You sure as hell ain't the malicious damage police. And you didn't come down here to talk to me about wrecking any bar.'"

I said, "Well, Frankie, we're going to talk about that later."

He said, "OK."

Following the visit from the cops, Roche underwent a series of surgeries in the following weeks. The bullet had torn through his large and small intestines, resulting in the scar tissue causing intestinal blockages. After several months in the hospital, Roche was finally starting to recover, and his doctors cleared him for travel. In light of this, Malidi and his partner flew down to Tampa again, but this time, they wanted to bring the wanted criminal back to Springfield and persuade him to cooperate.

Detective Malidi says, "He was in tough shape. I mean, he had a tough time walking. We put on a thing you put on a knee, where if you try to run, it straightens your leg out, so you'd have to run with a straight leg. We put that on him so he didn't have anything else impeding him. We brought him to the airport and got him on the plane."

After a few hours, the plane landed at Bradley International Airport, located approximately 20 minutes outside Springfield. The Springfield Police Department had notified the local police about the transportation of a wanted criminal, so they offered assistance. However, they may have gone a bit overboard.

"We come off the plane, there's like 50 troopers out there with guns and dogs," Malidi recalls." And I'm like, oh my God. I was, like, getting embarrassed. I'm like, what the hell? We went through the airport. It was like the parting of the seas. Everybody's looking at us like, what the hell's going on with this?"

Eventually, Maliti and his partner made it out of the airport terminal with Roche. They then transported him to Springfield in the backseat of their car and stopped at Wendy's to buy him a burger. Roche's hunger did not solely drive this gesture but also got him in a good mood. Afterward, they brought him to the station for interrogation and presented him with an opportunity. They suggested, "Hey, Frankie, you could work yourself a pretty good deal."

Malidia is discussing a potential cooperation agreement involving individuals accused of crimes providing helpful information to investigators in exchange for a reduced prison sentence. In this instance, the investigators were seeking answers regarding Bruno's death and whether Roche acted alone or was part of a larger scheme.

Unfortunately, the investigators did not receive the answers they sought, as Roche turned down the deal. He believed he could beat the case and remained silent, ultimately being shipped off to a state prison's medical ward. Roche returns to the region only to be jailed for three to five years for parole violations.

On December 12, 2005, FBI agent Brian Warren remembers that Roche needed many surgeries.

"He needed an incredible amount of medical services. There was quite a period where he was trying to recover, even to be available to face a criminal trial."

Enough time, it turned out, for local prosecutors to gather sufficient evidence to indict Roche for the murder of Al Bruno finally. Roche is facing a first-degree murder charge for allegedly blasting Bruno at close range with a .45-caliber handgun outside the Our Lady of Mount Carmel Society social club following a card game on a Sunday night. The district attorney's office has kept tight-lipped about the motive and potential accomplices in this highly-publicized mob hit.

Roche's trial on state-level murder charges was scheduled for April 2007, almost three years after his arrest.

Following Roche's indictment, Arillotta used two of his henchmen, the Geas brothers, to deliver a construction-site beating to Felix Tranghese. This was in response to Artie Nigro's order for Tranghese to be "put on the shelf." Along with the beating came a message, "This is from your friend in New York."

Frankie Depergola, the last man to see Big Al alive, was charged by the feds in 2006 with running a loan sharking operation under the Arillotta crew flag. Depergola was convicted and sentenced to two and a half years in prison.

Albert "The Animal" Calvanese, a burly and thick-handed 52-year-old, was caught up in a loansharking bust in November 2006 and subsequently given a four-year sentence in a federal prison. Before his imprisonment, he held an important position as a top earner and enforcer for the ambitious Springfield mafia leader Anthony "Bingy" Arillotta, who gained control of the city with violent force.

Calvanese admitted to his involvement in racketeering and loansharking in 2007, which were linked to a $20,000 juice loan given to an associate of organized crime, Mark McCarthy, a mortgage broker from the Springfield area. When federal agents raided Calvanese's home and apprehended him, they discovered a staggering $750,000 in cash, which was seized and divided between the FBI and the Massachusetts State Police.

Calvanese encountered problems the previous year when McCarthy ran into legal troubles. McCarthy was indicted for wire fraud about a shady real estate deal and faced jail time. He agreed to help the government build a case against Calvanese in exchange for leniency. A body wire on McCarthy captured the sound of Calvanese forcefully slamming his arm into a car door as punishment for not meeting payment deadlines. Calvanese also threatened to physically harm him if he did not repay the 20K that he had borrowed.

"You avoiding me, mother fucker? Get me my money, or I'll beat the shit out of you in front of your wife, you cocksucker. Do you think I'm fucking around here or what?" A car door alarm is heard dinging.

"I ain't avoiding you. I just don't have it."

"Go get my money, or I'll beat the fuck out of you in front of your wife, you mother fucker. Are you fucking around or what?" The sound of an apparent punch follows.

"Don't do that, Al. Don't do that."

According to federal prosecutors, Calvanese was "obsessed" with taking vengeance on McCarthy for his betrayal, which he expressed during a phone conversation with his wife while being monitored in a Boston jail. Authorities heard him discussing the fact that he wished McCarthy and his family were all killed, "even if the kids are innocent," Authorities also suspected that he may have planned to enlist the help of associates to track McCarthy's movements and potentially attempt to set-up a retaliatory hit before his testimony in court. As a result, they argued that Calvanese should be denied bail and remain in custody until his trial.

With both Anthony Arillotta and Albert Calvanese behind bars, Emilio Fusco, fresh out of prison, begins taking Amadeo and Ralphie Santaniello's rackets from them.

In the Spring of 2007, on the eve of Frankie Roche's trial, an unusual occurrence took place. Before jury selection, both the prosecution and defense lawyers requested a lengthy sidebar with the judge.

Upon returning to the bench, the judge said, " Okay, this case is continued indefinitely."

The defense team claimed to be tracking "new leads." As reporters trailed the assistant district attorney into the hallway, he curtly replied with a "no comment" before storming off.

According to Springfield FBI agent Brian Warren, Roche decided to cooperate the evening before the trial and give them everything he knew. Roche agreed to cooperate with state and federal authorities. He explained in detail that he had been asked to murder Bruno by Freddy Geas and that Geas had told Roche that the murder had been approved by "New York," which Roche understood to be the Genovese Crime Family.

While on the run from the authorities, only a day or two after killing Bruno, Roche was taken out of state and spent time in New York and Tampa, Florida. He met a woman with whom he eventually wed and had a child. However, when arrested, Roche did not fully consider its consequences on his newfound family.

FBI agent Warren recalls, "I think just being in prison and off the streets, he was becoming more mature and understanding of his predicament, and his new family was probably the big factor that made cooperating worth it. So, Roche let the prosecutors know he was ready to make a deal. He was very excited. The whole team was. And you look for these breaks in an investigation and get to that point where you'll hear the story."

The district attorney met with Roche in a proffer session to find out what he knew.

Officer Murphy also met with Roche a few times. He was struck by Roche's personality or lack thereof.

"Not a jovial guy by any stretch. He's not an emotional kid. If you ask him a question, he'll give you a direct answer. Just stone cold, a matter of fact, no emotions."

Right away, Roche admitted that he shot Big Al Bruno.

So, they asked, "Why'd you kill Bruno? What was it over?"

Roche said, "No, no, you got it all wrong. This had nothing to do with retaliation of the bar, any of that."

That's where he opened the floodgates and said, "I got paid by Freddy Geas to carry this out. His bosses in New York told Anthony Arillotta."

New York, the headquarters of the Genovese crime family. It became the long-awaited conspiracy that had been brewing. Things were finally falling into place, just as they had hoped. It was a momentous day. They aimed to climb the ranks. They knew that Frankie Roche was vital to reaching their ultimate destination. However, there was one obstacle. Roche was unaware that someone in New York had ordered the hit. He was the first domino that sparked the fire of the investigation.

Roche's failure to speak directly about killing Bruno with Arillotta or anyone in New York meant that the authorities only had enough evidence to go after one other person, namely Freddy Geas.

Shortly after Frankie Roche decided to tell his story, on April 19, 2007, Fotios "Freddy" Geas, a former inmate who had served time in prison alongside Roche, was federally indicted for murder for hire in connection with Bruno's assassination. Geas had previously been identified by the organized crime unit of the Massachusetts State Police as the "muscle" for the Springfield mob boss, Anthony "Bingy" Arillotta. Freddy Geas was apprehended in Naples, Florida, on a warrant for murder.

Freddy Geas was brought in for questioning at the station with the hope that he would follow in the footsteps of Frankie Roche and cooperate. The authorities wanted Geas to be the second domino to fall, but it became apparent that his strict code, rooted in his strong Greek heritage, prevented him from cooperating. He and his brother were so fiercely proud of their heritage and ability that they did not cooperate, never willing to "rat" on anyone. Geas was known for boldly stating that they were Greek and thus far stronger than any Italians and would never fold, even in the face of pressure to cooperate.

Despite countless attempts by investigators to offer him a deal, Freddy Geas never broke his code of silence and always turned them down. Dominoes would only fall with Geas, and the investigation would be stalled out, leaving no further leads to pursue. However, the prosecution refused to give up and had one more angle they could work, one that could still take them up the ladder to implicate Anthony Arillotta potentially.

However, Arillotta spent little time worrying.

"I'm not one of those types to worry about things. I'm not that type of person."

Even when Frankie Roche was arrested for shooting Al Bruno, Arillotta remained unfazed.

"I'm thinking, well, I never dealt with him. I never called him on the phone. I think I met him three times my whole life."

The next day, April 20, a third man, Brandon Croteau, was charged with the murder of Adolfo "Big Al" Bruno. Croteau, who is already serving a 15-year sentence for drug trafficking, was involved in planning the shooting and helping Roche get out of town afterward. The new defendant has denied any involvement in the murder.

Despite Arillotta's apparent lack of concern, perhaps he should have been a little worried. According to Frankie Roche, who had flipped, Freddy Geas had supposedly paid him $10,000 to carry out the shooting of the Springfield mob boss. As a result, Freddy was arrested and charged with Bruno's murder. This development brings Arillotta one step closer to potential consequences.

Arillotta recalls, "My mindset was I didn't focus on it, you know, every day you wake up and hope for the best, and the outcome is going to be what the outcome is."

A week later, on April 27, Freddy Geas, Ty Geas, and Anthony Arillotta face extortion conspiracy charges for their alleged involvement in an attempted shake-down of poker machine owners Carlo and Gennaro Sarno.

According to investigators, Ty Geas is believed to have served as an enforcer for Arillotta.

In June 2007, with Roche's cooperation, the Hampden County District Attorney's Office officially indicted Freddy Geas for the murder of Big Al Bruno. As the 40-year-old Geas is led out of the courtroom in handcuffs and shackles after pleading not guilty, Victor Bruno, the most high-profile of Bruno's five sons, rises from his seat in the audience and cries out: "Hey, Freddy!"

Geas turns back as Bruno gives an exaggerated wave. Geas simply nods in return. Bruno and his buddy, dressed in a tracksuit, quickly exit the courtroom.

The arrest of Freddy Geas made other people worried, including John Bologna, the bearded guy known for extorting the Mardi Gras strip club. More significantly, Bologna served as the right-hand man for Artie Nigro, the head of the Genovese crime family in New York. Freddy knew some things that could put Bologna in hot water, like the attempted hit on union leader Frank Dadabo, who miraculously survived being shot nine times. If Freddy cooperated with authorities, it could spell significant trouble for everyone involved.

In October 2007, Bologna began cooperating with the Government and provided them with concrete evidence of Arillotta's involvement in the Bruno murder. This crucial development allowed the Feds to build a case against Arillotta and Lil' Artie Nigro for the Bruno murder and other crimes.

However, it was enough for Brian Warren, a Springfield-based FBI agent, to prompt his following action. He contacted the FBI's New York division, which houses a crime squad investigating the Genovese family. It was an understanding that when you start hitting members of the Genovese crime family, you would be looking for their assistance.

Warren was curious about a specific member of the New York mafia named John Bologna. He was aware that Bologna spent many weekends in Springfield before the murder of Al Bruno. This led Warren to suspect that Bologna may have been involved in the crime. After sharing his suspicions with the New York FBI, Warren learned that they were also keeping an eye on Bologna and building a case against him for racketeering and extortion.

The US Attorney's office for the Southern District of New York then joined the investigation. They saw an opportunity to add murder to Bologna's list of crimes and potentially get him to flip. An agent and Bologna met, and we laid out all their evidence against him.

Surprisingly, Bologna agreed to cooperate within a week. This seemed too easy, as most cooperators require more time. For example, it took Frankie Roche three years to flip. This raised suspicions that something was up, and eventually, they found out what.

Without New York's knowledge, John Bologna had secretly worked as an informant for the Newark, New Jersey division for over 20 years. Surprisingly, while Bologna was visiting Springfield and attempting to take control of Al Bruno's rackets, he also provided information to the FBI. However, the Newark division didn't tell anyone in New York. Essentially, the Newark division had an informant living among and gathering intelligence on New York City's mobsters.

Some people in New York felt the informant should have been handed over to the New York division. This allowed Bologna to play both sides. For years, he had been feeding information to the FBI, not regarding what he did, but primarily what his enemies were doing.

According to Mark Lanfer, Assistant U.S. Attorney, he was not a fan of John Bologna. "Totally untrustworthy, total schemer. I mean, John Bologna was just a total schlub."

Lanfer explains that when Bologna was solely an informant, he manipulated the FBI for his own gain. However, now, as a cooperative witness, he couldn't simply give us snippets of information in hopes of us going after his enemies. To agree to be a cooperating witness, he'd have to tell them everything and be willing to testify at trial. However, John Bologna failed to grasp this concept fully. He believed he was smarter than everyone else and that flipping would allow him to skate by.

During Lanfer's questioning, Bologna didn't always tell him everything, just enough to keep prosecutors at bay.

However, the truth gradually surfaced, unveiling the identity of the individual responsible for ordering Al Bruno's murder. It was John Bologna who told the feds that Artie Nigro ordered the hit. This revelation from John Bologna suggests that Anthony Arillotta had been the one to put Artie Nigro's order to kill Al Bruno into effect.

On January 23, 2008, the Geas brothers and Anthony Arillotta were brought to trial for their involvement in an extortion conspiracy. The main witness for the prosecution is Emiliano Gonzales, the owner of Emo's Place on Locust Street, where the violent beating took place in 2003 before

Bruno's murder. Gonzales, who has a prior conviction for dealing drugs and is facing new charges, testifies that Arillotta and the Geas brothers used him to deliver threats to the Sarno brothers, which he secretly recorded. Roche pummeled another patron at the bar in 2003 and wrecked the bar after he was thrown out.

In 2004, Gonzalez met with the Geas' and Arillotta while wearing a wire. During the meeting, the men were caught on tape discussing video poker game locations in the area. The State Police suspected that this vending machine business, run by the Sarno brothers, was the victim of an extortion scheme. State Police had Gonzalez reach out to Arillotta and pretend to represent the Sarnos to mediate the dispute. According to Gonzalez, Arillotta told him he had the "green light" for everything.

During three meetings in May 2004, Arillotta was caught on tape demanding $4,000 to $6,000 in weekly profits from the Sarnos.

"We might go in and throw the machines," Arillotta told Gonzales on the tapes. "And if any of us gets arrested, any of us, we're gonna fucking run him over 85 times with a car."

The Sarnos have refused to testify in the case. They have invoked their Fifth Amendment right not to incriminate themselves.

"What happens to rats?" Assistant District Attorney Carmen Picknally asked Gonzales during questioning.

"They get killed," Gonzales responded.

"And what are you, sir?" Picknally asked.

"I'm a rat," he said, after admitting he wore a body wire to record conversations with defendants Anthony Arillotta and brothers Ty Geas and Freddy Geas.

"I had them handcuff me because of the patrons that were there. I didn't want them to get any suspicions," he said.

Gonzales said he was a member of Arillotta's "crew" until he was arrested with drugs in 1992 and went to prison for a decade.

The Geas brothers and Arillotta are acquitted after two days of deliberations. Ty Geas is freed; Freddy Geas remains held on the murder charges; Arillotta is slated for release later this month.

In January 2008, the government admitted that on August 19, 2004, Frankie Roche was taken into custody for unlawful flight to avoid prosecution after a warrant for his arrest was issued, and during the attempt to handcuff Roche, FBI Agent David Street's Colt M4A1 carbine, hanging from his sling, accidentally discharged a bullet. According to their statement, the plaintiff was resisting at the time. Roche's lawyer, Joseph Franco, demanded $10 million, leading to the federal lawsuit filed earlier this year.

"Claimant was handcuffed, on the floor, and was not resisting when an FBI agent discharged a bullet into his back," Franco wrote in a complaint.

Franco demanded a settlement, claiming that Roche was shot in the back and the bullet exited through his stomach, "doing extensive and permanent damage to claimant's organs and abdominal muscles and area." He argues that Roche will require permanent medical care. Ultimately, Roche settled for $150,000 for being shot.

Stephanie Page, an attorney representing Geas in the state case, strongly criticized the government's decision to settle with Roche.

"The federal government is paying off a mob hitman," she said. "Paying off is the polite way to say what lengths the government will go to buy the testimony of an admitted, cold-blooded killer to try to convict an innocent man."

On April 17, 2008, Frankie Roche, looking emaciated and sunken-eyed, took a stand during his plea hearing and uttered "guilty" to one charge of murder in aid of racketeering and abetting in U.S. District Court as part of a plea agreement. He confesses to being the gunman for $10,000. Instead of facing the possibility of the death sentence, Roche evaded it through a plea deal with prosecutors and has agreed to turn government informant. Instead, he will face a lifetime in prison and a fine of $1 million.

The official charging document submitted to the court reads like a complex puzzle, with strategically omitted key names. Roche admitted guilt to conspiring with unnamed members of the "Springfield Crew," a local faction of the Genovese crime family based in New York. However, a different version of the document, circulated to media outlets by the U.S. Attorney's office, alleged that Anthony Arillotta, Bruno's successor, sought authorization from the New York mob to have Bruno killed.

"Arillotta and others sought authority from the hierarchy of the Genovese family in New York, under the rules of La Cosa Nostra, to have Bruno killed," the second document states. That paperwork also identifies the New York higher-ups at the time as Pasquale "Scop" Deluca and Arthur "Artie" Nigro.

In light of Freddy Geas being held without bail regarding the murder case and Ty Geas striving for a legitimate life through the establishment of a trash-hauling company, Arillotta may need some new muscle upon his eventual release. Additionally, a filed report with Springfield's police detectives suggests that the ongoing rivalry between the Bruno and Geas factions still percolates beneath the surface.

Chapter 18

Knock, Knock

After being released from custody in June of 2008, Arillotta resumed his involvement with the Genovese crime family. However, his criminal endeavors were scaled back due to Nigro, his primary contact in New York, serving a prison sentence for an extortion conviction and Arillotta himself being on parole.

Despite these obstacles, Arillotta aggressively reclaimed everything that Emilio Fusco had taken from the Santaniellos, Amadeo, and his son Ralphie and even expanded his activities, including additional ventures in loansharking and marijuana trafficking.

In October 2008, Bologna, previously a dormant informant, was reactivated to reel in Arillotta and gather evidence by wearing a concealed FBI wire. Law enforcement had their sights set on adding Arillotta to the

Bruno murder indictment. Bologna set up a meeting with Arillotta at a Friendly's restaurant in Lee, Massachusetts, to discuss the pending federal case against Freddy Geas. Geas was initially the sole defendant charged with the Bruno murder in federal court in Springfield, but the case was later transferred to New York, and new charges were brought against multiple defendants.

Arillotta remembers, "He comes in, and he does his bullshit with the hug and the kisses. Then right away, Bologna said he was worried Freddy Geas might talk."

"It's just, things gotta get cleared up a little bit," Bologna stated. "It's gotta get cleared up a lot, cuz Freddy's gonna beat this case, cuz that other kid," Arillotta explained, referring to Frankie Roche, who confessed to shooting Bruno at the direction of Arillotta, Geas, and others.

"And I remember, I get up, whisper in his ear, 'I'm not talking about none of that stuff.' Because I always presumed that people were wired up. But I wanted to make sure this moron understood that I had no intention of talking about it. I just told him in his ear, 'I'm not talking about none of that stuff.'"

Arillotta added, "I mean, this kid is a liar. He had a personal beef with Bruno. He even said he shot him; that came right out in the newspaper. You understand this kid is just one of them nuts that acted like an idiot, you know, and um, did something stupid."

Despite Bologna's persistence, Arillotta refused to answer his questions. This only heightened Arillotta's caution, which eventually turned into full-on suspicion. He spoke with great care, stating, "Freddy's innocent. Frankie had a beef with Bruno, and the kid killed Bruno. Freddy's innocent. He's going to beat the case."

Arillotta repeated the phrase "Freddy is innocent" throughout the entire meeting, emphasizing his belief in Freddy's innocence.

A few weeks later, Arillotta got a call from someone who knew John Bologna. Anthony Arillotta was taken aback when the man said, "The guy with the beard went into the witness protection program."

Initially, the news did not register with him. He asked, "What?" but then realized it was John Bologna. Oh, this guy, he cooperated."

"Yeah, he went into the program. The feds came and got him. They packed him up in black SUVs, and they took him away."

The realization hit him like a ton of bricks.

"This guy knows about a few things I did that could get me locked up for a long time. Right then and there, I was like, boom. It was like the world was over."

Anthony was now faced with a dilemma - either take his chances in court and risk a lifetime behind bars or betray his mafia family. It was a defining moment for Anthony as his entire world seemed to crumble.

Around the same time Anthony was released from prison, "Villa Joe" Manzi was released and popped back on the Springfield underworld scene. He engaged in a violent beef with a group of former teenage employees who were involved in a drug operation under his leadership. Manzi's associates physically attacked the teenagers and even attempted to run one of them over with his car, resulting in a high-speed chase and a subsequent gunfight.

This incident led to the teenagers retaliating by firebombing Manzi's home, which ultimately burned to the ground. There have been rumors floated for years that Manzi may be secretly cooperating with law enforcement, as his criminal record lacks any drug-related charges.

The recent flurry of sealed documents by federal prosecutors in a mob murder case on January 27, 2010, has sparked speculation about the impending trial and the possibility of more defendants being charged. The prosecution has requested an April 5 trial date, which has been approved. Arillotta was secretly indicted on February 11, 2010.

After nearly seven years since Bruno's murder, the prosecution finally gathered enough evidence to charge Arillotta for the murder, albeit barely enough. When they brought forth the charges against Anthony Arillotta, they were based on pretty thin evidence. On a scale of one to ten regarding their confidence in his guilt, they would say it was a solid ten but only a three in provability. Why such a difference? John Bologna. The case is heavily reliant on the testimony of a very untrustworthy witness. It was unsettling and unpleasant, but unfortunately, that was what they had.

Upon discovering Bologna had flipped, Arillotta was fully aware it was only a matter of time before he was indicted. As a result, he was living each day to the fullest. The day before his arrest was especially full.

Arillotta reminisces, "It was just a great day before. As far as women went, my kids were eating, and I had a good-looking wife. I had a good-looking girlfriend. I was with them both that day. I was with my kids. I remember going to bed at night after being with one girl and then another. And then I'm home, and I got my little daughters, both lying on my chest. And you couldn't ask for a perfect setting."

However, the following day proved to be a little less perfect. On February 17, 2010, at daybreak, authorities from the federal, state, and local levels arrested him at his home on Chalmers Street.

"It wasn't like crashing the door in and yelling and screaming and with guns out. It was nothing like that. It was just knock, knock, and I hear you're under arrest. All right, that's it."

Arillotta was handcuffed by the cops and transported to the jail at the courthouse, where he was held until his arraignment. In the meantime, Arillotta dozed off for a nap.

"I wake up, and it's like that 1st second of waking up, and you're on a metal bed, and you're like, oh, oh. And you're thinking, the day before, I was just with a beautiful woman, my kids, eating good, and here I am waking up on a metal bed and probably never going to be with a woman ever again or see my kids like that ever again."

Then, finally, it was time for Arillotta's arraignment.

"I went in front of the judge, and my family and friends were there. And the judge asked the prosecutor, what am I facing? What's the maximum sentence? And they said, 'death by lethal injection.' And it was like, whoa. It didn't scare me. It was like reality. This guy just said they want to kill me."

A glaring omission caught his attention as the judge recited the list of crimes against Arillotta from his indictment.

"I was confused. Why wasn't I indicted for more crimes once this guy Bologna went in? The shooting of the union guy, Frank Dabado. John Bologna knew about that crime. John was involved with that from planning it. Why wasn't I indicted for that? Yeah. I really couldn't figure out what happened. I mean, he left it out."

Arillotta's focus was drawn to another aspect of the indictment: he was not charged in his home state of Massachusetts. Instead, they brought charges against him in the Southern District of New York.

Anthony Arillotta and Artie Nigro, the acting boss of the New York Genovese crime family, have been accused of engaging in a racketeering conspiracy as a "made" member of the Genovese Family. They are charged with substantive racketeering through a pattern that includes four acts: the killing of Adolfo Bruno, the extortion of James Santaniello, the conspiracy to extort Carlo and Genaro Sarno, and the operation of an illegal gambling enterprise.

Additionally, they are facing charges for aiding and abetting the murder of Adolfo Bruno, as well as for conspiring to extort and extorting James Santaniello. Four other men from New York have also been indicted, although not for murder.

According to a prosecutor's memorandum, Arillotta's pretrial confinement was deemed necessary as he had surpassed Bruno as the local boss of the "Springfield Crew" by mid-2003.

"Arillotta was the de facto leader as other senior made members, including Bruno, had been marginalized by Nigro," the memo reads.

According to Bruno's longtime defense attorney, the law only requires that the suspects harbored the belief that their target was an informant.

"I can tell you Mr. Bruno was not an informant. Law enforcement pursued him relentlessly, up until the time of his death," Springfield lawyer Vincent Bongiorni said.

Anthony Arillotta, the reputed mob boss of Western Massachusetts, had been in the notoriously gritty federal prison at the southern tip of Manhattan for about two weeks after being arrested on a murder charge. It's safe to say that he has completely fallen off the radar.

Arillotta was taken into custody on February 17 at his Springfield residence and transferred to a detention facility in Rhode Island before finally ending up at the Metropolitan Correctional Center in Manhattan. According to records from the U.S. Bureau of Prisons, he was still held there when he was arraigned on March 24.

Dressed in a black prison uniform, he appeared in court to face the charges alongside six other defendants, all of whom were named in a wide-ranging indictment for racketeering issued by a grand jury on December 29.

During the arraignment, Arillotta's attorney, Thomas Butters of Boston, pleaded not guilty on behalf of his client. Throughout the proceedings, Arillotta chatted quietly with Arthur "Lil Artie" Nigro, former Genovese family crime boss, and co-defendant in the alleged plot to kill Bruno. As the trial date was November 1st, the three defendants were escorted out of the courtroom without mentioning an argument for bail.

Arillotta appeared as "released" on the federal prison website the next day.

However, Attorney Butters maintains that Arillotta is still in custody, though he is unsure of his current location. Initially, a spokesperson for the Metropolitan Correctional Center promised to track Arillotta's whereabouts but later stated he could not explain further.

On the evening of April 6, 2010, a team of Federal, state, and local law enforcement officials gathered at a house located at 160 Springfield Street in Agawam. Their purpose was to secure the property and conduct a search for the body of a missing man from Springfield, who was believed to have ties to organized crime. The search of the property commenced quietly on Monday night, just days after jailed regional crime boss Anthony Arillotta virtually dropped out of sight in the federal prison system. Despite being classified as a missing persons case, sources close to the investigation revealed that the search in Agawam was specifically for Gary Westerman's remains. Further information showed that one of the tenants, Joseph Iellamo, was known to be acquainted with Arillotta.

The following day, a small squad of law enforcement officers had arrived to commence a thorough search of the residential area, suspected to be the site where the remains of Gary Westerman, a Springfield man who disappeared in 2003, might be found. Westerman was a convicted drug dealer with connections to organized crime, and according to court records, authorities suspect rival gangsters killed him. However, searchers had pretty precise information about where Westerman's body may have been located.

They dug one hole to uncover a skeleton, clothing, and jewelry.

Ty Geas turned to his older brother, Freddy, and sighed, "So, I guess my time is short here."

Reports in the newspaper were documenting the excavation to uncover Westerman's remains.

"It said they only dug one hole," Ty Geas remarked.

As law enforcement officials began their excavation of a wooded area in Agawam, seeking the whereabouts of a missing informant involved in organized crime, Emilio Fusco swiftly purchased a one-way ticket to his native land of Italy. Despite his lack of subtlety, Fusco was astute enough to flee the country on April 8th, just as reports surfaced that the FBI and state police had uncovered the precise location of Gary Westerman's remains.

On June 3, 2010, the Hampden County District Attorney, William Bennett, made an official declaration that the human remains unearthed in Agawam in April were those of a long-missing associate of organized crime, Gary Westerman. Bennett asserted, "I can confirm it was Gary Westerman, and I can confirm it was a homicide."

Arillotta guided the FBI to the Agawam, Massachusetts site, where he claimed Gary Westerman was killed and buried. After scouring the area, the FBI uncovered multiple bullet casings at the spot where Arillotta alleged Westerman was gunned down.

Following Arillotta's details, the FBI spent several days excavating the murder scene, where they ultimately uncovered the remains of Westerman. Among the recovered bones was his skull, cracked in a manner consistent with being hit by shovels, as Arillotta had described that he and Fusco had done. Arillotta informed the Government that he, along with Fusco and the Geas brothers, were responsible for the murder. With Arillotta's testimony as the primary evidence, along with recordings from prison, physical and forensic evidence, and phone records that supported his testimony, the Government brought charges against the other three individuals involved in the murder.

According to a spokesperson from the Bureau of Prisons' inmate information clearinghouse, Arillotta was recently released from federal custody. However, upon searching, his name could not be found in any New York state or Westchester, N.Y., county prisons.

"Someone gets released the day after his arraignment on a murder charge. I don't know how to react to it," said Nigro's lawyer, Murray Richman, of the Bronx, N.Y. "It's very puzzling."

In organized crime's treacherous and unpredictable realm, the slightest whisper can raise doubts about a member being a potential traitor. With his sudden departure from the federal prison system and the lack of anyone leaping to his defense, questions are swirling among both law enforcement and underworld circles. It is customary for law enforcement officials to neither confirm nor deny the identity of confidential informants, as their code of ethics dictates that they refrain from addressing the matter until the individual is forced out from underground through public court proceedings.

Bingy appears to have joined the ranks of informants.

Chapter 19

I Know About Bodies

Anthony Arillotta, reputed mob boss of Western Massachusetts, was noticeably absent from a pretrial conference in federal court on May 7, 2010. This absence further solidified his speculative status as a government informant. As the defendants and their legal representatives gathered in the courtroom in Lower Manhattan, U.S. District Judge Kevin Castel looked around with a perplexed expression.

"Is Mr. Arillotta here? Is there anyone here representing him?" he inquired.

After a brief pause, Assistant U.S. Attorney Mark Lanpher stood up.

"I think the court can excuse his presence," the prosecutor declared, effectively ending further discussion.

Shortly after being arrested in February 2010, Arillotta agreed to cooperate almost immediately. He was well aware of the Southern District's impressive track record, with a 99% success rate in their cases. They don't lose cases. They were known for their aggressive approach and faithful to the law, earning them the nickname the "sovereign district" of New York. They tackled the most significant and complex criminal cases, from terrorism to insider trading and organized crime. Arillotta knew the odds were stacked against him, and when his lawyer visited him in prison, he told him how he felt about the situation.

Arillotta was arrested in Springfield, Massachusetts, and was initially housed in a federal detention facility in Rhode Island, awaiting transfer to New York. He engaged a New York attorney to defend him if he chose to fight the charges; concurrently, he contacted another attorney, Thomas Butters, to explore the possibility of cooperating.

Anthony recalls, "My lawyer, John Mitchell, comes and sees me, and the first words out of his mouth are that New York is worried sick that Artie flipped. He was no longer in the system. I'm second on the indictment, so I had to make some sort of decision where I could live with it, and my decision was to look out for my guys in my area, send word to them, tell them what I'm thinking, and what I want to do and what they have against us and let them make a decision for themselves.

"I was locked up and had all the evidence come to me; my lawyer comes up to me and says Felix Tranghese is going to cooperate, and this guy, Ray Ruggiero, he was a captain in the Genovese family, he's another guy that knows about the murder. So, he's cooperating, so now we got four guys that put us in a direct murder."

Next, Attorney Butters asked for a one-week postponement of Arillotta's transfer to New York. If Arillotta cooperated, an attorney visit would be made in Rhode Island.

"I go, listen, this is the situation. I said, you know, I'm never going to get out of here. So, he's looking at me and asking, do you want to make a preemptive strike?

"He was saying things like, you got a hard decision. It's a decision you have to think about. Nobody's going to love your kids more than you do. No one's going to take care of your kids and your family more than you will. And he goes, it's not an easy decision, living the life you lived, but that's the decision that you got to think about. And this was like going in my head, back and forth, can I do that? One minute, I'm like, are you fucking kidding me? I can't do that. But then I'm thinking, well, wait a second. It's like if I don't do that, I'm never going to see my kids again. I'm never going to have freedom again. And I thought about it. That was the first time I said yeah. I go, that's what I'm thinking I want to do. So, he got up and whispered in my ear. He said, 'They're going to want bodies.' I said, okay, I know about bodies."

Seven years before Anthony Arillotta's indictment, he was in a vacant apartment building in the Bronx, taking the oath of Omerta. His finger was pricked, and a few drops of his blood were placed on a tissue, which was then set on fire. He was warned that any betrayal of this oath would result in his death, and any mention of this moment again would lead to his soul burning like the tissue.

However, by 2010, Arillotta contemplated breaking that oath and cooperating with the Southern District of New York. His soul wasn't burning, but it was deeply divided.

"Weird feeling. I mean, there are times when you want to wish you were dead, and then there are times you were like, fuck this. You're happy. I'm gonna move to Florida when I get out and start a new life. Fuck that. But then there are times you wish you fucking had a gun so you could put a bullet in your head. So, it's like mixed. It goes back and forth, you know?

"It's a very hard decision, and you know it's something that's not easy," Arillotta recalled. "You have to see what was going on before that for you to decide in that position. You have a death penalty case, and it comes to a point where you have to say, what's more important, your little kids, your family, or the mafia."

Within days, they heard again from Attorney Butters that Arillotta wanted to cooperate.

Shortly after his arrival in this District, the U.S. District Attorney had arranged two consecutive proffers for Arillotta on March 17 and 18, 2010. One notable aspect of this choice was that Arillotta had decided to cooperate before reviewing the discovery materials in the case or having the chance to assess the evidence against him thoroughly. Despite being aware of Frankie Roche and John Bologna's cooperation with the Government and the Southern District of New York's track record of successful prosecutions, Arillotta had yet to review the case or its chances of success meaningfully. However, he indicated that he wanted "out of the life" and recognized that the earlier he cooperated, the better.

Arillotta was open and forthcoming and proved to be one of the most significant cooperating witnesses against the Genovese Family.

On the day of Arillotta's first proffer session, he was still on the fence. Mark Lanfer had arranged the meeting at the US attorney's office in Manhattan, within the federal courthouse. The conference room was simple, with a basic table and chairs. The decor was outdated, the carpet stained, and windows you couldn't see out. It was a far cry from a lavish or inviting space.

Upon Arillotta's arrival, he was accompanied by Mark Lanfer, FBI agent Brian Warren, Massachusetts state police officer Thomas Murphy, and two other FBI agents. The US marshals escorted him to a chair, freeing him from his handcuffs. Lanfer then proceeded to outline the protocol for cooperation agreements. The deal was simple: Arillotta had to divulge everything if he chose to cooperate. No lies, only 100% the truth. He was expected to reveal all details about the charged crimes and any additional information that had yet to be charged.

"And I'm like, wow. I'm like, am I really going to do this and this and that? And I asked him, I go, could you give me some time?" Arillotta asked.

Arillotta was left alone with his attorney as everyone exited the room, seeking reassurance that he was doing the right thing. He picked up the phone and made a few calls, yearning for confirmation. First, he called his wife, who continued reaffirming, "I want you to do it."

Next, he called his girlfriend.

"I called up my girl. My girl says, wherever you go, I'm going to come with you. And whatever happens, she was by my side 100%."

And then Arillotta made one more phone call.

"So, then I called up some guys that owed me money because when I did get locked up, the money, right away, this fucking weasel bastard, the money stopped coming in. So, then I'm calling them up. I go, where the fuck is the money?"

At that moment, Mark Lanfer reentered the conference room and delivered a stern message: "You can't be collecting money no more."

Despite the reassurance from his wife and girlfriend, Arillotta remained hesitant to commit fully.

"I told my lord, I don't know if I can do this."

The entire room was on the edge of their seats, their nerves taut and their breaths shallow. The fate of the case rested on Arillotta's decision - to flip or not to flip. If he chose to cooperate, the case would get much more vital. But if he stayed loyal, they were stuck with using John Bologna as their star witness. The tension in the room was intense, almost suffocating. It was as if the air was thick with anticipation, each person holding their breath, waiting for the moment of truth. Finally, Mark Lanfer could take it no longer. He turned to Arillotta and asked, "So what are you going to do?"

As Arillotta pondered his predicament, he couldn't help but reflect on why he was in this position in the first place—not his crimes, but the betrayal of someone close—John Bologna.

"This guy, John Bologna, is coming up causing havoc in our area, reporting back to Artie, and asking them to do the things that they did," Arillotta recalls. "I was in the Bronx, and the acting boss of the Gambinos sees John Bologna sitting in the car with Artie. He says, 'What's JB doing here?

He's no good he's an informant.' Now, Bologna knows about stuff that can give me the rest of my life in prison: a murder, a shooting, all kinds of extortions.

"I was in Connecticut with the Patriarca family. It's the same thing. They come up to us and say, 'This guy John that comes up to your area is an informant.' That's two: a captain in the Patriarca family, a boss in the Gambino's, and then we had a faction in our area, the Genovese family, that had inside information that this John Bologna was no good.

"I approached Artie to clip him. Have the guy come up. You'll never see him again. I said, 'The guy knows a lot.'

"First, he downplayed it with the Gambino guy, he said, 'They're just jealous. That's good to know. If we want to get rid of him, we will kill him.'

"After that, he never sent John up to the Springfield area other than us meeting them in Albany or way up in Connecticut, and Artie was with him always. I think the reason that he did that was because I never got permission to kill my brother-in-law, Gary Westerman, and we were trying to kill some other people that Artie didn't give permission for that I did on my own. So he already knew that we were wild, so we clipped this guy. He asked me what happened to your brother-in-law, and I said, 'He took off to Florida; I think he went with another girl; he left my wife's sister.' So, he thought that we would clip John on our own.

"I think that was a big mistake by him putting made guys together with a guy that we were told was an informant. When you see the things that happen with Whitey Bulger, Greg Scarpa with the Columbo family, when you see these guys that are bosses, that are informants for years, and it

---

finally comes out that's what you think is happening today. You're thinking that if he's allowing this guy to be an informant, this could be another Whitey Bulger. Instead of being the informants, they put somebody else up to do the dirty work, to tell the Fed's stuff."

"I wanted to abuse him because I hated him. So, I said, 'You know, you got your prized informant. You guys all love him. But that piece of shit is the reason why all this shit happened in our area. I know that's your guy. I'm not bad-mouthing him. I just want you to know he's a dangerous scumbag, low life. But forget about that. I know he's your guy. I'm not saying anything like that. But if he's your guy and you guys love him so much and all this, how come I'm not indicted for shooting the union guy?'"

Mark Lanfer vividly recalls being in the room, with Anthony's words echoing in his mind: "There's another shooting. I don't understand why I'm not being charged for it."

Lanfer and his team were caught off guard. He thought, "Well, we'll tell you why you're not charged with it because we don't know about it. We don't know about any other shooting."

But Lanfer chose to remain composed and didn't say that out loud, not wanting Arillotta to know they knew nothing about it. Lanfer knew they had to act fast. "Tell us everything," Mark urged, his tone urgent. And that's when Lanfer decided to pull the trigger without hesitation. There was no going back now.

Confessing to a crime the feds didn't already know about, Arillotta had sealed his fate. There was no turning back. He told them everything, from how Artie Nigro, the boss of the

Genovese crime family, had ordered him to kill Frank Dabado, a union leader, to how his friends Freddy and Ty Geas had agreed to help. He revealed the gruesome details of how they shot Dabado nine times as he was entering his car and how John Bologna informed him that their intended victim had survived. And, as a final shocking revelation, Arillotta repeated Artie Nigro's chilling career advice, get better at headshots.

Arillotta got his revenge on John Bologna for his betrayal. Bologna's failure to disclose the Dadabo hit to prosecutors violated his cooperation agreement. Eventually, they tore up his deal and charged him with attempted murder.

As a result, he was forced to plead out formally. Furthermore, they charged the others with his information and jailed Bologna, but he never got out again.

Mark Lanfer continued to interrogate Arillotta, determined to uncover the motive behind Al Bruno's murder. It was evident that Artie Nigro and his right-hand man, John Bologna, had their sights set on taking control of Bruno's rackets. So, they needed Bruno out of the way. But what was their reason for killing him?

The most they've witnessed was a man being taken down and broken, and they demoted him. The thought of him being killed was never a thought. It was never discussed or even mentioned. Nigro and Bologna's only plan was to demote him. However, Nigro's perspective changed when he came across a document that altered his thoughts. This document originated in 2002, almost two years before the murder of Al Bruno. Bruno had a history of cozying up to local politicians, and that day, he attended a fundraiser for a city councilman in Springfield when an FBI agent walked in. Big Al Bruno had an engaging personality; over the years, he would speak with agents and have small talk.

During their conversation, the FBI agent and Bruno chatted for almost an hour. Bruno mentioned Emilio Fusco, a made member of the Springfield crew, at one point. Bruno expressed that he was upset that Emilio Fusco was made while he was in prison. As in all criminal cases, the judge received a pre-sentencing report outlining all the factors that should be considered when deciding Fusco's prison sentence. In the presentence report, one sentence stated that an FBI agent would testify. Al Bruno confirmed that Fusco had been made, which is the end quote.

The thing about pre-sentencing reports is that they're not confidential. The defendant has the right to read them. Upon reading what Bruno had revealed to the FBI, Fusco became enraged. Bologna informed Artie Nigro of the document, prompting Nigro to take action. He called a meeting of the Genovese crime family's governing council, and the trio met at a restaurant. They passed around the document, read it for themselves, and discussed what they should do. There is no greater sin in the underworld than speaking with law enforcement. It is a breach of the sacred oath of Omerta. Thus, the council unanimously determined that Al Bruno had to go.

The investigators in the proffer room had spent nearly seven years trying to figure out why Al Bruno was murdered. Now, they finally had their answer.

At the start of their first session, Mark Lanfer was hoping to find evidence against Artie Nigro for the murder of Al Bruno when he met with Anthony Arillotta. However, by the end, Lanfer had a shot at convicting Nigro for another crime - the attempted murder of Frank Dabado. This presented a new opportunity to bring down the boss of the Genovese crime family. But, the feds were not finished with Arillotta. They also sought details about another murder that occurred in November 2003, just three weeks before Al Bruno's death - the disappearance of a police informant in Springfield.

Officer Thomas Murphy recalls receiving a tip from an unknown caller.

"And the caller just goes, Gary Western is missing. Here's who did it. Arillotta and the two Geas brothers. Click, hangs up the phone."

When Anthony Arillotta decided to cooperate, he understood the gravity of his responsibility. He knew he must divulge every crime he'd ever committed, whether big or small. And so, on that pivotal day in 2010, Arillotta held nothing back during questioning.

As Thomas Murphy, the Massachusetts state police officer in the room that day, recalls, Arillotta's confession was delivered without emotion. "I know where a body's buried," he stated without emotion.

"I was like, please be Gary Westerman."

Gary Westerman was a low-level drug dealer and also worked as a police informant. However, in 2003, approximately three weeks before Al Bruno's murder, Westerman suddenly vanished. He was reported as a missing person, but authorities had reason to believe he had been killed. Despite their suspicions, there was no physical evidence, and there was no body. They hoped that Arillotta could point them to a body, which would be the most substantial evidence and significantly strengthen their case.

It would allow them to widen the scope of the conspiracy and bring forth the heaviest charges. This presented us with one final opportunity to take down the leader of the Genovese crime family and the entire Springfield crew.

Investigators have been asking about Gary Westerman's disappearance for nearly seven years. Finally, Arillotta had the answer they had all been waiting for. As it turns out, he and Westerman shared a long history, a connection forged over time.

"We met one time at Antonio's grinders down the south end. That's the first time I met him."

Gary was always around organized crime guys. He was a drug dealer, and initially, he had a swindler's demeanor.

They hit it off.

"He was a friendly guy with a good personality. He had, like, a charm to him, and so, we ended up becoming friends."

However, their bond worsened over time as Arillotta uncovered some information about Westerman that was not okay. At the beginning of November 2003, Freddy and Ty Geas were shocked to discover that Westerman was an informant for the Massachusetts state police.

"So, we just made a plan that said, let's kill Gary tonight. And that's how it happened. Let's kill Gary." And just like that, they began planning the murder.

Upon hearing about the bullets bouncing off Westerman's head, the question arose: were those same bullets still scattered in the yard? When Arillotta divulged that they had bludgeoned Westerman with shovels, a thought emerged: would an autopsy corroborate this claim?

And when Arillotta revealed that the body had been buried, it was decided that it must be dug up.

Utilizing a little-known legal tactic known as a "takeout order," they arranged for Arillotta to be temporarily released from prison for a rather morbid excursion. The FBI planned to drive Arillotta to Massachusetts and task him with locating the burial site. This was a crucial moment for Arillotta, as one lie could result in him losing his cooperation agreement and facing a lifetime behind bars. Furthermore, they'd lose their lead informant.

The team of prosecutors and investigators had no prior experience in searching for buried bodies. However, they were all determined to uncover evidence inside the hole. The search for Westerman's body was a team effort, with the Springfield police, Massachusetts state police, and FBI all working together. They spared no effort, setting up a large tent as their command center and bringing in multiple lighting arrays and generators to work day and night. As the FBI vehicle arrived with Anthony Arillotta, the crime scene was already busy with activity.

And with all that law enforcement at the scene, the FBI didn't think Arillotta would try anything. So, they allowed him to remain in his street clothes and removed his handcuffs.

At first, Arillotta directed investigators to the location where Ty Geas shot Westerman in the head, but the bullets bounced off. As they scoured the yard, they discovered bullet casings scattered on the ground.

"It's like, you got to be kidding me. Seven years later, and you didn't clean up after yourselves," recalls Massachusetts state police officer Thomas Murphy.

Arillotta then led them to the spot where they had used shovels to beat Westerman before dragging him to a nearby hole. Murphy vividly remembers the search.

"I walk back with him into the woods. There was one area where you could see a mild depression. He was looking at me and just jumped like a little kid. Like, jumped up and down right in the center of this depressed area I'm talking about. And he goes, 'This is the one I think you should try first.'"

Arillotta had completed his job, but the FBI's work was only beginning. They assembled a team to test the soil, using a unique pole to probe the ground. By inserting the pole, they could detect any disturbances in the soil composition, even years later. It dropped exceptionally quickly in the first location they put the pole in. They brought in a front-end loader, typically seen on construction sites, to excavate the area. Murphy recalls the machine carefully scraping away the top inch or two of earth. Special sifting boxes were used to sort through the dirt, ensuring that potential evidence would not be overlooked.

After hours of painstaking scraping and sifting, the front-end loader finally hit something other than dirt. It was Mr. Westerman's remains, which were unceremoniously placed in the hole headfirst. They first uncovered his sneakers, still clinging to his feet. A black Nike sneaker stood out among the debris.

At this juncture, the front-end loader was set aside, and the skilled archaeologist team took over, employing a gentler approach. The excavation proceeded at a painstakingly slow pace, with members using brushes and trowels to uncover the remains. It was a laborious process, but eventually, the body of Gary Westerman was fully excavated. Despite the passage of time, his body was remarkably intact, leaving no doubt that it was human remains. Even parts of his jeans were visible, along with other evidence found within the hole.

Gary went there to do a burglary, and in the hole was a ski mask, a Taser, and tools of the trade for a burglar. Along with these items, they also discovered a .38 caliber casing, which Anthony had previously described as the one used by Freddy Geas to shoot Gary in the head before burying him in a hole. Upon further examination, one of the most significant findings was a large bullet hole in the skull, accompanied by other fractures and injuries consistent with a brutal attack involving multiple gunshots and blunt force trauma.

"We've found bullet shells. We see some cardboard. We see a sneaker. We've got a leg!"

The ultimate pursuit is to find confirmation that your cooperator is telling the truth. He was being truthful when he confessed to being involved in the murder of Gary Westerman. How else could he have known the exact location of the crime? It would have been the easiest thing for Anthony to say, "Yeah, it was Emilio Fusco and Ty Geas who bashed him over the head with the shovel.". However, he chose to say it was Fusco and me. He displayed exceptional honesty in that aspect. His sincerity and lack of remorse were truly remarkable. He was an open book, unfazed by the gravity of the situation. He accepted it for what it was without any emotional reaction.

As the dig ended, the prosecution team was filled with a sense of confidence. They confirmed the authenticity of their key witness, Anthony Arillotta, who knew where the literal body was buried. With compelling evidence in their possession, they eagerly anticipated presenting their case to a jury. Additionally, they included a new charge for the murder of Gary Westerman in the indictments against Emilio Fusco and the Geas brothers, further strengthening their case.

One day, Mark Lanfer received a box from Freddy Geas's prison. The package contained CDs of Freddy's phone calls. The prisoners were aware that their calls were recorded, so they were cautious about what they said, but the CDs were still subpoenaed just in case.

Lanfer inserted the CDs into a player and began listening to the calls. Most of it was mundane and uneventful small talk.

"How are you doing?

"Okay."

"First before you're all right. How's that place? Okay?"

"Yeah, it's not bad at all."

However, one call caught their attention. Freddy called his brother Ty after the excavation.

"There's so much shit going on over here, and I don't know what's true, what isn't, man? What's going on over there?"

"Now there's all kinds of digging going on around this city and looking for something. And someone told me they suspect Ant was involved."

"Really?"

Ant meaning Anthony Arillotta.

"They dug one hole, it said, in this paper, and they have the bones or remains and forensic analysis."

"And Anthony, they keep saying he was on site helping them look for things or something?"

"They were, yeah. The news media kept on asking the FBI. The FBI says no comment. So, I don't know what the fuck's going on."

"Yeah, I'm just staying off the phone. I didn't want to even get into this conversation with you. That's where things are now. It looks like my days are short, yeah. So, I'm just enjoying the family. Yeah. I'm not going to act like a fucking animal, Ty."

A few months later, they charged Freddy and Ty Geas with the murder of Gary Westerman.

Felix Tranghese was arrested on July 23, 2010.

On July 29th, Emilio Fusco was apprehended in Sorrento, a small southern Italian town with a population of 16,500. The police disguised themselves as garbage collectors and utility workers and captured him.

Massimiliano Guidone, along with eight other investigators and "carabinieri," had been tailing Fusco to Santaniello, where he had been staying in a rented apartment in the tranquil Italian countryside. Guidone testified to the jury that he had spent six hours hiding in a nearby shed, monitoring Fusco's movements until he finally emerged and went to a local bar in the town square. After patiently waiting for the right moment, Guidone approached Fusco at a bus stop and took him into custody.

He was held at a jail in Avellino, Italy, while his legal team attempted to determine if he could potentially face the death penalty in the United States. According to his local attorney, Michael Jennings, the specifics of his extradition remain uncertain. In the past, the Italian government has refused to extradite natives to other countries where the death penalty is a possible punishment.

"It's unclear to me how the potential of a death penalty will play into this, if at all," Jennings admitted.

According to defense attorneys and confirmed by federal Bureau of Prison records and a noticeable absence in court, another high-ranking local gangster has recently switched sides.

Immediately after being arrested, Felix Tranghese decided to cooperate with the Government, mainly because he knew Arillotta had already turned against him. Following his arraignment in a New York courtroom in early August, the Bureau of Prisons listed Tranghese as "released" the next day.

Not only was Arillotta absent, but Tranghese was also noticeably missing during the most recent pretrial hearing on August 26, while all other defendants accused of murder were required to appear.

Freddy Geas's attorney, Frederick Cohn, said, "We didn't realize he had turned informant until the court date. But we weren't necessarily surprised. We were told we should expect that from him."

Despite seven men facing charges for the murders, only four will probably be present at the defense table. At the same time, the remaining three are anticipated to testify on behalf of the government. The prime witnesses for the prosecution against the Geas brothers, Artie Nigro and Emilio Fusco, are expected to be Anthony Arillotta, Felix Tranghese, Frankie Roche, and John Bologna. Multiple sources familiar with the investigation claim that Bologna has been a confidential informant for the FBI since the 1990s.

The era of Anthony "Bingy" Arillotta's reign as boss in Springfield spanned from the day Bruno was murdered until the signing of his cooperation agreement. With the recent departure of all made members of the Genovese crime family's Springfield faction, whether through force, prosecution under federal racketeering laws, or going in the U.S. Witness Protection Program, the landscape of the region's mob leadership is now desolate. According to law enforcement officials, this is unprecedented.

"For the first time in my memory, all we have left is a handful of bookies. Along with a bunch of older guys, we call the geriatric crew," states Lieutenant Thomas Murphy, a detective specializing in organized crime in the Greater Springfield area since the 1990s, as he describes the remaining cast of mob figures.

"You took all your made guys out in one shot. No one's taking the lead, or they're being very covert about it," Murphy recalled. There's nobody overly anxious to come to the forefront, pick up the ball, and run."

Murphy and others said, "Bruno was the 'old-school' mobster to take the helm."

In remembrance of his father, Victor Bruno, owner of the restaurant bearing his father's name, reflects on his father's legacy as a time-honored mobster who ruled with an iron fist yet generously contributed to charities, settled family disputes, recovered money for victims of financial disputes, and effortlessly navigated diverse social circles.

"A lot of these other bums. Do you think they ever did anything for Shriners Hospital? My father was more like a political figure," Victor Bruno said. "People liked being around him, whether it be district attorneys, judges, presidents of companies."

After spending 16 years behind bars for his involvement in loan-sharking, Rex Cunningham was released last year. He agreed that the murder of Big Al marked the end of an era. Cunningham, who prefers to be called a "bookmaker" rather than a gangster, was one of the first organized crime figures in the region during the 1990s to face a severe prison sentence for charges related to the mob.

"We had a tough group of guys, and Bruno was a legitimate tough guy," Cunningham said. "But it was a different world for us. We answered to the older guys, and the younger guys answered to us. And, if you did something wrong, you took a beating and went on your way."

"These days, things are different," Cunningham added. "There is no structure, no hierarchy, and little need to bet with your local bookie as offshore online gaming and casinos have exploded. Street lotteries have gone the way of the eight-track tape. And there are informants tucked in almost every pocket of the underworld.

"There's still money on the street. Everyone's still taking bets, but it's a free-for-all. And, there's a viper's nest of snakes and rats out there," said Cunningham, who refused to give testimony against his accomplices, even though he was facing a potential sentence of 30 years to life as part of his plea agreement. "Today, you can be your own mobster at your own risk, but with no one to answer to."

No members from the Springfield crew were probably made after 2010. This is due to the Genovese family's historic cautiousness triggered when word spread about law enforcement infiltrating the crew and Western Mass. Even those who appeared to hold senior positions within the crew were last known to be merely associates.

As a result of Arillotta's cooperation, the leadership of the Genovese crime family in New York was decimated, tarnishing the reputation of the Springfield regime in its entirety. This led to removing "capo" responsibilities from anyone in Western Mass and instead placing them in the hands of a Genovese administrator in Connecticut. Eugene "Rooster" Onofrio now oversees Genovese activities in Springfield, Massachusetts, a long-standing stronghold for the New York syndicate, as well as in Little Italy in Manhattan.

Ralphie Santaniello and his cousin, Albert "The Animal" Calvanese, took charge of the Springfield mob in Massachusetts, even though they did not hold official captain status and ultimately answered to Genovese leaders outside the state.

Ralph Santaniello and crew member Francesco "Frankie" Depergola were both being teed up for buttons when the Genovese crime family shut down membership. His father, Amedeo Santaniello, had regained his good standing within the underworld, allegedly acting as an adviser to his son and nephew, Albert Calvanese, as they put the crew back together after crippling infighting and government defections had greatly shaken the local mafia scene in recent years.

During the 2010s, an undercover FBI agent managed to infiltrate the inner circle of Eugene "Rooster" Onofrio, eventually rising to the driver position. Through an FBI surveillance wire, he was recorded boasting about his role as the "skipper" of Springfield and making plans to induct a group of Western Massachusetts mobsters into the Genovese crime family. A transcript of the wire reveals the 76-year-old Onofrio, living in New Haven, Connecticut, as the Genovese capo in charge of the rocky Greater Springfield area and the dwindling Little Italy neighborhood in Manhattan.

Onofrio is complaining to mob turncoat John "J.R." Rubeo about how "the books are closed" in the crime family and Onofrio's desire to get Springfield wiseguy Ralphie Santaniello "made" to ease travel pressures for him.

FBI WIRE:

Onofrio: "Everything's shut down right now."

Rubeo: "He doesn't put anyone up anymore?"

Onofrio: "Yeah, he does."

Rubeo: "Never."

Onofrio: "I do."

Rubeo: "He don't," referring to Danny Leo, a top Genovese boss.

Onofrio: "I already put a guy up from Springfield, Mass. You know, Springfield was given to me."

Rubeo: "Yeah, you told me."

Onofrio: "I got four, five guys up there. One I love to death."

Rubeo: "Why don't you move me up there? Can I make money?"

Onofrio: "I already got enough guys. I know this kid up there. I know he is a gangster, and I know he's got balls and heart. He, his name is already in. When they open up, I'm definitely putting him in because I can't travel from New Haven to Springfield all the time."

Rubeo's undercover work helped federal agents bring the infamous 2016 East Coast LCN case, which resulted in the indictment of nearly 50 Goodfellas involved in various racketeering crimes spanning New York to Florida. The bust also brought down prominent Springfield mob figures Ralphie Santaniello and Frankie "The Shark" Depergola, who have since pleaded guilty and are currently serving prison sentences. It was revealed that Santaniello, Depergola, and Onofrio were extorting a $30,000 loan related to the case.

After the case's conclusion two years ago, Rubeo was quickly placed into the Witness Protection Program. As for the current state of the Springfield crew, Albert Calvanese is alleged to serve as the sole leader.

One local mob old-timer was quoted as saying. "These guys now are wannabes compared to what used to be around here. Nobody outside Springfield gives these clowns the time of day. And many guys in Springfield won't either. It's a lightweight city these days in terms of organized crime, and it's being run by a bunch of lightweights."

Chapter 20

Brothers and Killers

Frankie Roche admitted pulling the trigger in the 2003 mob hit of Bruno and, on the eve of trial, has turned informant and entered the federal witness protection program. Anthony Arillotta, who assumed Bruno's leadership role in Western Massachusetts, was charged in connection with the killing but also became a cooperating witness.

"You have got the guy that helped engineer the removal and murder of Bruno and then became the top guy in Western Massachusetts, who then became a government witness. That is dramatic," Hampden District Attorney William Bennett said.

Bennett failed to establish any links between the current New York case involving the shooting of Bruno and the 125 gangsters who were arrested on charges related to organized crime by federal authorities in New York, New Jersey, Rhode Island, and Florida.

"This week's arrests and charges mark an important step in disrupting La Cosa Nostra activities in New England and other parts of the country as well as dismantling the organization," Richard DesLauriers, special agent in charge of the Boston FBI office, said.

Commenting on the arrests, Bennett said, "It reminds all of us that although the mob has been weakened, they have not been eliminated."

"The evidence at trial will show that the plot to murder Bruno began in earnest after it became known among the defendants and others that Bruno had spoken with FBI agent Cliff Hedges and confirmed that Emilio Fusco was a made member of the Genovese Organized Crime Family," a government motion reads.

As jury selection began on March 15, 2011, for a federal trial involving mob murders and racketeering in Western Mass, a pool of prospective jurors was gradually narrowed down due to hardships, prejudices, and religious beliefs. Over objections from defense attorneys, a federal judge in New York has allowed prosecutors to impanel an anonymous jury. The defense argued that seating an anonymous jury would unfairly portray their clients and put them at a disadvantage during the jury selection process.

"The Geas brothers have court-appointed counsel. They are alleged to be associates, not bosses, not capos. They don't have the means or the inclination to tamper with the jury," said attorney Frederick Cohn. "And it's my understanding that Ty Geas was waiting to be arrested for months while the government was fooling around with this."

Federal prosecutors in New York plan to summon gangsters hailing from here to South Florida to present to the jury the conspiracy to assassinate local mob boss Adolfo "Big Al" Bruno after he fell out of favor with the Genovese bosses. On trial for multiple successful and attempted murders are reputed mafia enforcers Fotios "Freddy" Geas, his brother Ty Geas, and Arthur "Artie" Nigro, the former acting boss of the New York-based Genovese family, the largest and most diabolical of the city's five Mafia crime families.

On March 16, 2011, the mob murder case opened in Manhattan, with Assistant U.S. Attorney Mark Lanpher telling a jury of nine men and six women that two parallel ascensions to power created a perfect storm of violence in two states.

"They are brothers, and they are killers."

Lanpher claims that Nigro is the puppet master behind nearly every crime listed in the extensive racketeering indictment. According to Lanpher, Nigro's rise within the Mafia began in 2001 when he was promoted from a soldier to an acting boss, coinciding with Bruno being appointed as captain in Greater Springfield. However, Nigro's attention soon turned to a young "earner" by the name of Anthony Arillotta, who was quickly recognized as a "rising star" within the Genovese family.

"Soon, Anthony Arillotta was getting face time with an acting boss in the Genovese crime family. Priceless," he told jurors.

Along with notorious brothers and seasoned bar fighters Freddy and Ty Geas, renowned in Western Massachusetts for their brute strength, Arillotta began taking marching orders from Lil Artie Nigro. These directives involved extorting more money from more businesses and funneling a share of bigger profits to New York, as revealed by the prosecution. This arrangement ultimately led to the murder of Bruno, who was shot six times while playing his usual Sunday night card game, just three weeks later.

"The Geas' and Arillotta had arrived. They were to be feared in Springfield," stated Lanpher.

Defense attorneys have portrayed Arillotta and Roche as liars and murderers in pursuit of lenient sentences. Additionally, one defense lawyer has linked the killing of Bruno to a personal feud with Roche, whom the defense has labeled as a "psychopath." During the trial, Ty Geas' attorney, Lee Ginsberg, offered an alternative motive for Bruno's murder. The night before Roche fatally shot Bruno, he publicly threatened to shoot another man at the bar, putting a gun to his head and announcing that he planned to kill Bruno as well.

Following eight years of law enforcement work, prosecutors had finally arrived at the pivotal moment: the trial for the murder of Al Bruno. However, it was not just Bruno's death. They also brought forward charges for the murder of Gary Westerman, who happened to be Anthony Arillotta's brother-in-law, as well as the conspiracy to murder Frank Dabado, who miraculously survived after being shot nine times. Arillotta was expected to testify against Artie Nigro, the leader of the Genovese crime family, and his testimony was crucial.

Arillotta remembered, "I could give a fuck less about Artie at this time."

He blamed Nigro for messing up a good thing, for ruining the once peaceful and highly profitable operations of the mob in Springfield.

"What they did to our area was completely destroy it with greed and bad decisions. Decisions about killing people, extorting people, bringing all the heat."

As a result, Nigro was not the only one facing charges in the ongoing trial. The focus was also on Freddy and Ty Geas, guys Arillotta cared about.

"I was hoping they pled guilty or whatever. I was hoping they cooperated, to be honest with you. I didn't feel good. I mean, that was my guys. I was with them. I did time in prison with Ty. I have a lot of memories of him there. Me and Freddy, we were on the streets since the early 90s, doing shit and a lot of fun times."

At this point, though, Arillotta had already decided to flip sides.

"I mean, it hurts. It sucks that I had to go through it. I wish they pled guilty and could have got twenty-something years, but once they didn't, they're not my friends anymore. If you're not my friend, then I am who I am. So, it's like, it was a shitty situation, but that's it. I mean, it was like, I made my decision. You guys made yours."

On March 17, 2011, Arillotta calmly took the stand and was careful to avoid making eye contact with Nigro or the Geas brothers, as he was forced to identify them for the jury. He shared with the jury his current living situation, "prison," and then proceeded to recount the changes in the organized crime scene in Springfield since the late 1980s.

Bosses had come and gone, with gambling, loan-sharking, and drug dealing being the norm.

Arillotta recounted how the street-savvy and violent Geas brothers helped him rise to a position of power in the local rackets in 2003, with the approval of Nigro, who gave the green light for Arillotta to take Bruno out of the mob's hierarchy.

On March 18, 2011, Anthony Arillotta provided jurors with chilling details of two cold-blooded murders and an attempted killing of a union official in 2003.

During the trial, he painted a grisly picture for the jury of the violent shooting of Gary Westerman, a brother-in-law of Arillotta.

Arillotta recounted the multi-year tear he and his supporters went on before and after his formal induction into the Genovese crime family.

On March 22, 2011, defense lawyers began trying to undermine the former Springfield mob leader's credibility.

Hochheiser calmly questioned him, "Do you maintain the same lack of emotion when you hit a dying man in the head with a shovel?"

"I dunno," Arillotta responded. "You're doing the act, and it just happens."

During the trial, Arillotta claimed that he coerced strip club owner James Santaniello into paying him $12,000 a month. He utilized the services of Springfield attorney Daniel Kelly, a former city councilor, to tote the payments from Santaniello to him and the Geas brothers for nearly two years. Other testimonies revealed that Kelly allegedly obstructed witnesses in criminal cases, leading prosecutor

Elie Honig to describe him as a "corrupt conduit for the mob" during his closing statement to the jury.

On March 24, 2011, Frankie Roche, the confessed hired hit man involved in the 2003 assassination of organized crime boss Adolfo "Big Al" Bruno in Springfield, took the stand to give his testimony. He confessed to the jury that upon his release from prison, he "slipped into a crew with murderous intentions."

Assistant U.S. Attorney Goldman put Roche on the witness stand, elicited his testimony, and prepared him to be grilled by the defense's cross-examination.

"I was most concerned that he was going to lose it on the stand, fight with the defense attorney, and say something completely crazy that would either show him to be a complete nut job or that he would fly off the handle and undermine his credibility. The evidence all showed what a hothead and crazy temper this guy has. He could fly off the hook."

Roche revealed that he had been considering cooperating with authorities when he was sent a letter from Daniel Kelly, the lawyer for the Geas' and Arillotta. Kelly passed it on through a fellow inmate of Roche's and, according to the letter, promised to orchestrate favorable testimonies from witnesses. The letter was presented as evidence during the trial. In the hopes of receiving a reduced prison sentence and $140,000 for his family's relocation expenses, Roche decided to become a government witness.

During cross-examination, Bobbi Sternheim, one of the attorneys for the Geas, asked him, "How soon do you hope to be out of prison?"

To which Roche replied, " Yesterday."

On March 25, 2011, Frankie Roche continued testifying in U.S. District Court.

"Did you hesitate when you pulled the trigger?" Freddy Geas' defense attorney, Harvey Fishbein, asked on cross-examination.

"Nope," answered Roche.

"You weren't nervous, were you?" the lawyer asked.

"Nope," Roche responded.

"You ever killed somebody before?" Fishbein continued. "First time? Your hands weren't even a little sweaty? Heart beating a little faster?"

"Nope," Roche stated again, his drooping eyes locked on Fishbein, who had previously interrogated him about his extensive record of arrests, reckless "Dukes of Hazard" pursuits, and evading law enforcement.

"Am I correct that at some point, you started approaching the car that he, Al Bruno, was getting into?"

"Yeah. I yelled out to him first when he started getting into the vehicle."

"And you had your gun out, right?"

"Yes."

"And it was a 45, wasn't it?"

"Yes."

"What kind of a noise does a. 45 make?"

"A lot of noise."

"How loud?"

"Very loud."

At this juncture, Harvey Fishbein strides dramatically towards Frankie Roche in the role of his character. Fishbein advances towards the witness stand with his hand formed into a gun.

"Boom"

"Little louder."

"Boom."

"Little louder than that."

"And you shot him again."

"Yes."

"Which time did you shoot him in the testicles?"

"Don't know."

"Which? Sorry."

"Wasn't the first. Wasn't the last."

"Sometime in between, you decided to shoot him in the testicles. Right?"

However, Roche was not allowed to respond to the last question. In that instant, Judge Costell's anger was on full display. Standing a mere few feet away from Roche, Harvey Fishbein practically screamed in his face. But the judge would not tolerate it. He swiftly interrupted Fishbein and sternly stated, "You may return to the podium and watch your tone." It was clear that Fishbein was attempting to provoke a reaction from Roche at that moment, hoping to catch him off guard, get under his skin, and make him look out to be a psychotic and sociopathic killer.

On March 29, 2011, under cross-examination, Tranghese testified that Bruno was put on the "pay no mind" list in 2003, according to Nigro's righthand man, a New Yorker named John Bologna, who was simultaneously working for the FBI as an informant, unbeknownst to the wiseguys at the time. Tranghese told jurors he was frozen out by Arillotta and the Geas' years later.

"I wasn't making hardly any money on the streets," Tranghese told Nigro's defense lawyer, Murray Richman.

"So why were you a gangster?" asked Richman, a veteran New York mob lawyer representing clients from the city's five crime families. "I don't mean to be funny, but are you saying crime doesn't pay?"

Tranghese testified that a gang of men that Freddy Geas brought to a construction site on Tiffany Street in Springfield in 2006 beat him.

"Freddy said, 'I have a message from your friend in New York,' before a guy jumped me from behind me, and then three or four of them started beating me for a few minutes," Tranghese said.

He denied anything happened when FBI agents knocked on his door the next day and told hospital personnel who diagnosed him with a cracked vertebrae that he fell off a ladder.

During the final arguments on March 31, 2011, attorneys made their closing statements, aiming at the key witnesses for the prosecution - government cooperators who confessed to committing murder and other crimes under oath in exchange for reduced prison sentences.

Frederick Cohn, the lawyer for Freddy Geas, dismissed the idea that his client was part of the mob think tank plotting murders as "a bunch of nonsense." He described Frankie Roche, the witness for the prosecution who admitted to shooting Bruno, as "impulsive, nuts and proud of it." Cohn emphasized to the jurors. "Those slime bags who testified, they have no loyalty. They sell out their wives, their children, you can't convict because of a general feeling of badness."

Once the prosecution concluded its case, which included testimony from 18 witnesses, such as FBI agent Brian Warren and union official Frank Dadabo, accompanied by solid evidence, the defense chose not to call any witnesses. This tactic is expected, as the prosecution must prove its case beyond a reasonable doubt in a criminal trial. Therefore, the defense often avoids presenting its case and instead argues that the prosecution failed to meet its burden. As a result, after the prosecution rested, the trial proceeded directly to closing arguments.

After three weeks of testimony, jurors in a federal court in Manhattan began their deliberations on April 1, 2011, at 3 p.m. Lead prosecutor Mark Lanfer anticipated a lengthy deliberation. Still, to his surprise, it only took about three hours.

On the following day, April 2, 2011, the jury unanimously found Fotios "Freddy" Geas, his brother Ty Geas, and the onetime acting boss of the Genovese crime family, Arthur "Lil' Artie" Nigro, guilty of murder, attempted murder of New York union official Frank Dadabo, racketeering, extortion, and other crimes. As a result, the three defendants will face life sentences.

Formerly viewed by the Geas brothers, who had endured the hardship of prison life and the harshness of the streets, as their path to prosperity and power, Arillotta undeniably emerged as the most incriminating witness against them, ultimately sealing their fate with jurors through his extensive and impactful testimony during the initial days of the trial.

After attending every day of the trial, Victor Bruno, one of Adolfo Bruno's sons, revealed that his reaction to the verdict was conflicted. The violent act that has consumed his thoughts since the shooting has left him with mixed emotions.

"I want to thank law enforcement for solving the murder, but yet it's a bittersweet ending," Bruno said on Friday. "I believe my father's murder could have been prevented."

Out of the seven charges, the accused were acquitted of only one: the murder to obstruct justice about Bruno. This means that the jury dismissed the idea that Bruno was killed because he was suspected of leaking information to law enforcement.

Victor Bruno believes the testimony and the jury's verdict on that count discredited the belief that his father was an informant.

Bruno stated, "That proved to be false," a belief he has held for a long time that has tainted his father's memory. Despite seven guilty pleas and convictions related to his father's murder, Bruno's most potent disdain was reserved for Arillotta, whom Bruno had once mentored before insidiously ingratiating himself with New York gangsters a year before seeking permission to kill Bruno.

"Anthony Arillotta was the master manipulator in this whole thing. He put it all together and was the first of the 'made' guys to sing," Victor Bruno said. "I hope the judge recognizes that and doesn't go easy on him."

While Victor Bruno acknowledges his father's chosen career, he emphasizes that Adolfo Bruno was a charitable man who maintained a sense of calmness within the criminal world.

"He made sure that on the streets, there was order," Victor Bruno said.

Massachusetts State Police's organized crime investigation unit, led by Detective Lt. Stephen Johnson, the work of state police and FBI agents effectively demolished two generations of gangsters through the guilty pleas and convictions in the case, according to Johnson.

"A lot of these guys were considered the up-and-comers in the Genovese family in Western Massachusetts; this took care of a lot of members of Al Bruno's generation and the younger ones," Johnson said. "Structurally, it decimated not just the leadership but the membership, and it'll eliminate a significant organized crime presence until they can rebuild themselves, and they'll do that cautiously."

Anthony Arillotta, John Bologna, Felix Tranghese, and Frankie Roche are federal Witness Security Program members awaiting their sentencing in undisclosed prison cells.

Chapter 21

Having a Bad Day

Dressed in navy blue prison garb, all three defendants, Freddy and Ty Geas and Artie Nigro, stood unwaveringly and maintained their innocence when given the chance by Judge Castel.

According to their attorneys, Nigro was a hard-working mason and devoted father; Ty Geas underwent a positive transformation after becoming a father to two young children, aged 6 and 2; and Fotios Geas simply requested to share a prison facility with his brother and use the 50 cents per hour wage of federal inmates to fund his commissary account.

The defendants' attorneys had made obligatory arguments on behalf of their clients, even though federal law mandated that the murder charges would lead to a guaranteed sentence of life in prison.

On September 13, 2011, Freddy and Ty Geas received a life sentence for their involvement in the 2003 murder of Adolfo "Big Al" Bruno, boss of the Springfield faction of the Genovese crime family, as well as the killing of Gary Westerman, a low-level associate, and a failed attempt on New York union boss Frank Dadabo's life. They were also found guilty of other murder plots and extortion schemes in Western Massachusetts.

Arthur "Lil Artie" Nigro, who was the acting boss of the Genovese family during the time of the crimes, was also convicted and sentenced to life. He sanctioned the hit on Bruno and ordered the attack on Dadabo over a union beef.

The Geas' were sentenced principally to four counts of life imprisonment and 240 months on two counts, also to run concurrently. Additionally, Freddy was ordered to forfeit $120,000. Nigro received a sentence principally consisting of three life imprisonments and 240 months for two counts, to be served concurrently. He was also directed to forfeit $234,000.

During the court proceedings, Judge Castel rattled off an exhaustive laundry list of previous criminal convictions for the Geas brothers, including serious assaults, drug possession, and theft leading up to the 2003 murders.

"I mean, you don't get to the spot where these defendants are by having a bad day or a bad period of life. This was a way of life," declared Castel during the sentencing.

During the court hearing, Elie Honig, the Assistant U.S. Attorney, emphasized to Castel that not only were the life sentences required by law but they were morally justified as well. As a veteran organized crime prosecutor in the southern district of New York, Honig stated, "All the murders were careful, deliberate, and well thought out; these were mob murders."

According to a statement from U.S. Attorney Preet Bharara, "The catalog of vicious and lethal crimes committed by these three defendants provides a stark reminder of the lengths to which the mob will go to protect their turf and exact revenge. With today's sentences, these men will now be put out of the mafia's ugly and violent business for life."

Roughly one month after the trial convictions of Nigro and the Geas brothers, Emilio Fusco was successfully extradited from Italy.

Six months later, on April 18, 2012, Fusco was accused of a racketeering conspiracy that included the Bruno hit, the gruesome killing of police informant Gary Westerman, and illegal activities involving sports betting and drug trafficking.

Special Agent Susan Kossler from the FBI gave testimony on a 1999 investigation into Fusco's criminal activities involving gambling and loan-sharking. Prosecutors presented several thirteen-year-old wiretap recordings as evidence, which sounded like a poorly-written script for a mob movie.

During opening arguments, defense attorney Richard Lind told jurors to be wary of Arillotta's testimony.

"He is a killer; he is a conniver; he is a cheat. He lies to virtually everyone," Lind argued.

Arillotta nonchalantly listed off the crimes he claimed to have committed with Fusco, "Murder, loan-sharkin', sports gamblin', and extortion."

The star witness for the prosecution, Anthony Arillotta, wrapped up four days of testimony in Manhattan on April 24, 2012, in his second trial for mob-related murder.

Victor Bruno, who has attended every day of testimony in both of his father's alleged killers' trials, scoffed at the idea that Arillotta should receive a lighter sentence in exchange for his testimony.

"He always had an exit plan. He was the master manipulator in all of this. Do I think he should get five years or time served? No, I do not. I think he should sit in the same cell with Freddy and Ty Geas," Victor Bruno said after the conclusion of Arillotta's testimony.

On April 25, 2012, the now skeletal, inked outcast of Springfield's criminal underworld testified against Emilio Fusco. He recounted how Fusco had contacted Freddy Geas, who then relayed the message to Roche regarding the whereabouts of Bruno the night he was executed.

The next day, on April 26, 2012, Felix Tranghese testified that he had presented a court document to acting Genovese boss Arthur Nigro at the request of Fusco back in 2003. "Artie gave me the order. Go back to Springfield and say Bruno had to be taken out, and it would be better if nothing was found," Tranghese revealed to the jury, hinting at a perfect plan where Bruno's body would simply disappear.

On May 3, 2012, Emilio Fusco was acquitted of the Western Massachusetts homicides of mob crime boss Adolfo "Big Al" Bruno and low-level associate Gary Westerman in 2003 after a 14-day trial and two days of jury deliberation in federal court in Manhattan. While he was found guilty of racketeering conspiracy, conspiracy to distribute marijuana, conspiracy to commit extortion, and interstate travel in aid of racketeering, the jury ruled out his involvement in the murders, direct participation in a shakedown of Springfield strip club owner James Santaniello, and any direct role in other extortion schemes as testified by witnesses for the prosecution.

Despite being acquitted of the 2003 murder plots against Adolfo "Big Al" Bruno and Gary Westerman in April, Emilio Fusco, a made member of the Genovese organized crime family, was sentenced to 25 years in federal prison by Judge Kevin Castel in Manhattan on October 12, 2012. His defense lawyer, Richard Lind, expressed frustration with the ruling, "I think it's unreasonable, and I think it's excessive." Fusco's involvement in the murders was determined by the judge, leading to his lengthy sentence.

Victor Bruno passionately argued against leniency in front of U.S. District Judge Castel, condemning the government's practice of offering lighter sentences to cooperating witnesses. In a haunting account, Bruno vividly recounts the final moments of his father's life.

"That night he was killed was a night that I play over and over in my head," he told Castel. "At 9:15, I got a call that my father had been shot. I saw him covered with blood and paramedics trying to resuscitate him," Bruno recounted, describing how he rested his head on his father's chest and begged him to stay alive.

"I cannot seem to forgive myself."

In his statement to Castel, Victor Bruno accused Arillotta of being "the real culprit" in his father's murder and that he would ultimately "win" if he received a significant sentence reduction. Castel deemed Arillotta an exceptionally credible witness and based his rulings in the Fusco case heavily on Arillotta's testimony and that of other cooperating witnesses.

On December 8, 2012, Felix Tranghese, an admitted accomplice in the 2003 Springfield plot to murder notorious mob boss Adolfo "Big Al" Bruno, who later became a government witness, was handed a four-year prison sentence by a federal judge in New York. Tranghese entered a guilty plea as part of a cooperation agreement with the government in 2010, confessing to six charges, including murdering to aid racketeering in Bruno's death, racketeering conspiracy, and extortion. In their sentencing report, federal prosecutors pointed out that Tranghese began cooperating "immediately" after being apprehended in the summer of that year.

Before his sentencing, Victor Bruno addressed the court, revealing that in 1982, his father had suggested Tranghese be officially inducted into the crime family. Additionally, he refuted the government's plea for leniency on behalf of their witness.

"Well, your honor, I want to ask the opposite, life, yes life, for taking my father's life, not a reward for the lies and useless information he provided," Victor Bruno said.

On March 1, 2013, Frankie Roche, the hired hit man responsible for carrying out the 2003 assassination of Adolfo "Big Al" Bruno, received a punishment of 165 months, equivalent to 13 years and nine months, with credit for time served. Roche would have faced a life sentence without striking a deal with the government. Despite his emotionless depiction of Bruno's gruesome murder, Roche cried as he addressed Judge Michael Ponsor during his sentencing.

"My involvement with and the carrying out of Mr. Bruno's murder came at a time in my life when I had no regard for my life or anyone else's," Roche said, reading from a letter he said he wrote the night before.

During the sentencing hearing, Victor Bruno spoke to the court, urging the judge to impose a life sentence for Roche. As the sole representative of Adolfo Bruno's family in the courtroom, he stated, "I know the government wants to send a message that if you cooperate, you get to go home, but that shouldn't be the message today."

He continued, "This man is a violent person. He will murder again. He's not reformed."

Roche, placed in the federal Witness Security Program, was escorted out of the courtroom by U.S. marshals without looking back.

On May 8, 2013, John Bologna, a Westchester-based gangster who pleaded guilty to helping incite the 2003 mob hit of Adolfo Bruno in Springfield, was handed an eight-year jail sentence by the federal court. Despite making a deal with the government, Bologna was repeatedly caught lying to the prosecutors.

At the sentencing, Victor Bruno was frustrated. He questioned Castel where the justice was in rewarding a defendant who had manipulated not only his fellow criminals but also the FBI handlers.

"John Bologna and Anthony Arillotta are cut from the same cloth," Victor Bruno said.

"He portrayed my father as an informant, which proved to be untrue, and it got him killed," he continued. "And today, he is begging for leniency?"

He compared the cooperating witnesses in the trial to "desperate rats jumping from a sinking ship."

As Bruno's killers faced their sentencing, Frankie "The Shark" Depergola had a meeting with wire-wearing informant Craig Morel, a wealthy tow-truck company owner and close friend. During their conversation, Depergola and Morel discussed Morel's impending shakedown coming his way.

"They are going to come after you. These guys are vindictive motherfuckers. Be careful what you say and what you do," Depergola told him.

Soon after, the conversation shifted to reflection, delving into Depergola's anger for Bruno.

"With me, everything I had, more or less, Al figured it was his, you know? And I mean it in a big way. I felt bad for the guy, though. He was a friend of mine, but you know, it was almost like a weight off my shoulders when he got killed. It was kind of like a way out. I mean, I got beat for $800,000 that prick took off me. You know what I mean? It's basically why I went away. He cleaned all of it out, not all of it, but I'd say he grabbed at least half of it. Some people die, you know? Believe me, I know how you feel. But, you know what, there was a way out after Al died, and I got out."

On March 4, 2014, Anthony Arillotta was able to secure his release from a life sentence in prison for committing two murders, three attempted murders, and engaging in six-figure extortions and other crimes. This was achieved by spending ten days on the witness stand, serving eight years in prison, and paying a hefty $2 million forfeiture order. With time served, he will still have to spend another four more years in prison.

According to his statements in two trials and proffer statements made to the Government, it is estimated that Arillotta profited around $2 million from his criminal activities spanning from the early 1990s until 2010. In light of this, the Government requests that the Court order a forfeiture of this amount during sentencing. While Arillotta only had a few immediate family members in the courtroom, Victor Bruno urged Castel to impose a life sentence on Arillotta despite his extensive testimony.

"Now you're executing your backup plan because you're not man enough or tough enough to take responsibility for your own actions. It was too much for you to handle. You were an ineffective and sloppy boss; most notably, your 15 minutes of fame is over," Victor Bruno said in an impact statement.

During his court statement, Bruno fiercely criticized Arillotta, someone he had known since childhood, with an intense gaze and consistent pointing. Throughout the entire speech, Arillotta remained stoic and unmoved.

"This guy, I grew up with him. I know him like the back of my hand. Your middle name should not be 'Jude.' It should be Judas," Bruno said, referring to the Biblical turncoat. "You ran to the government right away because you knew you were dead in the water. You became a rat, something you knew my father wasn't."

Arillotta recently addressed Victor's remarks.

"First of all, he is an informant; he's always been no good. He doesn't want to get it through his head that a 302 report came out that his father told the FBI information. I didn't order his death. When they brought that paper to New York, the Genovese family bosses ordered his death. That's why his father's dead. You're talking about Bruno's son; there was always a little rivalry. The father always had me around; if there was somebody to go hit or break someone's head, it was always me and my crew, never his son. When they talked about proposing and making a guy, a made guy, it was always me he was talking about, so there was a lot of envy with him. I wrote him letters from prison, trying to tell him. I get it. It was his father. That's who suffers. The family suffers when we get killed."

Arillotta addressed the court, expressing his remorse and apologizing to the Bruno, Westerman, and Dadabo families. Overwhelmed with emotion, he became quiet, deeply affected by his words.

"I joined the Mafia and chose the Genovese family over my own flesh and blood," he confessed emotionally.

As per the judge's ruling, Arillotta was ordered to forfeit $2 million and continue a sentence of 99 months, which equates to just over eight years. This was different from the outcome that Arillotta had hoped for. Despite having already served approximately four years behind bars, good conduct would only shorten his imprisonment by a minimum of three years.

"Up until that moment, with everything bad I've done, everything I've been through in my life, I never really had a sleepless night. I never stressed about anything in my life, ever. That night when I got that, I didn't sleep all night because I knew now my life was going to change. I just knew that the eight and a half years was going to fuck up my life as far as relationships with women, with my kids, with business, it was going to fuck up everything."

Despite being in prison, Arillotta was protected. He was locked up in Fairton Penitentiary's witness security unit during his incarceration, also referred to as, quote, "rat camp." This facility only housed inmates who had cooperated with the government, ensuring that Arillotta would not be targeted by his fellow prisoners for his involvement with law enforcement.

"There were about a hundred of us there. Everybody there was a notorious criminal. Like, you had mafia bosses, you had these cartel guys, El Chapo's guys. You had notorious Aryan Brotherhood prison gangs that killed 30-40 people in prison. Everybody there had at least a couple of bodies."

Cooperating has advantages, as the facilities for protected witnesses are considerably better than those found in conventional correctional institutions.

"It was great. I look back there; I mean, it was great doing time. For one thing, you work your way up; you get a single cell. That's huge. Anybody knows prison life; that's the number one thing. You could just disappear in your cell, close the door, and you could just be in solitude."

Amidst the quiet solitude, Arillotta delved into the depths of his being, embarking on a journey of self-discovery.

"I read the Quran, Bible, self-help philosophy, and yoga philosophy. I believe you come back to life in different lives and then different dimensions, and it's really interesting."

Arillotta says he even put those lessons into practice.

"I was doing yoga in there. I did a lot of meditation and found a lot of knowledge about life and everything. So, I kind of self-analyzed, self-fixed myself."

Chapter 21

Some Old Guy Died

According to an "old-timer," an inactive member with strong ties to the Genovese crime family's Western Mass crew, the current state of the mafia in Springfield, Massachusetts, is a disgrace.

"The so-called "new-school" mob leaders are nothing but a ragtag group of unrefined criminals, thugs, thieves, and braggarts."

This is a far cry from the glory days of the region's mafia, led by infamous figures like Salvatore "Big Nose Sam" Cufari and the Scibelli brothers, Franky "Skyball," Anthony "Turk," and Alfred "Baba." The last shred of respect for the organization, as noted by the old-school OG, died with capo Adolfo "Big Al" Bruno, the Scibellis' protégé who was ruthlessly killed on November 23, 2003, by his protege, Anthony "Bingy" Arillotta.

"These guys today are a total joke. The whole operation is a three-ring circus. You don't ask who the boss is; you ask who the next lead clown is, who's gonna sit on the seltzer bottle and make everyone laugh. To say this outfit is a shadow of its former self is an insult to shadows. Real men used to run this town, men you were proud to work for, men who could go across the entire goddamn country and find respect. What we've got now are a bunch of wannabes, a bunch of clowns, drug fiends, drug pushers, fake tough guys. It's a sad state of affairs. We're talking about the blind leading the blind here."

In 2017, Anthony Arillotta returned to his hometown after completing an eight-year prison sentence in a high-security federal facility and providing testimony in multiple trials against his former gangland bosses and mob associates. Rather than entering the Witness Security Program and assuming a new identity in a distant location, he chose to forgo the comfortable accommodations and remain in his familiar surroundings.

However, upon his release, the former boss of the Springfield mob crew found that he no longer had a home to return to, as it had been sold while he was in prison. Additionally, his wife had divorced him, leaving him with no choice but to move back in with his mother in the very same house where he had grown up. This stark reality served as a poignant reminder of the consequences of his actions and the toll they had taken on his personal life.

"You know, part of me was like, I'm coming back to my area. That's it. If I die in the streets here, I don't care. I'm not dying in prison, in a prison cell."

The "new administration" in the city has allowed his return without any issues, as Arillotta's testimony did not implicate any of them. Additionally, federal investigators had put Arillotta backed into a corner. Surprisingly, Anthony has been allowed to hang around the Our Lady of Mt. Carmel Society Social Club in the South End, where Bruno was gunned down, with the blessing of Albert "The Animal" Calvanese.

When questioned about his feelings while walking around the same area where he had committed these crimes and cooperated against dangerous individuals, he dismissed any nervousness.

He claimed, "Because there are no people around here. For the Italian mafia, there ain't nothing around here."

Despite this, he was asked if he feared retaliation from the mob, especially from Artie's associates in New York, who may come after him to send a message.

He confidently stated, "No, because they'd have to send a message to thousands of other guys before me. If they were going to kill anybody, there's a thousand guys that the Genovese family, New York, got to kill before they come this way. There's no fear at all. Nothing like that."

Upon his return, Arillotta also attempted therapy to openly discuss any matters on his mind.

"I was seeing this girl at the doctor, whatever you call them, and she goes, 'What are your two main thoughts?' And I was thinking, what do you think about? The two main thoughts were killing my enemies and beautiful women and hurting your enemies, thinking of ways to kill them or hurt them. I used to go to bed at night just thinking, I'm just going to go in there and kill them all, you know? What? And, you know, you're just thinking that way, and then you zone off and go to sleep. So, I told that to the fucking the shrink lady, and next thing you know, she canceled all my appointments and everything."

In the Fall of 2018, Freddy Geas was serving time at a maximum-security federal prison in West Virginia when the Federal Bureau of Prisons decided to move another Massachusetts mobster to Hazelton Penitentiary, the notorious Boston gangster James "Whitey" Bulger.

In 1994, Bulger was tipped off by a corrupt FBI agent that he was about to be arrested. So, he went into hiding. When Osama bin Laden was number one on the FBI's most wanted list, Bulger was number two until 2011, when his arrest made national news. The Boston mob boss who outsmarted and embarrassed federal agents for the last 16 years is a fugitive no more. The search ended in 2011 when agents found the mobster and his girlfriend living in an apartment building in Santa Monica, California.

The next day, Bulger was all over the news. Again.

Two inmates used a padlock attached to a belt to fatally beat infamous Boston Irish crime boss and long-time FBI informant Bulger on October 30, 2018. This vicious attack took place just hours after the 89-year-old Bulger was transferred from a protection unit in Florida and put into the general population.

Geas quickly became a prime suspect in the brutal attack that left Bulger dead in his cell, along with another Massachusetts native, Paul "Little Paulie" DeCologero. Geas' well-known distaste for "rats" has been a major factor in the Bulger massacre, as Bulger was one of the most treacherous informants in FBI history.

At 9 p.m., Bulger was locked in his cell with a fellow inmate from New York who had a 30-month prison term for gun possession. The night in the unit was far from calm, as one prisoner claimed that there was an hour-long chant about Bulger being a "rat."

At 6:10 a.m., the cell doors were unlocked, allowing the inmates to move freely within the housing unit before breakfast.

At 6:16 a.m., Bulger's cellmate left, and two other prisoners, identified as Geas and DeCologero, were seen on surveillance tape entering his cell and shutting the door behind them. They remained inside for seven minutes, during which they beat Bulger into a bloody pulp with a padlock and placed him in bed with a blanket pulled over his head. The killers reportedly tried to cut out his tongue and gouge his eyes out of his head.

A third inmate, Sean McKinnon, who shared a cell with Geas, acted as a lookout.

After two hours had elapsed, a prison staffer entered the cell and discovered Bulger's lifeless body. Despite their efforts of administering CPR and utilizing a defibrillator, the prison staff were unable to bring him back to life.

Bulger was pronounced dead at 9:07 a.m.

According to Geas' attorney, Dan Kelly, when he asked Geas about his remarks regarding his run-in with Bulger, Geas responded in his "typical Freddy fashion."

Kelly recounted, "He made a joke and said, 'Apparently, some old guy died, and now they think I did it,'" Kelly recalled.

Kelly added that Geas has not been questioned by the FBI regarding Bulger's death "because he just refused to talk."

"He wouldn't answer any questions even if I were there – he just doesn't answer questions," Kelly stated. "That's it."

Arillotta was a little shocked by the news.

"Yeah, I was surprised. I'm not surprised that he did it. I don't know. They came out, he got killed, and he did it. But, yeah, I was surprised by the event."

When asked if he believed that Freddy had killed Whitey Bulger, he affirmed, "Yeah."

"Why do you think Freddy killed Whitey Bulger?"

"It's kind of like the highest profile type of murder you can do, and I think that he likes that."

From the 1970s well into the 1990s, Bulger was notorious for ruling the South Boston rackets while serving as a top-echelon confidential informant for the FBI's Boston office. During this time, he also killed countless rivals and potential witnesses under the watchful eye of the FBI.

Freddy Weichel, an old-school, low-level Irish gangster in Boston Geas, was a former cellmate and close of Freddy Geas. Bulger framed Weichel for a murder he didn't commit. In contrast, it was a member of Bulger's Winter Hill Gang who killed Bobby LaMonica in 1980. Weichel, who existed on the outer fringes of the Irish mob, formed a strong bond with Geas while serving time in state prison during the 1990s.

According to private investigator Ted McDonough, "Freddy hated rats."

This speculation emerged after authorities suspected Geas of brutally assaulting Bulger on his first day at the Bruceton Mills prison in West Virginia.

McDonough stated, "Freddy hated guys who abused women. Whitey was a rat who killed women. It's probably that simple."

Springfield lawyer Daniel Kelly said, "Freddy is a dying breed."

Kelly, who has also represented Freddy's younger brother Ty, shared, "He has great disdain for informants."

"I'm not saying Freddy did this just because the media says so," said Kelly. "I'm just telling you what I know about him."

"Freddy is a man's man," said Kelly, recalling a time when Freddy was approached by Anthony Arillotta, a Genovese mobster who often utilized Freddy's skills for illegal activities, including another murder for which he was convicted. Despite Arillotta's attempt to persuade him through a secret "back channel" move, Freddy "didn't even blink an eye. He didn't flinch. He just said no."

The Geas family claims that the reason behind the Springfield gangster Freddy Geas killing the humiliated Boston Irish crime boss "Whitey" Bulger behind bars was in retaliation for the framing of Weichel for the 1980 murder. This revelation carries a significant impact.

In August of 2022, Freddy Geas, Paul DeCologero, and Sean McKinnon were indicted for conspiracy to commit first-degree murder in the death of Bulger. The charges alleged that Geas and DeCologero repeatedly struck Bulger in the head while McKinnon served as a lookout, according to the indictment.

Arillotta clarified that he doesn't regret testifying against Freddy and Ty Geas.

"We were close. We did things together that no other people would have done as far as the violence. So, our friendship went a different way. It's like a sick and twisted way about it. Could that have meant that in the future, we would kill each other? Turn on each other? Probably could have happened."

When asked if he had any communication with those guys?

"Well, I had a communication with Freddy. That's all I'm going to say."

"When?"

"About a year ago. It wasn't bad either."

"Who initiated it? Did you or him?"

"A mutual friend. And it wasn't go to hell, I'm rotting in prison while you're out. No, it wasn't. It wasn't bad at all."

"And you sent word back?"

"He's got my number. Put it that way. The number I got right now, he's got."

"So, you're on okay terms with Freddy?"

"I'm not saying I'm on good terms. Okay? I'm not saying nothing. I'm just saying you asked me if I had communications. Yes, I did. Maybe he'll call me. I don't know."

"If he said come visit, I'm going to put you on my list. Would you go out there?"

"Of course."

"Same with Ty."

"Yeah."

Was Big Al an Informant?

According to court testimony, Bruno's fate was sealed when federal authorities unintentionally revealed key details suggesting that Bruno had confidentially shared information about the Genovese family with the FBI. This information was disclosed in a pre-sentence report that was presented to a Massachusetts federal judge to assist in determining the appropriate punishment for Emilio Fusco, a mobster who was convicted in 2003.

The question remains: was Big Al Bruno an informant?

The incriminating words were just one paragraph from a lengthy federal probation officer's report. However, they served as undeniable proof for the Genovese family that Bruno had broken his most sacred Mafia oath: he had talked to law enforcement.

Law enforcement officials expressed shock that a careless leak from the government led to a Mafia rubout. A former federal prosecutor remarked, "Obviously, Bruno's name should not have been in the PSR as the source of the information. It's like putting a bulls-eye on the guy's chest."

Another organized crime agent stated, "It looks like everyone messed up. The agent shouldn't have given Bruno's name to the prosecutor; the prosecutor shouldn't have repeated it to the probation department, and the probation officer shouldn't have included it in his report."

According to FBI Agent Cliff Hedges, the actions of law enforcement in documenting the movements of mafia members were simply part of their job. He believes that if Bruno had refrained from speaking to FBI agents, he could have spared his own life.

"I don't know what he was thinking. Why he felt the need to tell me about it, I have no clue," Hedges said. "But I get it. It was the final straw."

The inclusion of a document believed to be filled with lies attributed to Big Al in Fusco's pre-sentencing report was seen by Bruno's family as the primary motive for his execution, according to their beliefs. Fusco and Tranghese strategically utilized this intelligence document in Fusco's official court record to advocate for Bruno's murder, with Tranghese personally delivering copies of the document to New York and passing it around.

In 2003, Bruno's enemies flaunted this court document in organized crime circles, from Western Massachusetts to New York City, insinuating that the already vulnerable mob boss had developed a disturbingly close relationship with an FBI agent. At its worst, it sparked suspicions that he was an informant for the mob.

For years, there has been uncertainty surrounding whether Bruno had provided information to the FBI. Despite repeated inquiries, the FBI's response has always been underwhelming, with a standard statement of "neither confirming nor denying" any potential involvement. However, according to Agent Hedges, Bruno was not an informant to his knowledge. Instead, the agent believes that Bruno, a notorious gangster, may have grown too comfortable associating with law enforcement officials he knew well.

Hedges further adds, "In fact, I always believed the contrary to be true since he was always a target in every organized crime case I worked."

According to the FBI 302 report, Hedges submitted a detailed account showing Bruno did engage the agent in conversation. Their discussion included Bruno asking about the well-being of the agent's family, his own golf game, a future trip to Florida, and his belief that the FBI was targeting the wrong criminals. Hedges quoted Bruno as saying, "Why is the FBI not targeting the Puerto Rican drug dealers in the South End?" Hedges wrote, quoting Bruno as saying, "This type of investigation is giving my son Victor, a restaurant owner, some bad press, and now nobody wants to go downtown with the gangs and the recent fights."

As stated in Hedges' report, Bruno continued to declare, "If you guys would turn your heads for a few weeks, we would take care of them." He reflected on the good old days, remarking, "Cliff, I can remember when we could leave our doors open and not worry about our women. Not anymore."

According to Hedges, he had arrested Bruno multiple times in the 1990s for bookmaking and associated crimes. Over the years, he had served countless notices to Bruno that he had been picked up on wiretaps. Despite these encounters, the two men maintained a cordial relationship.

Hedges described Bruno as an old-school gangster who viewed arrests and visits from law enforcement as a cost of doing business.

"Guys like him and Skyball," Hedges mentioned, referring to the late Francesco "Skyball" Scibelli, who was once the boss of the Springfield Crew, of which Bruno eventually became the chief until he died in 2003. "For lack of a better word, they were gentlemen."

Hedges denies Bruno served as his informant but asserts that Bruno may have grown too comfortable in their relationship to his detriment.

"It was unfortunate that he felt the need to say the things he said to me inappropriately, to an FBI agent, knowing that I have a sworn duty to report that, and that's exactly what I did," Hedges alleged. "Was I surprised he said it to me? Absolutely. I was shocked, especially in front of all of those people. Everybody there knew me because I was working the public corruption case, and everybody obviously knew him."

"As a result, the repercussions of Bruno's sensitive disclosure to an FBI agent landed in his own lap," Hedges stated.

"If anyone did anything wrong here, it was him," Hedges exclaimed. "As a human, I felt bad when I heard he was killed. But when I heard his son Victor Bruno was blaming me for his death, I said, 'Wait a minute, brother, this was not my fault.' This was just me being a diligent agent."

Hedges declared, as affirmed by the report that he finished the discussion by informing Bruno that another undercover informant disclosed to the FBI a "real and current threat" to Bruno's life.

After the dust settled, the once-powerful Springfield crew and the notorious Genovese crime family were never the same again.

Going back decades to the prohibition era, the Genovese had an established, organized presence and operation in this area, but it all crumbled afterward. Their downfall created a vacuum up here that they haven't recovered from. At its peak, the Springfield mob boasted six made guys, each overseeing dozens of associates. However, after law enforcement finished them, not one made guy remained. Instead, the area is now filled with pretenders, posers, and jerk-offs trying to make a name for themselves on social media.

The Genovese crime family never regained its foothold in Springfield. New York must be humiliated. The fact that mob guys rolling over, ratting to authorities, and betraying their own kind is a huge blow. It's no wonder New York wants nothing to do with this area. This must be the biggest black eye that they've ever had.

Springfield has become the "City of Betrayal."

A Letter from the Daughter of Freddy Geas

"When I was little, I was under the impression that my dad was never around because he was in the army. I didn't know the truth until I was in eighth grade. It was then when I began reading news stories with my dad's name in the headlines. Words like "Mafia," "extortion," "heists," "criminal," "enforcer," and "murder" were plastered across my computer screen. That's when I quickly found out my dad led a double life.

"My dad, Freddy Geas, is going to be spending the rest of his life in federal prison. If we look at this scenario through the eyes of the system, you could say justice was achieved, but if you look at this scenario through a daughter's eyes, it was the most unfair, devastating event that has ever happened to me. I learned that what is fair is not always just, and what is just is not always fair.

"I remember it like it was yesterday, the first time my dad had to leave. I turned the corner of the staircase, and he was in the bathroom brushing his teeth. When my dad looked over at me, he started to cry, and I didn't understand why he was so upset. I had never seen a grown man cry before.

The look on his face was as if his whole world was falling apart.

"One of the hardest things I had to do and continue to still do is explain my father's situation – because the person I am talking about isn't my dad. He is labeled in Western Massachusetts as a brutal criminal, but when I'm sitting across the table from him during our visits, I don't see a monster; I see a flawed man that's paying for the choices he made. My dad is intelligent and one of the best people I know. I know who he really is behind all of the obligations that were expected of him because of the organization in which he was affiliated.

"I have no intention of paying tribute to my dad or praise the man he was. My intention is not to defend him or clear his name. But in a twisted world where everyone is categorized so specifically, I wanted to take the opportunity to remind everyone that we are all human beings. We do not fit perfectly into these divisions of good or evil. At any point in time, things can change.

"All people have the capacity to feel hurt, loss, suffering, joy, freedom, love, and compassion. At one point or another, most people have experienced some of life's highs and lows, some more than others. Although people look, dress, feel, and act very differently from one another, when you look beyond someone's exterior, they are quite similar. Our circumstances may be different, but when it comes down to our core, we are essentially the same.

"One of the evilest things we do is dehumanize one another. If you turn on the news or flip through the newspaper, you will come across millions of atrocities happening around the world, and at the heart of each one, there is someone to blame. What people often forget is that this is someone's brother, sister, father, or mother.

"Today, I look at the same person, Freddy Geas, my father, that all these other people see. I've been looking at this person for 23 years, the person all these people think they know, but I see someone different. The person I know is the father that would tuck me in at night and tell me funny stories until I fell asleep. He was the person that taught me how to throw a baseball and got me my first pair of soccer cleats.

"When I look in the mirror, I see his smile because I have the same one."

-Taylor Geas

A message from Freddy Geas:

"I'm angry, hurt, and disappointed every time I think about Anthony's betrayal."

A message from Ty Geas:

"Arillotta is a rat, and he better hope he never goes back to prison."

Also, by Author Nicholas Parisi

Mafia Confession: "King of Bootleggers" Murder

This is a must-read for anyone fascinated with Mafia history. It is a rare inside account of the rise of the "Springfield Crew" during Prohibition in Massachusetts, its ties with the Genovese Crime Family of New York, and its evolution into the present-day Mob.

www.ingramcontent.com/pod-product-compliance
Lightning Source LLC
Chambersburg PA
CBHW062047270326
41931CB00013B/2969